War and Intervention in Lebanon

Despite the bitter conflict that divided Jerusalem and Damascus, a fascinating process of indirect – through the United States – and tacit understandings emerged with regard to Lebanon in the 1970s. This derived largely from the Israeli deterrence posture which held in check Syrian military involvement in Lebanon. This book, first published in 1987, traces the development of the Israeli and Syrian involvement in Lebanon between 1975 and 1985, and of the deterrence dialogue which evolved between them. It also places this dialogue within the larger context of the overall Israeli-Syrian deterrence equation. *War and Intervention in Lebanon* is a fascinating and relevant work, of great value to those with an interest in International Relations and Middle Eastern history, politics and diplomacy.

War and Intervention in Lebanon

The Israeli-Syrian Deterrence Dialogue

Yair Evron

Routledge
Taylor & Francis Group

First published in 1987
by Croom Helm Ltd

This edition first published in 2013 by Routledge
2 Park Square, Milton Park, Abingdon, Oxon, OX14 4RN

Simultaneously published in the USA and Canada
by Routledge
711 Third Avenue, New York, NY 10017

Routledge is an imprint of the Taylor & Francis Group, an informa business

Publisher's Note
The publisher has gone to great lengths to ensure the quality of this reprint but
points out that some imperfections in the original copies may be apparent.

Disclaimer
The publisher has made every effort to trace copyright holders and welcomes
correspondence from those they have been unable to contact.

A Library of Congress record exists under LC control number: 87002851

ISBN 13: 978-0-415-83091-1 (hbk)
ISBN 13: 978-0-203-49298-7 (ebk)

WAR AND INTERVENTION IN LEBANON

The Israeli-Syrian Deterrence Dialogue

YAIR EVRON

CROOM HELM
London & Sydney

© 1987 Yair Evron
Croom Helm Ltd, Provident House, Burrell Row,
Beckenham, Kent BR3 1AT
Croom Helm Australia, 44–50 Waterloo Road,
North Ryde, 2113, New South Wales

British Library Cataloguing in Publication Data

Evron, Yair
    War and intervention in Lebanon: The Israeli–Syrian
    deterrence dialogue.
    1. Lebanon — Politics and government — 1975 –
    I. Title
    956.92′044   DS80.95
    ISBN 0-7099-1451-2

Filmset in English Times by Pat and Anne Murphy,
10 Bracken Way, Highcliffe-on-Sea, Dorset
Printed and bound in Great Britain by Mackays of Chatham Ltd, Kent

Contents

To RUTI and ROI

Preface

Research for this book began indirectly in 1980, when in the pursuit of my ongoing interest in Israeli deterrence policy I began research on more specific instances of Israeli–Arab deterrence 'dialogues'. My focus was increasingly directed on the Israeli–Syrian strategic relationship and especially in regard to Lebanon. During my research I was fortunate in being able to interview Israeli decision makers and officials. All of them were interviewed while not in Government. These interviews were of considerable help in preparing Chapters 2, 3, and 4. The following decision makers were kind enough to be interviewed: the late Yigal Allon, the late Yisrael Galili, Mordechai Gur, Shimon Peres, Yitzhak Rabin and Yitzhak Berman. Officials interviewed included Amos Eran, Reuven Merchav and Gideon Raphael. I have also discussed briefly some specific aspects of the subject of this book with Simcha Dinitz and Mordechai Gazit. Finally, I have conducted various interviews with other ex-Israeli officials who preferred not to be named. I am grateful to all of them.

While in the United States, I was fortunate to be able to conduct interviews with Joseph Sisco, following his retirement from government, and with several American officials who were involved over the years in the Israeli–Syrian–Lebanese triangle.

I would like to thank the following for commenting on parts or the whole of the manuscript or for giving me helpful advice during the research and writing of this book: Arnan Azariahu ('Sini'), Avraham Ben-Zvi, Dan Horowitz, Aharon Klieman, Moshe Maoz, Yehoshua Porath, Janice Stein and Saadia Touval. Their comments were invaluable.

A grant from the Jaffe Center of Strategic Studies, Tel-Aviv University, during the initial stage of the research is hereby gratefully acknowledged, as is a grant from the Leonard Davis Institute for International Relations, The Hebrew University of Jerusalem.

During different stages of the research and writing of this book I was fortunate in having the opportunity of discussing different aspects of the book with learned and helpful audiences. I have benefited from discussions conducted at departmental seminars of the Department of Political Science at Tel-Aviv University, the Dayan Center of Middle-Eastern Studies, also at Tel-Aviv University, the Department of International Relations at the Hebrew University of Jerusalem, the Seminar on Israeli Security at the *Yad Tabenkin* Research Institute, and from a special seminar at the International Institute for Strategic Studies in London.

I would also like to specially thank Warwick Sharp for his considerable contribution in carefully reviewing, editing and correcting the manuscript, and in also giving much helpful advice. Margaret Cornell was of great help in her meticulous scrutiny of the manuscript and in providing many important editorial comments. Finally, my research assistants, Nitzan Goldberg and Omri Yakir, were very helpful.

Introduction

The disastrous conflict among the ethnic and religious communities in Lebanon has already attracted considerable international scholarly attention. The involvement of external powers, primarily Israel and Syria and to a lesser extent the superpowers, culminating in the 1982 War and the subsequent direct American intervention, has also stimulated some academic interest in the issue. Nevertheless, it seems that the multidimensional nature of the Lebanese conflict, and especially the role of the external powers, requires additional scientific investigation. This book focuses on the policies and strategies of Syria and Israel, the main external actors in the Lebanese quagmire. As their involvement began to expand in the mid-1970s, the two states observed each other's moves with inevitable suspicion. However, despite the deep conflict that divides Jerusalem and Damascus, there gradually evolved a fascinating process of indirect and tacit understanding between them. This development derived mainly from the Israeli deterrence posture, which delineated the limits of Syrian military involvement in Lebanon. Gradually Syria also defined its own deterrence thresholds. This set of understandings held firm, under considerable stress, until 1982 when it broke down under the impact of the Israeli-initiated war.

The 1982 War was a significant international event, and requires extensive historical treatment in and of itself and as an input to the study of Middle Eastern politics. Furthermore, the aftermath of the war, the long and messy process of the Israeli withdrawal, and the re-emergence of Syria as the most important external actor in Lebanon, are also of importance to any follower of international and Middle Eastern politics. Since Israel's withdrawal in 1984–5, the system of tacit understanding between the two countries in regard to Lebanon has re-emerged, though with some modifications.

While the respective policies of the United States and the Soviet Union are not discussed here as independent subjects, the crucial role of Washington as a mediator between Jerusalem and Damascus, and as a constraint on Israeli policy at some junctures, forms part of the historical account.

There have already been several studies of the Lebanese Civil War and of Israeli and Syrian involvement in Lebanon, but no analytical account of the gradual development of this involvement, or of the direct interactions between the two states, has been fully presented. Thus the first focus of this book is a historical-analytical discussion of Syrian and Israeli policies in Lebanon from 1975 to 1985. The second focus is the evolution of the deterrence relationship between them. The specific Israeli deterrence thresholds delineated in Lebanon, and some corresponding Syrian deterrence thresholds, constitute one cluster in this relationship, and the one which is discussed here in greater detail. It is analysed, however, against the backdrop of the overall deterrence equation — beyond Lebanon — which had developed between the two countries since the beginning of their conflict.

Hence, the book is mainly targeted at the International Relations community and within it at those interested in deterrence theory and its applications, as well as at the Middle Eastern studies community.

Events in Lebanon cannot, of course, be explained solely in terms of the involvement of external powers. On the contrary, the actions of the external powers were generally in response to internal developments. It is the basic assumption of this book that the nature of the Lebanese political system and its inherent instabilities had a profound impact on the successes and failures of the policies of the external actors. Thus, while Israel and Syria serve as the focus of attention, it has been necessary to relate to Lebanese internal political events throughout the narrative.

Indeed, the question of Lebanese internal politics is the starting-point for this book. Consequently, Chapter 1 describes the basis of Lebanese political instability and goes on briefly to narrate the development of the Civil War. In Chapter 2, the background to Syrian and Israeli policies in Lebanon is presented: their interests, their respective perceptions of Lebanese domestic developments and their assessments of each other's role within the context of the Lebanese Civil War. Chapter 2 also deals with the gradual evolution of the Israeli–Syrian deterrence dialogue concerning the limits of Syrian military intervention. This intervention is discussed both within the context of the Israeli–Syrian strategic relationship and as a factor affecting and being affected by internal developments in Lebanon.

viii

Chapter 3 focuses on the complex interrelationships between developments within Lebanon and Israeli–Syrian strategic relations there during 1977–81. Five specific instances will be discussed: the Nabatiyya encounter; the Litani Operation; the 1979 air confrontation; the 'missile crisis' of 1981; and the escalation of the Israeli–PLO conflict of the same year. These encounters are analysed against the background of the understandings reached between Israel and Syria in regard to the limits of military intervention.

By 1981, Israel had begun to change its perceptions of developments in Lebanon, especially concerning the usefulness of the Syrian military presence in that country. In parallel, the use of military power for the accomplishment of far-reaching Israeli political objectives was seen as increasingly feasible and desirable. These perceptual developments resulted partly from personal changes in the main group of decision-makers, as well as from new inputs into their calculations. Among the latter, the Israeli–Egyptian peace treaty created a new strategic environment in the Middle East, which made Israeli decisions on the use of force easier to reach. These developments, and the consequent momentous decision to launch the 1982 War, are discussed in Chapter 4. The chapter includes a discussion of the Israeli war objectives, some explicit, others ambiguous, and outlines the main military moves. The discussion of these moves serves to underline the politico-strategic objectives of Israel and Syria. The siege of Beirut and the intricate Israeli–Syrian–Lebanese–American interactions leading to the withdrawal of the PLO and Syrian forces from Beirut are described and analysed.

By the autumn of 1982, Israel had emerged as the ostensible winner of the war, but already the objectives that it had set itself seemed less and less tenable. Within months, the whole situation began to change and by mid-1983 it was crystal clear that the costs of the war were considerable, whereas the benefits appeared to fade into thin air. The war ended only in early 1985 with the final Israeli withdrawal and the re-emergence of Syria as the most important external actor in Lebanon. Chapter 5 concentrates on the aftermath of the war, and concludes with a discussion of the re-emergence of a system of mutual specific deterrence in Lebanon.

Over the past three decades deterrence theory has focused on nuclear deterrence and only recently has its relevance to conventional deterrence between regional powers received more attention. Furthermore, while the theory has become more refined and nuanced, the number of empirical studies of deterrence has remained limited. Indeed, most of the empirical studies have been about the failures of deterrence rather than its successes. The successful Israeli–Syrian deterrence relationship in Lebanon is therefore of interest not only in itself, but also in relation to the application of deterrence in general. Chapter 6 discusses the development of the largely successful Israeli–Syrian deterrence relationship in general and in Lebanon, and considers the specific conditions under which it succeeded and also those under which it twice partly failed — in 1973 and again in 1982.

The deterrence experience in Lebanon indicates that this particular pattern of behaviour could serve as a valid instrument for the regulation and management of conflicts. The research task is to identify the conditions for success or failure, and how they can be positively manipulated by the deterrer. This has been analysed in the chapter.

The Lebanese Civil War 1975–76: A Brief Historical Account

THE LEBANESE STATE[1]

Lebanon is traditionally identified with Mount Lebanon. Yet, when France received the Mandate over Syria and Lebanon after World War I, it introduced a major change in the borders of Lebanon. Le Grand Liban was created. To the traditional area of Mount Lebanon, where the Maronites constitute a clear majority (with the Druze second in importance), were added large tracts of land in the south, east and north. The change ultimately proved to be the major factor in the decline of Maronite political power. The areas newly appended to Mount Lebanon were inhabited in great part by Muslims: in the south and east, the Beqa, primarily by Shi'is, while in the north, in the area of Tripoli, Sunnis were more dominant. Since World War I modern Lebanon has witnessed a continual gradual change in its demographic make-up. At the time of the formation of le Grand Liban, the Maronites constituted about half the population. In subsequent years, the proportion of Maronites has diminished significantly. This decline has been due primarily to the extensive Maronite emigration (mainly to the United States and Latin America), and also to the higher Muslim birth-rate.

When Lebanon received its independence in 1943, the elites from the different communities agreed to the creation of a peculiar, yet very realistic, political system, based on the recognition that Lebanese society is divided into several religious communities, and that religion is the main locus of communal identity. Moreover, the argument took into consideration the fact that the various communities also differ along other important lines, and recognised that the political system should accept and incorporate these differences. In fact, the arrangements of 1943 were deeply rooted in a political system whose origins can be traced to the regime created in Mount Lebanon after the 1860 civil war. At that time, the *mutasarifiyya* (Governorate) of Mount Lebanon was given privileged status under a non-Lebanese Christian governor, who was to be assisted by a council consisting of four Maronites, three Druze, two Greek Orthodox Christians, one Melchite, one Shi'i and one Sunni Muslim.[2] The roots of Lebanon's confessional political system date back to the nineteenth century.

The 1943 national pact agreed upon orally by the Maronite and Sunni elites recognised the predominant position which the Maronites should assume in the political life of Lebanon. Accordingly, the most powerful political position, the presidency, was given to a Maronite. Similarly, the role of Chief of Staff of the armed forces was also allotted to a Maronite. However, the constitution created a delicate system of checks and balances, which, while giving the predominant position to a Maronite, also delegated slices of political power to other communities. Thus, the Prime Minister had to be a Sunni Muslim, the Minister of Defence a Druze, and the Chairman of the Parliament, a Shi'i. In this way the important governmental positions were held by representatives of the various religious communities. The actual functioning of such a system depended on continued agreement among the communities' elites. The system could not be maintained by the imposition of the will of one community only, but was dependent on the elites' recognition of their shared interests.

Until the collapse of law and order in Lebanon with the outbreak of the Civil War in 1975,[3] the political system, despite being under continuous pressure, nevertheless functioned successfully, and even made possible a measure of personal and social liberty unparalleled in any Arab state. Lebanon has enjoyed a free press, freedom of expression and freedom of political organisation to a degree almost equal to that of the Western democracies. Lebanese development has not been without its irony: rapid economic modernisation and an advanced educational system (for part of the population) have been the awkward bedfellows of a semi-feudal system of economic and political power.

INHERENT INSTABILITIES

The Civil War and the subsequent instability result from several processes indigenous to Lebanon, but which have become increasingly intractable due to the pressures of external actors. Several factors must be taken into account, although it is difficult to assess their relative importance.[4]

Firstly, it is important to survey the forces resulting from the heterogeneous ethnic and religious character of the country, and from social processes, that gradually undermined erstwhile political structures. The Maronite community has existed since the fourth century, and moved to Mount Lebanon in the eighth–ninth centuries. The Druze community emerged in Mount Lebanon at a later stage. Until the nineteenth century the two communities co-operated with each other, and indeed from the late sixteenth century created a viable political system, the Imarah of Lebanon. However, animosity between them broke out in the mid-nineteenth century when general intercommunal fighting broke out.

French aid to the Christian Maronites in 1860 contributed to the development among the Maronites of an increasingly European, and particularly French, orientation; indeed they tended to regard France as their external backer. Moreover, an extensive system of education, again largely French-oriented, developed in the Maronite community, transforming its educational levels, and consequently its general world outlook.

Even prior to the end of the Ottoman Empire, the Maronites entertained aspirations for the creation of a separate political entity, and to this end had developed strong links with external non-Ottoman powers. They welcomed the creation of the French Mandate over Syria and Lebanon with enthusiasm, seeing in it the promise of political self-fulfilment. However, the extension of Lebanon's political boundaries introduced a major change in the composition of the population. The Maronites ceased to be the majority and became one minority in a country of several religious and ethnic minorities. The decline in the Maronite demographic status has accelerated since World War II.

The Sunni community, which was concentrated in Beirut and in the region of Tripoli in north Lebanon, accepted the Maronites' leading role only after obtaining an agreement which, as already stated, allowed the Sunnis the second most

3

important position in the political system. Indeed, the understanding reached in 1943 was really a compromise worked out by the Maronite leader Bishara al-Khuri and the Sunni leader Riad el-Sulh. Once this compromise was settled, the leaderships of the two communities formed a coalition to underwrite the system, and enabled Lebanon to remain united, in the face of internal and external pressures, until 1975. Indeed, the Maronite–Sunni coalition was critical throughout the duration of the regime.

The traditional animosity between the Maronites and Druze persisted in modern Lebanon, but remained dormant for many years, while the Druze were allowed their share in the political system. However, this underlying tension also broke out once the system came under increased pressure.

Since the establishment of le Grand Liban major demographic and social processes have taken place. The Maronite community, other Christian communities, and upper-class groups within the Sunni community, rapidly raised their levels of education, and since the 1960s, have also enjoyed unprecedented material affluence. Beirut became the centre of banking for the entire Arab Middle East, and much of the income from oil was invested there.

Notwithstanding the economic success enjoyed by some parts of the population, other sectors, primarily those belonging to the Shi'i community in the south, remained poor and uneducated. In the demographic context, the Maronites and other Christian communities grew at a much slower pace than the Muslims, and this was particularly evident with respect to the Shi'is. The rate of emigration to Western countries also contributed to the change in the relative size of the communities, since many more Christians than Muslims emigrated. By the 1970s, the Shi'i community had grown in size to become the largest single minority in the country, close to a third of the population.

These economic and demographic trends were highly visible and were perceived with apprehension from two opposing points of view. The Maronites were concerned lest their political position be adversely affected by their relative decline. On the other hand, the Muslims, and primarily the Shi'is, became increasingly restive because of the growing gap between their economic level and that of the Maronites. Indeed, in order to defend their political position the Maronites have refused to allow another census since that conducted in 1932, on which all the demographic calculations which served as the basis for the 1943 pact were founded.

The economic system in Lebanon has always been *laissez faire*. Only limited attempts have been made to encourage the development of social services of any kind, which might have served as a corrective to the country's deepening social and economic problems. The only attempt to alleviate the social inequalities occurred during the presidency of Fuad Shihab from 1958 to 1964. In that period, several social and economic programmes were undertaken. For example, the Litani irrigation project was established and the Qarun artificial lake dug. The beginnings of a somewhat more equitable social system seemed to be emerging. However, in subsequent years, many of these programmes were abandoned. The lack of governmental intervention benefited the more active and educated sectors of the population and increased the economic gap from which the Shi'is were suffering. Their frustration was deepened by the Israeli strategy of retaliation (to be discussed below), which hurt the Shi'is, the main population grouping in the south, more than the other communities. Many moved north and settled in shanty towns around Beirut. In addition to their old frustrations, this migration involved the new experience of living in a large and difficult metropolitan area.

However, despite their numbers, the Shi'is remained without significant economic and political power. They were also disorganised, although this began to change in the 1970s when one of their religious leaders, the Imam Mousa al-Sadr, laid the foundations of a Shi'i political organisation. Thus, on top of the traditional conflict between Maronite and Druze, and the inherent tension between Christians and Muslims in general, there emerged another set of tensions — that of a frustrated community, unable to match economic and political power to its demographic growth. Once the Shi'is began to organise and to articulate their demands, a change in the *status quo* became difficult to resist.

The intercommunal tensions were also reflected in another strain within the Lebanese body politic. This concerns the national self-identification of the various groups within the society. On the one hand, there were those who searched for a separate Lebanese identity, with an invariable emphasis on a Western-oriented cultural approach. On the other hand, there were many groups which sought their national 'redemption' in some kind of 'Arabism'. These differences emerged from the heterogeneous religious and ethnic character of the population, and were also connected to the rise of militant Pan-Arabism in the 1950s and 1960s. While there were, of course, many variations to both approaches, a broad dichotomy coloured the political scene.

The 'Lebanese' orientation, promulgated primarily by the Maronites, has had several emphases. Not without support was a Christian thrust, arguing that Lebanon should be a Christian–Maronite state. Simultaneously there was the contention that, because of the pluralistic structure of the society, Lebanon should maintain a separate identity, distinct from the Arab world. One aspect of this approach calls for the continuation of Maronite hegemony and of the confessional political system. Only Maronite hegemony could protect the separate identity of Lebanon. Other national-cultural variations developed in the 1920s conceived of the Lebanese entity as the culmination of all the cultures developed in Lebanon beginning with the Phoenicians. They also stressed the 'Mediterranean' nature of Lebanon.[5]

'Arabism', on the other hand, emphasises the common destiny and culture that Lebanon shares with the other Arab states. Not surprisingly, most of its adherents have been Muslims.

The clash between 'Lebanese Nationalism' and 'Arabism' does not necessarily follow the divide between Christians and Muslims. Many Christians, in particular the Greek Orthodox but also other Christian denominations, identify themselves as Arabs. Some have even adhered to Pan-Arab ideas. Similarly, Muslims from various quarters have emphasised that Lebanon must find a special and separate role within the Arab world.

Side by side with an 'Arab' orientation, there has also been another school of thought claiming that Lebanon was a part of Syria, and which supported *Syrian* nationalism. The Parti Populaire Syrien (PPS), founded in 1932 by Antoun Sa'adeh, called for the re-establishment of Greater Syria, to include most of the Fertile Crescent and even Cyprus.[6] The PPS opposed Arab nationalism, but was equally opposed to Lebanese separatism. In any case, its influence dwindled over the years and the party itself modified its ideology. Yet notions emphasising the Lebanese–Syrian connection, while usually part of an 'Arab' approach, have remained prevalent among some political sectors in Lebanon.

In addition to these pressures — religious, ethnic, social, economic and ideological — on the political system, the Palestinian issue became critical for Lebanon after the 1967 War. During the 1948 War, tens of thousands of Palestinian refugees fled from northern parts of Palestine to Lebanon and Syria. Many of them were gradually integrated into Lebanese society. The majority, however, lived in refugee camps, relying on aid supplied by the United Nations Refugee Welfare Agency. Palestinians became more and more active in Lebanese intellectual and political life, but until 1967 were not allowed to organise themselves politically, and most retained their second-class status. The change came with the 1967 War, and the subsequent rapid growth of the Palestinian organisations. *Fath* itself, the main Palestinian organisation, moved its centre of activity to Lebanon in the early 1960s, but initially operated there underground; in any case, until 1968 the size of the Fath and its operations was miniscule. The other leading Palestinian organisation, the Palestine Liberation Organisation, was essentially created by Egypt in 1964 following the first Arab summit meeting. However, following the 1967 War, and the merger of the Fath and the PLO, the now united PLO was perceived by many in the Arab world as a major factor in the fight against Israel. Moreover, the salience of the Palestinian issue increased greatly. Against this background the Lebanese Government found it increasingly difficult to oppose the enhanced power of the PLO in the country.

In the strong Arab countries like Egypt and Syria, the Palestinian organisations were allowed no freedom of action. But in the two small vulnerable countries, Jordan and Lebanon, the regimes faced enormous difficulties in their attempts to control the Palestinians.

The PLO quickly exploited the opportunities opened to it in Lebanon. Its main activity was concentrated in the refugee camps, where it succeeded in the formation of an extensive infrastructure. Simultaneously, its military arm began a campaign of terrorist operations against Israeli settlements near the Israeli–Lebanese border. This campaign was on a smaller scale than the one conducted by the Palestinian organisations from Jordan, and indeed Israeli attention at the time focused mainly on the eastern, and not the northern front. However, the continued irritation along the Lebanese border led Israel to a series of retaliatory strikes aimed at south Lebanon. Although

7

the main targets were the refugee camps where the Palestinian organisations had established their headquarters, bases and facilities, a lot of collateral damage was caused to the areas and population around these camps. Thus, for the first time since 1948, Lebanese citizens and property were hit by Israeli forces. The tough Israeli response led to the beginnings of a major Shi'i migration northwards.

The Lebanese Government tried to control the situation by limiting the activities of the Palestinians, in this way reducing the punishment rendered by the Israeli reprisals. However, strong Lebanese action against the Palestinians aggravated strains between Christians and Muslims or, more accurately, between those with a 'Lebanese' orientation and those identifying primarily as 'Arabs'. The Muslims were not necessarily devoted supporters of the Palestinian struggle against Israel. However, because of the basic cleavage on the question of national identity, and the symbolic nature of Palestinian operations as a manifestation of Arabism, they felt compelled to resist the attempts to curb the Palestinians. The Lebanese Government's policy of constraint of the PLO also met with strong resistance from other Arab countries. The authorities therefore tried to follow a middle-of-the-road policy, limiting the emerging Palestinian semi-autonomy and anti-Israel activities, but not to the extent of crushing PLO power in Lebanon. In 1968, the Lebanese army went into action against Palestinian units and enforced some control over several refugee camps, but failed to impose an effective administration. Further clashes ended with the Cairo Agreement of 1969, according to which the Palestinian organisations accepted a number of restrictions on their freedom of action. They were, however, allowed a semi-autonomous regime in the refugee camps and were thus able to convert some camps into major bases for indoctrination and training and springboards for attacks on Israel. The Palestinians also agreed to refrain from attacking Israeli settlements from across the Lebanese border, but were permitted to infiltrate the border and to operate from inside Israel. The Palestinian organisations gradually transgressed these understandings.

A further major change occurred in 1970, following the termination of the presence of Palestinian organisations in Jordan. The leadership and many activists and fighters fled to Lebanon, and soon established themselves in Beirut, in the surrounding refugee camps, in the refugee camps in the south, and also in the north around Tripoli. Thus, once Jordan was 'lost' from the Palestinian point of view, Lebanon became the best alternative. A weak regime, dependent on a delicate political consensus between various communities, some of whom supported PLO operations, was unable to take firm preventive action. Gradually, the Beirut Government was obliged to conclude that it was incapable of imposing tight restrictions on the PLO. It therefore limited its control to central Lebanon and to some functional aspects of PLO behaviour. South Lebanon came under increasing Palestinian influence; by the mid-1970s, the PLO, to all intents and purposes, controlled large parts of southern Lebanon. PLO activities against Israel did not cease, nor did Israeli retaliation. The Shi'is continued to suffer most from these Israeli actions, but they received no response to their demand that the central government take measures aimed at easing their problems.

The delicate yet durable co-operation between the Maronite and Sunni elites surmounted all these difficulties. It was only when this relationship split up that the country's tensions and inherent instabilities finally converged to bring about the devastating Civil War.

The weakness of the Lebanese central government encouraged the creation of independent militias for the self-defence of the particular communities. On the one hand there were the various Maronite political groups each with its own militia: the Kataib Party (*al-Kataib al-Lubnaniyya*) — the Phalanges, led by the Jumayyil family;[7] the National Liberal party led by Camille Chamoun; and the group led by Suleiman Faranjiyya, who at this time, in the early 1970s, still served as the President of Lebanon. These three groups were the fulcrum of the *status quo* forces that opposed all political change and also tried to constrain as much as possible the activities of the Palestinians. The three political leaders, Pierre Jumayyil, Chamoun and Faranjiyya, co-operated during the Civil War in defence of these political objectives.

In addition, other political elements, primarily from within the Maronite community, also supported the continuation of the *status quo*. The Maronite clergy establishment was active on the side of the Maronite militias. Indeed, the head of the order of Maronite monks, Father Sharbal Qassis, was a central figure in the Maronite political effort. More extreme in their opposition to the 'Arabisation' of Lebanon were some smaller Maronite groups. One such group was the 'Protectors of the Cedar', which completely rejected the Arab elements in both the politics and the culture of Lebanon, and saw the country as one continuous political and cultural entity going back to the Phoenicians. In 1976, together with Father Qassis (who later was replaced by Father Bulus Na'amam), the leaders of the three main political groupings formed the Lebanese Front which became the representative political body of the forces supporting the *status quo*. On the other hand many, primarily Muslim, groups were seeking a change in the *status quo*. They included the Nasserites with their militia — the *Murabitun*, the Communist Party, the PPS and the Progressive Socialist Party. The emerging leader of this camp was Kamal Junblatt, the Druze feudal leader, who led the Progressive Socialist Party. These groups together formed a loose coalition — the National Front. The final break in Lebanese stability came when the traditional Sunni leadership lent its backing to this coalition.

THE CIVIL WAR

It is difficult to point to one event which can be termed the beginning of the war. Two events, however, have been referred to by many observers. Some writers begin their account with the clashes in Sidon in March 1975, in which Palestinians and Lebanese Shi'is rose against the representatives of the central Government. The second, perhaps more widely accepted, account begins with the attack by a group of Palestinians, probably belonging to the Popular Front for the Liberation of Palestine,[8] on a Maronite gathering attended by Pierre Jumayyil, in 'Ayn al-Rummana, on 13 April 1975. This attack led to fierce retaliation by the Phalangists in Beirut. The fighting in Beirut rapidly intensified with the Kataib matched against various Muslim and Palestinian militias. Most prominent among the latter was the PFLP. Within days, there were also outbreaks of fighting in Tripoli. The Civil War that followed can be divided into five main phases.[9]

Phase I: clashes in Beirut and beyond: April–December 1975

In the first few months the fighting mainly centred on Beirut and involved the Christian militias, primarily the Kataib, against the various Muslim militias. The leading Palestinian militia, Fath, was only partly and informally involved in the fighting, as was the PFLP; more active were the smaller Palestinian organisations. During the early period, the other Christian parties and militias backed the Kataib, but were not heavily involved in the war. The only Christian leader to withhold his support from the Maronite front was Raymond Eddé, a Maronite leader and the son of Emil Eddé, the President of Lebanon in the 1930s.

On 23 May 1975, in an effort to restore order, President Faranjiyya appointed an all-military cabinet, under the chairmanship of Brigadier Nur al-Din al-Rifa'i. The forces opposed to the *status quo* refused to accept the new cabinet, and the fighting spread. Under pressure, Faranjiyya was forced to appoint his political opponent, Rashid Karami, a Sunni political leader from Tripoli, as Prime Minister.

Karami voiced the view of many in the anti-*status quo* forces in demanding constitutional reform. There were, however, many variations in these demands. The Shi'i leader, Imam Sadr, for example, and the Greek Orthodox Metropolitan opposed the militancy of the Muslim militias, insisting that the constitutional reform must be slow and gradual and could only be achieved through a peaceful dialogue. The Maronite leadership by and large opposed the proposed reform.

During the summer, the fighting was somewhat reduced, only to be renewed in parts of Beirut in September. By the end of the summer Beirut was a divided city, with the eastern sector under the control of the Christian groups, while the western part was held by various Muslim and leftist groups.

In this initial phase of the war there were several Syrian diplomatic and military interventions. These will be discussed in detail below; suffice it to note here that, following the collapse of several cease-fires and the failure of attempts to mediate in the crisis by domestic parties, as well as by external actors such as the Vatican and France, the traditional leaders of all camps increasingly realised that the key to renewed stability lay in Damascus. This realisation became clear following the new escalation in the fighting during December which closely corresponded to the rejection of proposals for constitutional reform by the 'Maronite Summit', which convened on 31 December.

Phase II: the Palestinians join the battle: January–March 1976

Up to January 1976, there had been some direct Palestinian involvement in the fighting and the logistical support given to the National Front was even considerable, but by and large, Fath did not fully commit its combat units to the war. In early January, however, full-scale fighting broke out between Fath and the Christian militias. The latter laid siege to the camps of Tel-al-Za'tar, Jisr al-Basha and Naba'a, while the Palestinian organisations attacked Damur.

Beirut was quickly engulfed again in heavy fighting, and violence spread to many other parts of the country. By late January, about two-thirds of Lebanon had come under the control of the Palestinians and the Muslim militias. The military situation had turned against the pro-*status quo* forces. Against this background (and with intensive Syrian mediation), a new constitutional reform was drafted, which received the endorsement of the pro-*status quo* forces. The final document was prepared during the visit of Faranjiyya to Damascus in early February.

The Prime Minister, Rashid Karami, also declared his endorsement of the document. The new formula stipulated that some of the fundamental elements of the political system should be maintained — most crucially, the division of the three most important positions on ethno-religious lines. Thus, the Presidency was to remain in the hands of the Maronites, the premiership would be retained for the Sunnis, and the position of Chairman of Parliament for the Shi'is. Moreover, the important executive positions would continue to be divided according to unchanged principles. However, some important modifications were also introduced: membership of Parliament was now to be divided equally between Christians and Muslims, and a constitutional body was to be created to which both the President and the Prime Minister would be responsible. These two modifications, coupled with changes in the majorities needed for election of the President and the Prime Minister in the House of Representatives, would have made the political system more responsive to the demographic, social and political changes which had taken place in Lebanon since independence. The proposal also envisaged new social reforms.

However, the National Front and the PLO came out against

the compromise plan. Their ostensible objective was a complete revision of the constitution and the abolition of its confessional basis. The PLO was probably hoping to have more freedom of action and greater influence within an 'Arab' Lebanon which would be mobilised for a continued struggle against Israel. It felt that complete victory was within its reach. The fighting escalated and the situation continued to deteriorate. In addition, the Lebanese army, which, despite lending some support to the Christians, had generally tried to stay clear of the fighting, began to disintegrate. The first split developed in January with the rebellion of Lieutenant al-Hatib, who formed the 'Lebanon Arab Army' which co-operated with the Muslim militias. Shortly afterwards Brigadier Aziz al-Ahdab, the Muslim Sunni commander of the Beirut military district, led a *coup* against President Faranjiyya, demanding his resignation.

The new year also saw changes in the external political context. By February–March, there were many indications that Syria was moving its political support which had in any case been equivocal from the Muslim–PLO coalition to the pro-*status quo* forces. This change of posture also involved the use of military units under Syrian control. (Syria's policy will be analysed in Chapter 2.)

Phase III: Syrian intervention: April–May 1976

In April, units of the Palestinian organisation based in Syria, al-Sa'iqa,[10] under Syrian control and together with some regular Syrian units, began lending large-scale, open military support to the Christian militias. With the Syrian intervention the reversal of the military situation began and the possibility of a Christian military defeat was diminished.

On 10 April, a meeting of most of the traditional leaders came to the decision that Faranjiyya must be replaced as President six months prior to the due date. Section 372 of the constitution had been revised to that effect.

The now more active Syrian influence also resulted in the Parliament's election on 8 May of a new Syrian-backed President — Ilias Sarkis. Sarkis belonged to the Shihabi political grouping and was more acceptable to the Muslim communities than many of the other Maronite leaders. Faranjiyya ignored this decision, however, and continued to claim to be President until September.

Phase IV: the Syrian invasion: June–September 1976

The pretext for the Syrian invasion was the shelling and siege of two small Christian towns, Andakat and al-Qubaya, by units of al-Hatib's Lebanese Arab Army. The towns appealed to Syria for protection. It is clear, however, as will be explained in Chapter 2, that the invasion was motivated by a much more complex set of considerations.

The Syrian forces initially numbered some 6,000 men, but this soon swelled to 13,000, with about 400 tanks. These forces fought against PLO and National Front militias, and succeeded in taking control of the centre of Lebanon. In three columns, they pushed towards Beirut, Sidon and Tripoli, but encountered unexpectedly heavy resistance, primarily from Palestinian units.

The Maronite leadership welcomed the Syrian intervention, while Junblatt and Arafat turned to the Arab world, asking for its support against Syria. The Arabs acceded to their demands and applied pressure on Syria to halt its intervention, but without success.

In the meantime, the Kataib initiated the establishment of autonomous self-management for the emerging *de facto* Christian canton, centred on Junieh. Throughout June and July the Christian pressure on Tel-al-Za'atar continued, this time with the aid of Syrian artillery. On 8 July, Christian militias with Syrian backing also attacked other Palestinian strongholds near Tripoli. The Syrians meanwhile strengthened their hold in the Beqa.

Phase V: Arab response: The Ryadh and Cairo conferences

Arab responses to developments in Lebanon[11] were primarily dictated by their attitudes towards Syria. The internal actors in Lebanon were only a secondary consideration. The positions of Egypt and Saudi Arabia were the most important and relevant in respect to the Syrian involvement. The tension between Egypt and Syria — always in existence but relatively dormant — escalated following the signing of the Second Sinai agreement in 1975 on the withdrawal of Israeli forces from the western part of Sinai in exchange for various Egyptian political concessions. Hence, Egypt was determined to limit Syria's activity and influence. Saudi Arabia's concern was precisely the deepening

Egyptian–Syrian rift. The Saudis were sceptical about the Syrian role in Lebanon. On the one hand, they were not over-disturbed that Syrian attention should be diverted to Lebanon; on the other hand, they were not happy about increased Syrian influence, especially at a time when Syria was improving relations with Jordan.

Egypt hastened to help the PLO during the spring of 1976, by which time it was clear that the Palestinian organisation had succeeded in halting Syrian inroads into Lebanon. Indeed, two weeks after the invasion took place Arafat went to Cairo to meet President Sadat. Iraq had served warning on the Syrians in April when it stopped the flow of oil through the pipeline across Syria, and in the summer it joined Egypt in diplomatic efforts to halt the Syrian military advance, the main obective being to mobilise opposition to the Syrian intervention on the part of Saudi Arabia and the other oil-producing countries.

Under Arab pressure Syria agreed to a meeting of the Arab Foreign ministers on 9 June to deal with the situation in Lebanon. This ended with a call for a new cease-fire and the dispatch to Lebanon of an inter-Arab peace-keeping force, which was to operate under the auspices of the Arab League. After intensive negotiations with Syria, Faranjiyya and several Arab countries, a five-nation force was organised. Syria's agreement to the dispatch of the force was partly the result of Arab pressure, and partly in the hope that it would be able to crush PLO resistance before the force arrived. During July Syria also continued to improve its relations with Egypt, thus signalling its readiness to join — on certain conditions — the moderate bloc in the Arab world, and to distance itself from the extremist countries — Iraq, Libya and Algeria. The peace-keeping force included units from Libya, Sudan, Algeria, Saudi Arabia and Syria; Egypt preferred not to participate. The advance units began to arrive in Lebanon on 21 June.

By the late summer, it was apparent that Arab pressure, coupled with Syrian interest in reaching an understanding with the moderate Arab bloc, would eventually force Syria to halt its military activity in Lebanon. At the same time it was obvious that the ability of the Arab states to impose an immediate effective cease-fire was negligible. Syria therefore decided to use the time gap before reconciliation with the other Arab countries and launched a final military push. In September and October 1976, it was able to hit effectively at the PLO, and was thus in a better starting position for negotiations.

After much diplomatic haggling about the form and size of an Arab meeting to deal with the situation in Lebanon, it was finally agreed to hold a mini-summit which would prepare the ground for a general summit meeting. Convened in Riyadh in mid-October, the mini-summit was attended by the heads of state of Egypt, Saudi Arabia, Syria, Lebanon and Kuwait; the head of the PLO, Yasir 'Arafat, also took part. On 18 October, the meeting reached agreement to impose a cease-fire which was to be supervised by an Arab Deterrent Force (ADF). It was also agreed to enforce the Cairo agreement of 1969.

The Riyadh conference heralded the formation of a new *ad hoc* coalition comprising Egypt, Syria and Saudi Arabia. This coalition dominated the eighth summit conference convened in Cairo, which endorsed the Riyadh Protocol. (Iraq, Algeria and Libya rejected or ignored the Protocol.)

The Riyadh understanding and the Cairo summit conference legitimised Syria's continued military presence in Lebanon. Syrian units made up most of the ADF, and the only factor restraining the freedom of Syrian activity was an ADF supervisory committee which included representatives from other Arab countries.

The Syrian military operations put an end to the Civil War. By late 1976, after the Syrian entry into Beirut, relative calm descended on Lebanon. The tensions remained, but the ferocity of the violence subsided.

NOTES

1. On the emergence and structure of the Lebanese political system see, *inter alia*, Leonard Binder (ed.), *Politics in Lebanon*; Kamel Suleiman Salibi, *The Modern History of Lebanon*; Michael Hudson, *Conditions of Political Violence and Instability*; idem, *The Precarious Republic: Political Modernisation in Lebanon*; Leila Meo, *Lebanon Improbable Nation: A Study in Political Development*; Meir Zamir, *The Formation of Modern Lebanon*. Helena Cobban, *The Making of Modern Lebanon*.

2. See H. B. Sharabi, *Governments and Politics of the Middle East in the Twentieth Century*, p. 106.

3. There has already appeared a limited volume of literature on the Civil War. See, *inter alia*, Adeed Dawisha, *Syria and the Lebanese Crisis*; Itamar Rabinovich and Hanna Zamir, *War and Crisis in Lebanon 1975–1981* (in Hebrew); Itamar Rabinovich, *The War for*

Lebanon 1970–1983; David Gordon, *Lebanon: The Fragmented Nation*; Walid Khalidi, *Conflict and Violence in Lebanon: Confrontation in the Middle East*; David Gilmour, *Lebanon: The Fractured Country*; Roger Owen (ed.), *Essays on the Crisis in Lebanon*. Helena Cobban, *The Making of Modern Lebanon*.

4. Different views of the causes of the disintegration of Lebanon have been suggested. See fn. 3. Some emphasise internal developments while others point to external pressures. However, consideration of the various developments in the years leading up to the war in 1975, and since then, leads to the inescapable conclusion that the primary reasons lie in the breakdown of the consensus among the leading communities — Maronites (and other Christians), Sunni, Druze and Shi'i. External forces, including the PLO, only aggravated domestic processes.

5. On the ideological developments see, *inter alia*, Albert Hourani, *Arabic Thought in the Liberal Age*, Chapter XI; *idem*., 'Ideologies of the Mountain and the City: Reflections of the Lebanese Civil War' in his *The Emergence of the Modern Middle East*, Rabinovich, *The War for Lebanon*. Foremost in the intellectual movement emphasising 'Phoenician' and 'Mediterranean' variations were Michel Chiha and Charles Corm. However, as a practical statesman, Chiha also sought for co-operation with the Muslim communities. For an interesting first-hand account of this movement by an Israeli, see Elihu Eilat, 'The "Phoenician Zionism" in Lebanon' (in Hebrew), *Katedra*, No. 35, April 1985.

6. L. Z. Yamak, *The Syrian Social Nationalist Party, An Ideological Analysis*.

7. For a study of this party see J. Entelis, *Pluralism and Party Transformation in Lebanon; al-Kataib 1936–1970*.

8. The PFLP had been formed in December 1967 under the leadership of George Habbash.

9. For accounts of the various stages of the Civil War see, *inter alia*, Dawisha, *Syria and the Lebanese Crisis*, Gordon, *Lebanon, The Fragmented Nation*, Rabinovich, *The War for Lebanon,* Khalidi, *Conflict and Violence in Lebanon*.

10. Al-Sa'iqa was founded by the Government in Syria in April 1968 and has been under Syrian control ever since.

11. For an analysis of inter-Arab relations during this period, see, *inter alia*, Avraham Sella, *Achdut Betoch Perud* (in Hebrew).

Table 1.1: Composition of the Lebanese population 1865–1979

	1865[a]	1956[a]	1979[b] assuming 1932 percentages persist	1979[b] assuming changes in demographic trends since 1932
Maronites	171 800	424 000	650 000 (29%)	400 000–500 000
Druze	28 560	88 000	150 000 (6.3%)	180 000–200 000
Sunnis	7 611	286 000	470 000 (21%)	500 000–600 000
Shi'is	9 820	250 000	400 000 (18%)	500 000–600 000
Greek Orthodox	29 500	149 000	230 000 (10%)	150 000–200 000
Greek Catholics	19 370	91 000	150 000 (6.3%)	100 000–150 000
Armenian (Orthodox, Catholics)		79 000	150 000 (6.2%)	100 000–150 000
Protestants		14 000		
Jews		7 000		
Small minorities		23 000		

Sources:
  a) David Gordon, *Lebanon: The Fragmented Nation*, pp. 41–2. In addition there were in 1956 about 200,000–300,000 Palestinians.
  b) Arnon Sofer, 'Ochlusia Vekalkala BiLevanon' ('Population and Economy in Lebanon'), *Maarachot*, No. 7, July 1982.

2

Syria and Israel in Lebanon: Interests, Policies and Deterrence Dialogue

In 1976 Israel and Syria became involved in a complex process of redefining their respective political and strategic interests in Lebanon. This process led to Syrian intervention, but only in the light of a careful assessment of possible US and Israeli reactions, which included diplomatic contacts aimed at reducing American and Israeli apprehensions. Syria and Israel exchanged tacit indirect and direct signals and messages comprising both threats and indications of readiness to 'accept' certain military actions by the other side. On the whole, Syria was the more active, because of its deep political involvement in Lebanon. Israel was more inclined to react to situations, concentrating as it did on a posture of deterrence.

SYRIAN POLICY[1]

Relations between Syria and Lebanon have always been close and complex. The division between the two countries has traditionally been contested by the Syrians, as well as by powerful forces within Lebanon. The great debate inside Lebanon between Lebanese and pan-Arab orientations was partly reflected in the debate between those who saw Lebanon as part of Syria, and the 'Lebanon-first' Europe-oriented school of thought, most closely associated with the Maronites.

Amir Faisal, son of the Sherif Hussein of Mecca, who acted as the King of Damascus in 1918–1920, had demanded the inclusion of Lebanon within his kingdom. According to his definition, Syria's 'natural' borders incorporated what are today

Syria, Lebanon, Israel and Jordan. Lebanon was considered to be the north-western region of that large unit. The Christians in Lebanon opposed his plan and warmly welcomed the French as the mandatory power, and the subsequent creation of le Grand Liban (at the prompting of Maronite leaders).

When Syria and Lebanon attained independence, the debate about the nature of the relationship between them continued. Virtually all Syrian regimes have adhered to the view that an integral unity exists between the two countries.[2] In practice, however, they did not attempt to translate this view into reality. Indeed, 'Greater Syria' remained a Hashemite rather than a Syrian concept, although at times it has also been used by Syrian spokesmen.

The Ba'th regime which came to power in 1963 emphasised Pan-Arab ideology rather than the more limited concept of unity between Syria and Lebanon. Ironically, this approach somewhat reduced Syria's ideological claims regarding Lebanon. However, the Ba'th ideology sharpened some Syrian–Lebanese tensions. In the first place, it increased the division within Lebanon between the 'Arabist' and 'Lebanese' approaches. It also widened the gap between Syria's extreme etatist regime (with its socialist rhetoric and some socialist practice) and Lebanon's liberal, almost purely *laissez faire*, regime. The Syrian Ba'th regime quickly consolidated its political power and imposed severe and ruthless dictatorial control, whereas Lebanon's delicate political system allowed much freedom of expression and other liberties.

Apart from their ideological differences and Syria's traditional ambitions, the connections between the two countries have indeed broadened. Beirut served for many years as an important point of transit for Syrian trade. Lebanon is one of Syria's major trading partners, and many Syrians have found work in Lebanon (by the mid-1970s, an estimated 400,000 Syrians were working in Lebanon). The scope of these links forced the two countries to maintain close and non-conflictual relations. Syria also maintained contacts with many Lebanese political groups which shared all or some of its political objectives.

President Asad's pragmatism led Syria to adopt a cautious policy towards Lebanon. While Damascus would not have been averse to the imposition of total control, or even *de facto* annexation, of Lebanon, Syria faced other pressing problems in the mid-1970s, primarily the conflict with Israel and the unresolved problem of the Golan Heights. Thus, until 1975, it refrained from active open intervention in Lebanese affairs. Moreover, it was searching for new openings in its overall foreign policy, the most important being the hesitant beginnings of a diplomatic dialogue with the United States following the series of meetings between Kissinger and Asad in 1974 in which the Israeli–Syrian disengagement agreement was worked out. This important development did not contradict Syria's continued close relationship with the Soviet Union. It did, however, provide the potential for much more flexibility in Syrian foreign policy.

Until 1976 Syria generally lent its support in Lebanon to the PLO, and to Muslim and radical groups. However it maintained a subtle and flexible policy enabling the maintenance of connections with the Christians despite the deep differences between the Ba'th regime and the Christian community.

It should be stressed that Syrian policy is best viewed not through the prism of objectives and the means for their implementation, but as a continued effort to maintain optimal control over various sub-state and state actors in the environment. Such control should preferably be indirect, as direct control usually proves to be too costly. If effective indirect control is impossible, then direct control should be tried. In any case, the emergence of independent actors that threatened to limit Syrian flexibility was to be strongly opposed. The PLO was precisely such an actor.

Indeed, the main threat posed by the anti-*status quo* forces in Lebanon in the mid-1970s was Syria's potential loss of control of events there. The breakdown of the *status quo* threatened to bring the country to the verge of anarchy and, were these rebel forces to obtain effective control, there was the possibility that Lebanon would pursue policies prejudicial to Syrian interests. There was also the danger of catalytic behaviour by the PLO and related groups that might have dragged Israel and Syria into a direct military confrontation, while Israel enjoyed a clear-cut 'strategic superiority'. The Syrian leadership knew only too well how such catalytic strategies could be employed in the Middle East. Syria had pursued a similar strategy itself in the period 1964–7 and had eventually 'succeeded' in involving Israel and Egypt in a war that neither side sought at that time. The Syrian leadership seems to have learnt from these experiences that the way to forestall such developments is to eliminate capabilities for potential independent catalytic action. If Syria was to go to war, it would be only when it considered it opportune.

A Lebanon controlled by the PLO and its associates threatened other grave consequences for the Syrians. For example, in order to diminish its dependence on Syria, the PLO might decide to depend more heavily on other, even rival, Arab states, such as Iraq or Egypt. In that context, it should be added that Iraqi activity in Lebanon, both within and outside the PLO, increased considerably during the 1970s. Pro-Iraqi factions within the PLO achieved control over parts of some Palestinian refugee camps. Similarly, Iranian activity among the Lebanese Shi'is also threatened to diminish Syrian influence.

Consequently, in the mid-1970s the Syrian regime pursued a convoluted course regarding Lebanon. On the one hand, Syria supported the PLO and other Muslim radical elements in Lebanon which were considered useful as troublemakers against Israel and were also perceived as increasing Syrian influence over events in Lebanon. On the other hand, it seems that Syria would have preferred the political system to remain intact and controllable. Thus, Damascus sought to end the Civil War in order to preserve the *status quo*, albeit in a modified form.

There is another dimension to the Syrian regime's approach to Lebanon. Officers belonging to different minorities, and most prominently to the Alawite community, have always played a central role in Syria's armed forces and an increasingly important role in the Ba'th Party. Following the military *coup* of February 1966, Saleh Jedid and Hafiz al-Asad, both Alawites, became the two dominant political figures in Syria. Extensive efforts have been invested in securing influential positions in the armed forces for Alawites and members of other minorities. The upshot of a series of *coups*, attempted *coups* and purges, is that the Alawites have increased their power relative to the other minorities and to the Sunni majority.[3] This disproportionate representation of Alawites within the high ranks of the officer corps and in the security services has bolstered the regime's confidence, while prompting Sunni resentment.

In order to pre-empt active Sunni opposition, the regime has maintained a posture of Pan-Arabism. While this ideology seems to have considerable popular appeal, the regime continues to rely on the minorities for the main body of its support. This ambivalence *vis-à-vis* its constituency seems to have developed the regime's sensitivities towards other minorities both in Syria and in neighbouring countries.[4] The attitude of Damascus towards the Maronites is a case in point. One notable illustration of that relationship on the family level has been the connection between the Faranjiyya and Asad families which began long before the outbreak of the Civil War. The Asad regime has also been sensitive to the attitudes of the Christians who comprise about 14 per cent of Syria's population.[5]

The ambivalence which also characterised Syria's attitude and actual policies towards Lebanon in general, and during the Civil War in particular, has led to the emergence of two interpretations among observers of Syrian behaviour in Lebanon. One school emphasises Syria's traditional ambitions towards Lebanon and argues that Syria perceived the Civil War as a major opportunity to increase its influence over Lebanon. To that end it assisted certain Lebanese groups in order ultimately to bring about the country's disintegration and annexation. The other school argues that Syria's most important objective in Lebanon was to maintain unity and stability; the Civil War threatened dangerous changes in the *status quo* which could adversely affect Syrian interests.

Syrian decision-making

Very little is known about the inner workings of the Asad regime. Similarly, it is difficult to probe the process of decision-making in foreign policy. Dawisha[6] has suggested that between May 1975 and January 1976 decisions were taken by an *ad hoc* committee comprising Asad, the President, Abdul Halim Khaddam, Deputy Prime Minister and Minister of Foreign Affairs, Major-General Naji Jamil, Deputy Defence Minister and Chief of the Air Force, and Major-General Hikmat Shihabi, Chief of Staff of the Armed Forces. The first two were also the foremost members of the Ba'th Party. Jamil also held an important position in the party and Shihabi was a party member.

From January 1976 this *ad hoc* committee was expanded into a nine-member forum. In addition to the original four members, it included Mahmoud al-Ayyoubi, Prime Minister until 1 August 1976, Abdulla al-Amhar, Assistant Secretary-General of the Regional Command of the Ba'th Party, Muhammad Jaber Bajbouj, Assistant Secretary-General of the Regional Command of the Ba'th Party, Colonel Muhammed al-Kholi, Chief of

Security in the Air Force, and Zuhair Mohsen, the Palestinian leader of al-Saiqa. Most of the new members also held important positions in the Ba'th party.

Although these bodies were apparently deeply involved in the process of consultations, nevertheless it seems we can assume that Asad was the ultimate decision-maker. At the same time, different and contradictory considerations confirming the intervention had probably been weighed up by the Syrian leadership at the time. One probable consideration was to use the situation in Lebanon as a vehicle for the implementation of the traditional objective of Syrian–Lebanese unity. Another consideration was probably that the costs of intervention were high and could involve Syria in a costly and unwinnable situation. Syrian hesitation suggests that the second view was widely held. The eventual decision to intervene was reached only when the costs of non-intervention seemed clearly to outweigh the costs of intervention.[7] Yet when the intervention took place, it also served some of Syria's traditional ambitions in regard to Lebanon.

One must be careful not to identify the two interpretations of the Syrian intervention with attitudes regarding the Palestinian issue. Intervention in Lebanon could in principle have served either side in the Civil War. Initially, in 1975, the Syrians extended cautious aid to the PLO. Then, in 1976 the Syrian intervention was more favourable to the interests of the Maronites. Yet the Syrians were careful all along to maintain some balance between the different communities. Thus when they later again aided the PLO and its allies, they refused to become party to a basic change in the Lebanese political system. In retrospect, it appears that had it not been for the growing opposition of parts of the Maronite community from 1978, the Syrians would have continued a policy of co-operation with that community. Indeed, even during their co-operation with the Muslim–Palestinian alliance, they persisted in attempts to gain control over the PLO and to this end planned to remove Arafat from his position as PLO leader. Syria's relations with the PLO remained tense, and its behaviour during and after the 1982 War, as set out in Chapters 4 and 5, served as a clear notice of its indifference to the Palestinian plight, and of its dual perception of the PLO as an instrument, when under Syrian control, or as a threat, when acting independently. Indeed, possibly the least accurate interpretation of Syria's actions is that propagated by the regime's spokesmen, attributing its policy to an altruistic desire to help the Palestinians in Lebanon in their hour of need.

ISRAELI INTERESTS AND STRATEGY

The Israeli position on Lebanon has always been dictated by the dynamics of the Arab–Israeli conflict and by the role played by Lebanon in that conflict. The Arab–Israeli conflict has been viewed almost exclusively through the strategic-military prism, and by and large this has also been true of the Israeli–Lebanese relationship. However, rudiments of the policy towards Lebanon have marked it as a rather special case. The basis of these particular aspects of Lebanon policy relates to the ambiguous political and cultural identity of Lebanon.

The existence of a Maronite community claiming to have a separate identity was recognised by the Zionist leadership even before the establishment of the State of Israel, and indeed, at that time, contacts were established between the Political Department of the Jewish Agency and some Maronite political personalities. It should be emphasised, however, that for both sides these contacts were of only minor importance. The Maronite community, a strong non-Muslim, non-Arab semi-national entity, which it was assumed would sympathise with Zionist aspirations, was considered as a useful regional link. Indeed, in the late 1930s, Emil Eddé, the then President of Lebanon (under the French Mandate), indicated his sympathy for Zionism. However, many Maronites did identify themselves as Arabs and were in any case suspicious of Zionism and later of Israel.

Apart from a pragmatic interest in cultivating relations with any group or entity in the Middle East, the Israeli approach to the Maronites had some stronger intellectual and emotional undertones. These sprang from notions of a renaissance of the relations in the ancient world between the Phoenicians and the Hebrews, represented in modern times by the Lebanese and Israelis. There has long been a tradition associated with Zionist thought in which ideas have been advanced of a non- or post-Jewish 'Hebrew' nationalism, directly connected with the ancient Hebrews. Judaism, according to this school of thought, was created at a later stage.[8] The ancient Phoenicians were themselves close relatives of, if not identical with, the ancient Hebrew civilisation. It is interesting that, while these ideas reverberated

25

among small intellectual groups only, they apparently also formed part of Ben-Gurion's political and conceptual outlook.[9] The political translation of these ideas has been the notion of an Israeli–Maronite alliance. Thus Ben-Gurion notes in his diary:[10]

> The weakest link in the Arab coalition is Lebanon. The Muslim rule there is superficial and could be easily shattered. It is necessary to establish a Christian state there whose southern border would be the Litani. We shall then have an alliance with her.

From the point of view of the history of political ideas in Israel, three notions were involved in Ben-Gurion's formulation: the 'Hebrew' approach described earlier; the notion of an alliance in the Middle East of non-Muslim, non-Arab political entities (which in a different form could be described as an 'alliance of minorities'); and an activist approach, seeking to change the political and possibly even the territorial structure of the Middle East.

A heavy caveat must of course be added. Ben-Gurion, while perhaps fascinated by all these ideas, conducted foreign policy in a cautious and cynical manner. Notwithstanding his own numerous references to grand designs and forward strategies, he refrained from translating them into actual policy. His immense pragmatism was evident in the case of Lebanon also, and was given strong expression in the mid-1950s at a time when proposals for a new Lebanese policy were receiving government attention.

Ben-Gurion resigned from the premiership in late 1953. Once clear of the leadership, he felt free to suggest plans whose implementation would not be his responsibility. In early 1954 Syria was in turmoil following the downfall of its ruler Adib Shishakli and signs of approaching Iraqi intervention. Ben-Gurion prompted the then Israeli Prime Minister Moshe Sharet to utilise the unstable situation and to encourage the Maronites to partition Lebanon and to proclaim a Christian, non-Arab state.[11] Sharet rejected the idea. In a letter to Ben-Gurion he pointed out that the Lebanese Christians were not united and did not constitute a majority; that in any case most of the Maronites accepted the idea of a Christian–Muslim partnership as the lesser evil; and that they agreed to Lebanon joining the Arab League, assuming that, in this way, the Muslims would relinquish their aspirations to reunite with Syria. Sharet added that he did not exclude the possibility that Lebanon would one day be partitioned, but that partition would only result, if at all, from a major wave of instability in the Middle East. Israel, he urged, should certainly not attempt to initiate the partition. Finally, Sharet argued that he would favour Israel assisting Maronite separatist activities, but only if these activities were initiated and undertaken by the Maronites themselves. The initiative and direct responsibility should not rest with Israel.[12]

An even more ambitious plan was proposed in 1955 by the then Chief of Staff, General Dayan.[13] He envisaged a Maronite officer launching a *coup* and calling upon Israel to intervene militarily. Israel would move in, annex the territory up to the Litani, and create an alliance with the new Lebanon. The idea was rejected by Sharet and the Cabinet.

Ben-Gurion returned to his grand designs during the preparations for the British–French 1956 Suez strike and 'Operation Kadesh' (the Israeli attack on Egypt). During the Sèvres Conference, when plans for the operation were discussed with French and British officials, he set out some of his ideas about the future structure of the Middle East. Among other things, he suggested that Lebanon should relinquish some of its Muslim regions and become a Christian state.[14]

The ideas of an 'alliance of minorities' and of 'Hebrewism' were not shared by the majority of Israeli leaders, but the special identity of Lebanon and its relevance for the broader nature of Arab–Israeli relations has been more widely recognised. Some perceptive leaders saw in Lebanon the living demonstration of a formula which could also apply to Israel's role in the Middle East. The very character of Lebanon denies exclusivist Pan-Arab notions. An independent Lebanon whose affinity to Arab culture and nationalism is ambiguous was therefore a demonstration of the inapplicability of Pan-Arab exclusivism.

Despite the currency of all these ideas, little was executed, even by Ben-Gurion, on an operational level. The view argued by Sharet as Foreign Minister, and later as Prime Minister, prevailed. According to the Foreign Ministry evaluation of the situation in the mid-1950s, Lebanon was coalescing into one nation of Christians and Muslims, and was becoming a more integral part of the Arab world. At the same time it was argued that contacts in Lebanon should be sought and cultivated whenever possible. Indeed, low-level clandestine contacts have been maintained with the Maronites since the 1950s.

This restrained policy was manifested in 1958. The Civil War in Lebanon led to renewed contacts between Israel and various Christian groups in the country. Some arms were delivered to Christian villages in southern Lebanon and to Christian militias in the Beirut area. However, the extent of this assistance was limited and of little consequence.[15]

The strategic-military dimension 1969–75

The grandiose conceptions of an Israeli–Maronite alliance were ultimately not decisive in the formation of Israeli policy towards Lebanon; of prime importance rather were the logic and dynamics of the general Arab–Israeli conflict.

The Arab–Israeli conflict has also been viewed in Israel largely through the strategic-military prism. This comprises two levels: first, 'basic security', that is, deterrence and defence in the case of a full-scale war, and secondly, 'current' security, that is, deterrence and defence against limited terrorist attacks. On the first level, the Israeli interest was that Lebanon should not become part of a war coalition against Israel, nor serve as a base for the forces of another Arab country involved in a war against Israel. On the second level, the Israeli interest was that terrorist attacks against Israeli targets should not be carried out from Lebanese soil.

Until 1967 Lebanon itself was considered of little military significance. Its military capability was weak and its political system complex and potentially unstable. Indeed, the Israeli–Lebanese border was completely quiet between 1949 and 1967. After the 1967 war, the Palestinian organisations, primarily Fath, began establishing themselves in Lebanon.

However, for a year following the war, there was no terrorist action across the border.[16] On 17 May 1968, mortar shells fell on Manara, an Israeli kibbutz. Another period of calm was followed by some small-scale activity in late October. In the meantime, the Palestinian organisations increased their activity in Lebanon. When an Israeli El-Al passenger plane was attacked in Athens, Israel — acting on the assumption that the attack was engineered by the PLO in Lebanon — retaliated heavily by attacking Beirut airport, destroying 14 Lebanese civilian carriers. A few days later, Katyusha rockets were fired on Kiryat

Shmoneh for the first time. Calm returned to the border until the spring of 1969, when shooting was resumed. The Palestinian fighters were concentrated in the south-eastern part of Lebanon, an area sparsely populated and with geographical features convenient for small-scale operations. It is hilly, thick with shrubs and heavily wooded. On 30 July 1969 the Israeli air force was used for the first time in a strike at targets in south Lebanon — a practice later used extensively.

In the period 1967–70, Israel was forced to contend with threats and security problems much graver than those facing it from Lebanon. There was continued small-scale fighting along the Jordan river, and from March 1969, the War of Attrition raged along the Suez Canal. In comparison to these two fronts, the northern border was considered calm. This situation changed only in late 1970. The War of Attrition was terminated, and following the Civil War in Jordan the border with that country was also quietened. Events along the northern border became relatively much more visible. Moreover, as a consequence of the defeat of the PLO in Jordan in 1970, the headquarters of the Palestinian organisations moved to Beirut. Since then, arms and explosives have been stored in Lebanon, military instruction and planning conducted there, and terrorist activity originating from Lebanon has increased. Admittedly, Iraq and Libya, and to a lesser extent Algeria and South Yemen, have also served as centres of Palestinian activity. However, Lebanon was the main one.

Palestinian operations against Israel from Lebanon took three different forms. One was strikes against Israeli targets abroad. The second and most irritating was the infiltration of small terrorist teams from south Lebanon into northern Israel. In some cases the penetrations were conducted from the sea: terrorist teams would leave bases in Lebanon and land on Israeli shores. The third was shooting and shelling across the border.

Israeli retaliation followed quickly, and took several forms: artillery shelling of Palestinian bases, penetration of Israeli ground units into south Lebanon to strike directly at terrorist bases, and air strikes. One of the more outstanding actions was the spectacular commando raid on Beirut international airport in 1968. Another commando action was conducted in 1973 when PLO headquarters were attacked.

The developing situation led to the emergence of one vital security interest for Israel — the neutralisation of south Lebanon and its conversion to a buffer zone. Israeli concern was to deny the PLO access to Israeli settlements in the border area. This interest lay within the framework of 'current security'.

Of similar importance was the Israeli interest in denying the presence in south Lebanon of the regular army of a hostile Arab state. This was considered as a threat to 'basic' security. The obvious possibility was that of a Syrian military deployment. South Lebanon could be used as a springboard for a Syrian attack against Israel or for launching a variant of a stationary war of attrition.

Following 1967, and even more after 1973, an additional strategic consideration emerged concerning south Lebanon, namely, to keep it open for a possible Israeli offensive designed to outflank heavy Syrian deployment in the Golan. An Israeli advance could move through south Lebanon into the Beqa, and proceed from there in an outflanking sweep towards Damascus and even central Syria.

The 1975 Civil War

The Rabin Government, which came to power in mid-1974, focused its attention on two main contexts: Israeli–US relations and further attempts at Israeli–Egyptian accommodation. When the Civil War broke out Israel was in the midst of the painful breakdown in March–April 1975 of the negotiation of the Sinai II agreement with Egypt. American 'reassessment' at this time clouded relations with Washington. Moreover, uncertainty about future Egyptian moves gave cause for deep concern. Thus, Israel had to concentrate all its foreign and defence policy efforts on these two crucial areas. Against this background, the Syrian and Jordanian contexts were considered to be of lesser importance, and Lebanon occupied an even lower ranking in the list of Israeli priorities.[17] As we shall see, the American and Egyptian issues remained central in Israeli calculations throughout 1975–6, and in some ways remained so up to the 1982 War. The American 'connection' has usually acted as the main direct constraint on Israeli decision-makers. Egyptian–Israeli interactions have also acted as a constraint, but in a tacit and indirect way.

Furthermore, the Civil War increasingly diverted PLO attention from the border with Israel to the Beirut area. Thus, until September 1975, when Sinai II was signed, Israeli interest in and concern about developments in Lebanon was limited and relatively marginal.

With the signing of Sinai II, the Israeli political and strategic position improved considerably. Relations with the United States regained their previous warmth and closeness (although there persisted some elements of unease); Egypt appeared to be moving closer to a 'political' rather than a 'military' approach to the conflict; and last but not least, the division within the Arab World was deepened. Syria came out strongly against the Sinai agreement and hastened to consolidate its newly emerging association with Jordan. At the same time, its relations with Iraq deteriorated.

In this context, the heavy fighting in Lebanon and the signs of Syrian interference led to increased Israeli attention to developments there. Of particular importance was the emerging Syrian intervention, and Israel's reactions to developments in Lebanon must be seen in the light of its perceptions of Syrian attitudes and behaviour.

Syria has always been viewed as the most hostile and radical of Israel's Arab neighbours. Indeed, following its vehement rejection of Sinai II, Syria was perceived as intent on forming an aggressive military alliance against Israel. Furthermore, Syrian intentions in Lebanon aroused deep suspicion. It was seen as the patron of the Palestinian organisations and the radical groups, and as scheming to bring Lebanon under its influence and possibly also under its control.

The deteriorating situation in Lebanon, and the threat of Syrian military intervention, presented Israel with a complex political and military challenge. A special forum was created in order to deal with the Lebanon issue. This enabled the top decision-makers to conduct a relatively systematic and rational analysis of events and to seek appropriate solutions. The participants in these consultations included Prime Minister Rabin, Foreign Minister Allon, Defence Minister Peres, Minister without Portfolio Galili, Chief of Staff Gur, and several officials. Among the latter the head of the *Mossad* (the main Israeli intelligence service) and the head of the Military Intelligence Service (AMAN) were regular participants. In addition, there were one or two officials from the Defence and Foreign Ministries.

The Israeli policy and decision-making process in regard to

Lebanon during this period, and throughout 1976, can be characterised in the following ways:

(i) Politico-strategic priorities were clearly defined. The Israeli–US and Israeli–Egyptian contexts were seen as most important and as dictating behaviour in other less critical areas.

(ii) There was an attempt to identify direct security threats that might emanate from Lebanon and appropriate remedies were investigated.

(iii) The policy and strategies adopted were primarily 'reactive'. Israel reacted to developments initiated by domestic groups inside Lebanon and by Syria. It refrained from undertaking major initiatives, primarily because the area was not deemed to be of critical importance, and also because it might have involved an undesired military confrontation.

(iv) The main strategy adopted was that of deterrence (to be more fully analysed later in this chapter and in Chapter 6). Within this context, Israel anticipated possible future strategic developments and sought to deter or contain them.

(v) The deterrence strategy was heavily affected by the broader political context.

(vi) Although its policy was largely 'reactive', Israel was ready to respond positively to overtures from domestic groups within Lebanon and to undertake limited initiatives of a more activist nature. However, these initiatives were of relatively minor significance and would have incurred only small costs had they failed.

(vii) The process of decision-making was rational and cautious, and was conducted in an effective and successful way. It lacked, however, assessments of the long-range consequences of current policies and strategies.

(viii) The 'reactive' approach formed the context within which the deterrent strategy was applied.

An additional characteristic of the decision-making process was the relatively high degree of unanimity among the main decision-makers. All the top decision-makers were agreed on Israel's priorities and on the need to avoid the dangers of military escalation on secondary security issues. Also, the US and Egyptian contexts were seen to be of great importance. There were, however, some differences among them both in terms of their assessments of long-range developments and the desirable level of intensity of Israeli involvement in Lebanese events.

Rabin was careful to avoid deeper commitments to groups within Lebanon. Allon occupied a unique position in that he attempted to assess long-term implications of the growing Israeli involvement in Lebanon and was ready to propose deeper political involvement. He had always argued that Israel should cultivate relations with ethnic and religious minorities in the Middle East, and now emphasised the possibilities arising from contacts with the Maronites. However, at the same time, he also insisted that Israel should not rely solely on the Christian connection in its activity in Lebanon. Taking the long-term view, Israel had to establish contacts with the Shi'is, whom he considered of vital potential importance within the Lebanese context. Moreover, he noted that the Maronites' political options were limited and that they had an interest in maintaining relations with Syria as well.

On the question of the deterrence of Syrian activity, the top decision-makers were again unanimous. There was, however, one interesting difference between them and the Chief of Staff. Rabin, Peres and Allon were readier to delineate Israel's deterrence thresholds and to make deterrence less ambiguous and consequently more binding on Israel. Gur, on the other hand, suggested a more flexible posture that would not commit Israel to any threshold. Yet, all the decision-makers tended to see deterrence more as a vehicle for lowering the threat of escalation rather than as an instrument for increasing its probability. For example, Allon, while seeking an increased role for Israel in Lebanese internal developments continued to stress the imprudence of the use of military force for such purposes.

Finally, in 1976 the group of decision-makers underwent a process of 'learning' concerning Syrian interests and behaviour. In particular, they were also to take account of changed Syrian policy vis-à-vis the Maronites and the US in early 1976. Their assessments of Syrian policy became increasingly more subtle in the course of time. This experience served as a useful background for handling Syrian intervention in 1976 and the Nabatiyya affair to be described in Chapter 3.

SYRIAN DIPLOMATIC AND MILITARY INTERVENTION AND ISRAELI REACTION

Between the outbreak of the Civil War and January 1976, Syrian concern about developments in Lebanon continued to increase. Although they transferred arms to the Muslim–PLO coalition, they nevertheless sought to prevent the deteriorating situation from destroying the political *status quo*. To this end they applied various means.

The Syrian modes of intervention and influence fell into five categories: (i) diplomatic intervention and pressure; (ii) the supply of arms or the threat to withdraw such supplies; (iii) threats, explicit or tacit, of military intervention; (iv) actual intervention with non-regular units under Syrian command; and (v) intervention with regular Syrian forces.

Apart from the Syrian regular forces, there were two military formations at the disposal of Damascus: the Palestine Liberation Army (PLA), part of which was deployed in Syria (other units outside its borders were not under Syrian control), and the al-Saiqa, which, while under the command of a Palestinian, was completely under Syrian control.

Syria's first act of diplomatic intervention immediately followed the formation of a military government in Beirut on 23 May 1975. Khaddam and Jamil went to Beirut and persuaded President Faranjiyya to ask Karami to form another government.[18] This action indicated Syrian opposition to strong steps by the forces supporting the *status quo* to destroy the opposition.

As the situation deteriorated during May and June, Syria decided to increase its mediation efforts. On 28 June, Asad with his Lebanon committee (Khaddam, Jamil and Shihabi), decided to send Khaddam again to Beirut. Khaddam was instrumental in the formation of a new coalition government with the participation of both Rashid Karami and Camille Chamoun, which succeeded in restoring a measure of calm to Lebanon. Syria's short-term objective was met and the process of disintegration halted.

On 28 August fighting again broke out around Zahle, and in September spread to Tripoli. Syria launched a mediation initiative aimed at stabilising the situation. The Syrians decided to intervene militarily also in order to back their diplomatic efforts. Direct military intervention appeared out of the question because of the significant external constraints. Hence, the intervention was limited to the use of Syrian-commanded PLA units, and interestingly it was confined to the Tripoli area. Tripoli was considered of special interest to Syria because of its proximity to Latakiya — the Alawite region in northern Syria; in addition, it was the area most distant from Israel. The use of units that could not be described as being Syrian or Syrian-controlled, and the distance from Israel, made an Israeli reaction less likely. In any case, the PLA units were withdrawn shortly afterwards.

The fighting which began in Zahle and Tripoli soon spread to Beirut. Syria's mediation efforts intensified with the despatch of Khaddam and Shihabi to Beirut. After seven days of intensive negotiations they succeeded in bringing about the formation of the Committee for National Dialogue with the participation of both Junblatt and Pierre Jumayyil. The committee tried in vain to effect a successful dialogue between the two sides.[19]

September also witnessed a major change in Syria's perception of the Arab–Israeli context with the signing of the Sinai II agreement, providing for the further withdrawal of Israeli forces from part of the Sinai. This was another step in the process of Israeli–Egyptian *rapprochement* which eventually reached fruition with Sadat's visit to Jerusalem. Syria viewed the agreement with the utmost concern and its leadership rightly suspected that Egypt was now ready to move independently to an accommodation with Israel and to neglect its commitments to other Arab states, primarily Syria. The agreement also heightened Syrian anxieties that Israel, feeling more confident in the south, might flex its muscles on the front to the north and northeast.

These Syrian perceptions dictated an even more active policy in Lebanon to pre-empt developments there which might be utilised by Israel, such as the disintegration of Lebanon and the further strengthening of the radical and independent (of Syria) Palestinian and Muslim forces. Simultaneously, Syria, feeling more isolated within the Arab world because of Egypt's independent move, was seeking to mobilise more support in its conflict with Israel. The PLO in Lebanon was therefore a natural ally. The Syrian despatch of PLA units to Tripoli thus corresponded with developments in the regional context. However, it seems that Syria persisted in its refusal to back a breakdown of the *status quo* in Lebanon.

From the beginning of the Civil War, Israeli sympathies naturally lay with the Maronites. However, they did not lead to an Israeli initiative in their defence. Indeed, Israeli sensitivity to developments in Lebanon increased only following the first sign of Syrian military involvement. It should be added that the Israelis were rather sceptical of the Maronite military capability. Already in 1975, Israeli decision-makers reached the conclusion that if all the forces opposed to the *status quo* were to unite, they would be able to defeat the Maronites.[20]

In reaction to the penetration of PLA units into the Tripoli area in September, Yigal Allon, the then Foreign Minister, stated, 'We do not have to intervene in what is happening inside Lebanon as long as the conflict is confined to the Lebanese people themselves'.[21] This cautious and somewhat oblique reference was followed by a more explicit statement. In late October he addressed the point more squarely:[22]

As long as the quarrels in Lebanon are confined to the Lebanese community, I don't think that Israel can or should do anything. But her defense interests along the northern border may be touched if another, a foreign army intervenes — such as the Syrians. In such a case, Israel should preserve her moral right and her military might to protect her security interests in the border zone.

Chief of Staff Mordechai Gur pointed out several weeks later that a Syrian movement into *south* Lebanon would constitute the opening of another hostile front against Israel.[23] Prime Minister Rabin also referred to the possibility of Syrian intervention, stating that,[24]

Israel has an interest in the existence of Lebanon in its present political form. Any attempt to take over Lebanon will constitute a situation which adversely affects our security. It is not impossible to assume that Syria might try to utilize the situation in Lebanon for her own purposes.

As to the likely Israeli reaction he stated on another occasion: 'Israel cannot remain indifferent in the event of foreign intervention. What it will do and whether it will do anything is not a subject for *a priori* threats or talk'.[25] The Defence Minister Shimon Peres was also reported to have stated that, in the event of a Syrian invasion into Lebanon, Israel would undertake all steps necessary to ensure that it would not be hurt.[26] Gur returned to the issue when he pointed out that the introduction of an Arab army, and 'especially a Syrian one', into southern Lebanon would have paramount military significance, and that to such a situation Israel will have to find the 'appropriate' response. He went on to draw a distinction between the implications of Syrian intervention on the one hand and a multi-Arab force on the other. The first possibility was considered to be much more serious.[27]

These statements contain tentative suggestions of some of the main themes of Israel's policy. First, they reflect Israeli caution about domestic developments inside Lebanon. Israeli leaders recognised that their ability to affect the domestic situation there was very limited. Secondly, there was no inclination to adopt a more 'activist' policy. This particular tenet of Israeli policy was to evolve later and to undergo major modifications. Third, a 'military' intervention in Lebanon's domestic developments was completely ruled out. Fourth, Syrian behaviour was viewed with great suspicion. Fifth, it was emphasised that Israel's main security interest was in south Lebanon. At the same time, general Syrian intervention in other parts of Lebanon was considered to affect Israeli interests adversely. Finally, the possibility of an Israeli military intervention were Syria to intervene was hinted at, but in an oblique and ambiguous way; in this too the Israeli posture was to undergo modifications.

The PLA intervention in Tripoli, Israel's threatening signals from September to December, and the generally increased tension between Israel and Syria during that period, led to active American efforts to defuse the situation. The US sent messages to Israel and Syria warning both against direct military intervention in Lebanon. These warnings, as much as the Syrian and Israeli cost/benefit calculations, led to their respective decisions not to intervene militarily at that time. The same period also witnessed the beginnings of Syrian–American contacts concerning the situation in Lebanon, the fruits of which became manifest only a few months later.

From October to the end of December 1975 the fighting in Lebanon escalated and no breakthrough was achieved in the various negotiations for a political solution. The Syrian mediation efforts continued, and in early October Rashid Karami went to Damascus to discuss the situation. Contacts between the Maronites and the Syrians also continued. Syria decided to exert military pressure again through the limited use of Palestinian forces from the Syrian-controlled a-Saiqa organisation. By late

October, units of that organisation were deployed in Beirut.

As part of Syria's mediation efforts, President Asad met in Damascus with Karami and 'Arafat, and in December with Pierre Jumayyil. At these meetings he carefully sought reforms in the Lebanese political system which would nevertheless maintain the fundamentals of the *status quo*. He pledged to Jumayyil his opposition to any change in the constitutional system.[28] This demonstrated once again Syria's close relations with the Maronite groups, despite its simultaneous interest in cultivating relations with the PLO. At the same time, concerned with Christian threats to partition Lebanon, Khaddam warned that Syria would intervene militarily to prevent partition.

This warning immediately heightened Israeli concern. Nevertheless, in its response Israel had to take account of two major constraints on its use of force: concern about American reaction at a time when Israeli–American relations were improving following the tensions of the previous year; and — of equal importance — the appreciation that Israeli military action might orient Egypt towards a renewal of military activity. The Israeli Government was committed to moves conducive to a political understanding with Egypt. A major escalation in Lebanon might interfere with these efforts.

Moreover, Israeli interests in Lebanon, with the exception of current security interests related to south Lebanon, were as yet ambiguous. Even the *current* security concerns were seen as essentially secondary to the US and Egyptian contexts. Finally, the Israeli Government was not at all keen on a major military engagement only two years after the costly 1973 War.

Apart from all these calculations was the *basic* security interest relating to suspected Syrian intentions to convert Lebanon into another 'confrontation' state. However, concern with this interest was qualified. Israeli decision-makers were convinced that the military balance with Syria, or even with Syria and Jordan, favoured Israel, and that the role of Lebanon itself was insignificant. Only the presence of Syrian forces in south Lebanon would be of military significance. This assessment was generally accepted by all Israeli decision-makers.

In this respect it is interesting to note that the four top decision-makers not only had wide strategic and military experience,[29] but also tended to approach the problem in a rational and pragmatic manner. They were not impressed by tendentious arguments about imminent threats from the north and north-east. Moreover, Chief of Staff Gur was also opposed to undue military entanglement in Lebanon.

It seems, however, that Israel was guided by the view that a *major* Syrian incursion into Lebanon would have compelled the employment of Israeli forces in south Lebanon. In order to prevent the development of such a situation, Israel articulated its deterrence posture in a more elaborate way. On 9 January 1976, in an apparent response to Khaddam's warning, Peres stated that Israel could not remain indifferent to Syrian intervention.[30] Rabin stressed that the intervention of a foreign force would constitute a threat to Israel's security and 'we cannot accept that'.[31]

In addition to verbal messages, Israel also adopted two other sets of deterrence signals. First, and in what was to become a critical channel of communication, it delivered a message to Syria via Washington,[32] in which it voiced its 'concern' about possible Syrian intervention. The second set of signals was by means of military moves 'in the field'. Thus, *Ma'ariv* reported that 'a strong vigilance can be felt among IDF forces along the border'. These two channels of communication became standard procedures, used simultaneously with public announcements by Israeli decision-makers.

In the first half of January, the Christian militias went on to the offensive in Beirut and attacked several Palestinian strongholds. In reaction, the PLO reinforced its forces by moving most of its units from southern Lebanon to the Beirut area, and reversed the initial Christian successes. These developments threatened Syria's diplomatic efforts, and it decided to back its diplomacy with a show of force. It is significant that this was done apparently after a careful assessment of possible American and Israeli reactions. As Asad put it:[33]

We discussed the possibility of war, and found out that there was such a possibility but not by necessity, for reasons that I do not wish to elaborate in detail . . . All the same, the war remained a possibility but it also remained possible that war would not break out. So we decided to enter and rescue the resistance.

This carefully oblique reference suggests that Asad assumed that if the show of force were to be limited and not conducted by regular Syrian forces, it would not provoke an Israeli military response — an assumption probably based on an analysis of Israeli deterrent threats and the American posture. He might have interpreted the Israeli deterrent threats as referring only to the use of Syrian regular forces. He also possibly received American signals from which he could have inferred that a limited show of force would be 'acceptable'.

In justifying the use of force, Asad referred to the plight of the 'resistance', meaning the PLO–Muslim opposition. In fact, however, when the Syrian decision was taken, the PLO had already succeeded in reversing the defeats of early January. It appears, therefore, that the Syrian regime was concerned with the generally deteriorating situation rather than the state of one party to the conflict. On 18 January 1976, PLA units under Syrian command entered Lebanon. Soon afterwards, Syria presented its proposal for constitutional reform, which was accepted by the Maronite leaders.

The PLA intervention heightened Israeli concern. It was assumed that this was the prelude to direct Syrian intervention — an impression which was strengthened for a short while by an unconfirmed report of the participation of regular Syrian units. By late January the situation had been somewhat clarified. First, it became evident that the size of the force was limited (only about 1,200 men), and that no Syrian regulars were among them. Secondly, the PLA units took no action. In addition, Kissinger issued a strong statement against any foreign intervention — a warning probably directed at both Israel and Syria.[34] Finally, the Lebanese internal situation appeared to be improving with the Maronite acceptance of the Syrian proposals for constitutional reform.

Israel's reaction to the introduction of the PLA units was to adopt a cautious deterrence approach. It repeatedly emphasised that it did not intend intervening in Lebanese internal affairs. In addition, it somewhat reduced the ambiguity of its deterrence posture. A distinction was drawn between the introduction of regular Syrian units and those of the PLA (even though they were under Syrian control).[35] Israel also emphasised that, in its assessment, Syria had understood the Israeli deterrence threat and had been deterred from intervening in Lebanon.[36]

In late January, Rabin went to Washington on a state visit. Two aspects of that visit are related to the situation in Lebanon. First, the Lebanese question, although discussed, did not play a central role in his negotiations with President Ford and Secretary of State Kissinger. More significant was the question of the continuation of the 'political process' between Israel and Egypt, and between Israel and Jordan. The possibility of negotiations between Syria and Israel was also raised, but in this context there was no mention of the possible implications of the Syrian role in Lebanon. The relatively low profile given to the Lebanese question is a further indication that, at the time, Israel saw its interests there as limited. The Lebanese situation and even the threat of Syrian intervention did not as yet play a central role in Israeli politico-strategic considerations.[37]

The second interesting feature of the visit concerned the elaboration of the Israeli deterrence posture at the highest possible American level. Rabin indicated to his American interlocutors that, if asked, Israel would assist the Christians with arms. He added that, were Syria to invade Lebanon, Israel 'cannot allow her to control south Lebanon, and we shall have to place our security border on the Litani river'.[38]

Thus, by late January, if not earlier, the United States was aware of two distinctions which Israel had drawn in its general deterrence posture vis-à-vis Syria in Lebanon: first, the distinction between Syrian regular forces and other units under Syrian control, and second, the critical importance of Israeli security interests in south Lebanon as against their lesser importance in Lebanon in general. Both distinctions had been suggested before, but their communication at a meeting between heads of state gave them additional force and clarity.

A third distinction was also tentatively emerging. This concerned the weapons systems employed by the PLA units. The Israeli press cautioned against PLA use of heavy weapon systems such as tanks.[39]

In February and March, Syria increased its efforts to secure a cease-fire in Lebanon and to mobilise all the factions to accept its proposal for constitutional reform as well as the centrality of its role in Lebanon. These efforts failed owing to the opposition of the Muslim—leftist—Palestinian coalition. Moreover, the disintegration of the Lebanese Army, owing to the attempted coups by al-Hatib in January and al-Ahdab in March, described in Chapter 1, both of which threatened the survival of the political system, forced Syria to adopt a strong posture on the side of the forces supporting the status quo. The new alliance between the Christians and Syria began to consolidate during this period.

The Syrian—Christian connection was also influenced by

Israel's posture and behaviour. In early 1976 the Maronite leadership began sending signals to Israel about the likelihood of co-operation. The possibility of Israeli intervention in Lebanon probably increased Syria's desire to restore order there. Similarly, the continued Israeli deterrence signals compelled Syria to adopt a very cautious strategy in order to reduce the likelihood of Israeli intervention. Moreover, it was reasonable to assume that Syrian intervention on behalf of the Maronites, and against the PLO, would not provoke an Israeli counter-action. Thus, not only was Syria's main objective best served at that time by an alliance with the *status quo* forces, but such an alliance also lessened the threat of Israeli military intervention.

In mid-March, when Al-Hatib's units moved towards the presidential palace with the objective of forcing Faranjiyya to abdicate, Syrian-controlled units drawn from the Saiqa and the PLA intervened and saved him. The escalation of the conflict between Syria, the National Front (under the leadership of Junblatt) and the PLO, forced Syria to increase its military presence. During the second half of March more Saiqa units penetrated into Lebanon, some of them deployed in West Beirut. Simultaneously, Syria imposed a naval blockade on Tyre, Sidon and Tripoli in order to stop the flow of arms to the PLO and the National Front. This action came in the context of a copious flow of arms from Israel to the Christian militias, which together tended to redress the balance of military power within Lebanon.

Israeli–Maronite contacts

In the meantime, a new dimension of the Israeli involvement in Lebanon assumed greater salience. The Maronite groupings sought contact with Israel in 1975. Indeed, limited political contacts between Israel and groupings within the Maronite community were established already in early summer 1975.[40] In late 1975, four Maronite delegates came to Israel and met Defence Minister Peres.[41] This was followed by subsequent meetings at various levels and with different representatives. During the first few months of these contacts, the Maronite group most closely involved was the Chamounites.

The contacts took on greater significance in late March 1976, when Chamoun himself met Rabin.[42] Shortly afterwards, at a meeting of the Israeli forum in Lebanon it was decided to extend support to the Christian militias in the form of arms and ammunition. Significantly, and as a sign of caution in the relationship with the Christians, it was also decided that the militias should pay for these supplies, even if the actual payment were postponed.[43] From very early on, the Maronite representatives asked for several types of aid from Israel. They enquired about deliveries of arms, ammunition and fuel. They also aired the possibility of an Israeli military intervention in order to forestall threatening developments in Lebanon. Most significant was the emerging recognition by both Israel and the Maronite leadership of the two sides' coincidental interests.

In late March–early April, and only when the connections with Chamoun's militia had become more firmly established, the other major Christian group — the Ka'taib — joined the contacts with Israel. Thus, Israel began the cultivation of simultaneous contacts with different Maronite political parties and militias.[44]

Among the Israeli decision-makers there was a feeling of satisfaction that another ethnic group in the Middle East sought direct, close contact with Israel. As mentioned earlier, Israeli analysts and policy-makers had always assumed that there was potential in cultivating relations with the Maronites (although the importance and significance attached to it varied according to the perceptions of the different decision-makers), but this was the first time that the established Maronite leadership had sought such contacts and contacts of such broad scope. However, Israeli policy on the Maronite connection was constrained by several factors. There was a reluctance to become too deeply involved in the domestic affairs of Lebanon, because it was assumed that deeper commitment would lead to military entanglement, and that this might cause Israel political and strategic costs: Israeli–American relations might be strained, the move towards an understanding with Egypt could suffer a reverse, unity in the Arab world could increase, and a war with Syria might ensue, and over issues apparently unrelated to Israeli vital security interests. Furthermore, there was the assessment, mentioned for example by Allon, that Maronite interests were complex and also included contacts with Syria.[45] In other words, there was a clear perception of the constraints within which the Maronites themselves were operating. This Israeli assessment was possibly formed partly as a result of the stance taken by the Ka'taib, which was more restrained in its relationship with Israel, and which held open the possibility of a Maronite opening towards the Syrians. On that issue, Faranjiyya undoubtedly was of the same mind as the Ka'taib. The policy implication of these Israeli assessments was to cultivate the relationship with the Maronites, but to avoid any deep commitment to them. In practical terms, this was expressed in a decision to supply them with arms and ammunition, but to make it clear that they were obligated to rely on their own defence. This policy might be succinctly expressed as 'Israel will help the Maronites to help themselves'. Indeed, in early April 1976 the Christians expressed their disappointment that Israel was not operating militarily in south Lebanon. Such an operation promised to divert the attention of the anti-*status quo* forces that were applying pressure on Christian strongholds in central Lebanon.

The Israeli deterrence posture against Syrian military intervention was perceived by Israel as a substantial contribution to the Maronite cause.[46] As will be discussed below, Israel modified this posture when it became increasingly clear that the Syrians were in fact aiding the Christians.

Israeli caution about the Maronite relationship increased in one respect during 1976. It became clear that Maronite reports and information were on many occasions unreliable and exaggerated. Their lack of unity and internal rivalry gave pause to the Israeli decision-makers and dictated a policy of caution. The Israeli inclination to avoid deep commitment and to concentrate only on extending help and aid, on the one hand, and to transmit deterrence signals on the other, was reinforced. Indeed, Israel was also careful to refrain from demanding from the Maronites explicit anti-Syrian behaviour which might have exposed them to massive Syrian reaction. Furthermore, Allon also recognised the overlapping of Maronite–Syrian interests; thus unrealistic Israeli demands could not be accepted by the Maronites.[47] Israeli decision-makers also occasionally referred to long-range ideas raised by the Christians regarding the preferred ultimate outcome of events in Lebanon. The Israelis assumed that partition could be a useful outcome but they considered it unrealistic in view of international constraints, and the division within the Christian community itself.[48]

In adherence to its assessment that its security interests in Lebanon were centred in the south, Israel did increase its commitment to the Christian grouping living in that region. The population of south Lebanon is comprised primarily of Shi'is. However, in the area close to the eastern part of the Israeli border, there is a concentration of fourteen Christian villages. Until March 1976, the south was relatively free from the Civil War. In March, however, anti-government units under the command of Lieutenant Hatib, arrived in the south and began harassing the Christian population. Some of the villages turned to Israel for assistance. This aid came in two forms. Israel extended medical aid, and allowed the south Lebanese to work in Israel and obtain vital supplies there. This was the well-known 'Good Fence' policy. The second aspect was the transfer of arms and ammunition. The Israeli relationship with the south Lebanese Christians deepened in August 1976 with the arrival in the south of Major Sa'ad Haddad, who was posted by the Lebanese Government to take command of the Lebanese army units deployed there. Within a short time Haddad, with the help of Israel, organised a local militia and created a buffer zone between the PLO and the Israeli border. Israeli involvement in the Haddad area gradually increased and evoked an Israeli commitment deeper than that extended to the Maronite enclave in Beirut and to the north-east of the city. By November 1976, Israel decided for the first time to use artillery shelling to help Christian villages in the south which came under pressure.

March–June 1976 — Emergence of 'Red Lines' System

Although profound suspicions about Syria's ultimate objectives in Lebanon persisted, Israel nevertheless gradually became convinced during March that the Syrian intervention was in fact directed primarily against the Muslim–leftist–PLO coalition. Admittedly, Israeli leaders assumed that Syria would eventually reorient its policy towards the National Front coalition against the Christians, and pursue its vision of a Greater Syria. In the meantime, however, it appeared to be aiding precisely those groups with which Israel itself had connections. Moreover, it appeared likely that the Syrians would deliver a blow to the PLO.

Another important factor at this time was the continued strong Israeli disinclination to become deeply involved in domestic Lebanese affairs. Requests by the Maronite leadership that it should become involved militarily in the fighting were rejected by the Israeli leadership. This left the 'Syrian option' as the only viable alternative for the *status quo* forces. The combination of these different factors created a framework within which Israel became increasingly prepared to accept Syrian intervention *provided the latter was directed against the PLO and the Muslim coalition.* The Israeli deterrence posture therefore became more flexible.

In early March, Allon met Kissinger and, among other things, discussed with him the Lebanese situation.[49] By mid-March, Washington began to communicate Syrian intentions to Israel, and added its own assessment of these intentions. Within a few days, Kissinger was pointing out that it was Washington's impression that the Syrian intention was to act as a stabilising force, defending the Christians and the Lebanese Government and blocking the PLO. By 23 March the situation had been clarified somewhat by Syria's communication to Washington of its view of the situation. Khaddam stressed that the situation in Lebanon was deteriorating rapidly and he indicated the possibility of Syrian military intervention to forestall a general collapse of the Lebanese state.

It was clear that Syria was seeking US support through its Washington contacts for Israeli acquiescence in Syrian military intervention, should this become necessary. Syria also repeatedly pointed out that it was being invited to intervene by President Faranjiyya, Chamoun and the Phalangists. The Americans immediately turned to Israel for the latter's response to the Syrian communication. They indicated the possibility of developing a joint American–Israeli strategy. They also pointed out that Syria had a more vital interest in Lebanon than Israel. Throughout these negotiations with Israeli, they repeatedly warned Syria against a unilateral move.

In response to American queries about the Israeli tolerance threshold on Syrian intervention, Israel communicated to Washington on 24 March a set of conditions which could be described as 'red lines'. It indicated that it did not wish to intervene militarily but would have to do so if Syria intervened unilaterally. However, the definition of Syrian action was wide enough to allow for some such intervention. The conditions were the following:

(i) Syria should not intervene in a declaratory and open way.

(ii) The intervention forces should not exceed one brigade.

(iii) The force should not employ tanks, artillery or surface to air missiles.

(iv) Syrian aircraft should not operate in Lebanon, nor Syrian naval units in Lebanese waters.

(v) Syrian units should not move south of a line running 10 km south of the Beirut–Damascus highway.[50]

The communication added that, in case of violations, Israeli military actions would be directed at capturing strategic positions vital for the security of northern Israel. The movement of Syrian forces south of the geographical line indicated above might lead to Israeli operations beyond the activity suggested previously.[51]

An analysis of the tolerance thresholds included in the Israeli communication reveals some interesting features. To begin with, there were restrictions on different aspects of military involvement: size of forces, type of weapon systems allowed, and geographical delimitation. Moreover, the Israeli reaction in case of violations of the 'red lines' would be limited to strategic assets directly linked to the security of northern Israel. There was no threat of operations beyond that. However, a violation of what appeared to be the most important Israeli tolerance threshold — the geographical limitation — might provoke a reaction beyond the limited range suggested. Even then, it appeared that the threat of direct strikes against the Syrian forces was not clearly identified.

Damascus responded via Washington to Israel's definition of the 'red lines' by defining the size of forces to be involved, but the Syrian definition was vaguer than the Israeli communication. At one point a whole division was mentioned. In general, however, Damascus stated that it would despatch forces no larger than those required to control the situation. The geographical limitation was also defined differently: namely, Beirut, some areas in the Beqa, and certain mountainous zones where fighting was going on. In any event Syria was not going to send forces to the south.

Throughout these crucial Israeli–American communications, Kissinger urged that US and Israeli positions should be coordinated. He claimed that the United States was continuously warning Syria against unilateral intervention without advance American (and by implication Israeli) approval. Israeli decision-makers, however, assumed that the Americans had in fact already signalled to Syria their approval of a limited Syrian

47

intervention. This was indeed probably the case. One might only add that Israel itself gradually moved to a similar position, but was careful to signal to Washington a somewhat tougher stance with regard to Syrian intervention.[52]

Apart from a specific signal to Syria via Washington, Israel also sent messages by way of public references in the mass media. These declarations were more ambiguous than the ones communicated via Washington.[53] For example, Rabin stated in mid-April:[54]

> military intervention to an extent that I will not describe, will oblige Israel to act in order to ensure its security. The consideration of when and how to act is directly connected with Israel's security needs and emanates from those security needs. Israel has a distinct 'red line' beyond which it will have to take action, but I cannot specify here what is the exact significance of the 'red line'.

Syrian efforts during February–March were not sufficient to coerce the PLO–Muslim coalition to accept the political compromise. On 9 April Syria moved to employ its last instrument of influence. Commando and armoured Syrian units entered Lebanon via the Damascus-Beirut highway and began deployment inside the Lebanese border. The first reports referred to a force of 400 men; later reports gave higher figures. In any event, this was a major step signalling Syria's firm commitment to impose its concept of order in Lebanon. The move was executed only after Damascus learned via Washington about the Israeli 'red lines'. Syrian penetration was limited to a few kilometres only, and only light artillery and APCs were involved.

The Israeli reaction was low-key. Israeli concern was apparently focused only on the south. The recognition by Israel that the Syrians were in fact aiding the Christians was publicly voiced by Rabin, who declared on 13 April that 'Matters have developed in such a way that today the Syrians are the saviors of the Christians'.[55] The Israeli deterrence thresholds were thus in process of being communicated to Damascus via Washington, and also directly through public references by the decision-makers. An interesting feature of the difference between the two types of communications was that the first set were more explicit, and included the specific tolerance thresholds (the so-called 'red lines').

Syria's actions in Lebanon in May clearly revealed its political and military preferences. Syrian-controlled units fought on the side of the Christians. The Christian leadership welcomed this intervention and the Syrian political initiatives certainly helped the forces behind the *status quo*. Israeli leaders remained deeply suspicious about Syrian long-term objectives. But for the time being, and within the context of short- and possibly even middle-term objectives, Israeli decision-makers became convinced that Israel and Syria had not only conflicting interests but also a set of coincidental interests in Lebanon. These sets of considerations were clearly expressed by Rabin:[56]

> The Syrians today favor a Muslim–Christian compromise solution, which puts the number of members of Parliament at fifty-fifty and which stipulates a change in the jurisdictions of the President and the Prime Minister. This is opposed by the PLO, most of the Muslims and the left. The reason why the Syrians support this compromise solution is the desire to maintain the existence of a united Lebanon without totally abandoning the Christian community and its rights, while maintaining a balance that will prevent serious and severe developments — something that could cause the rise of left-wing extremists in the Arab world because, and this might seem strange, as soon as Lebanon became an extreme leftwing Arab state then in order to avoid Syrian control it would have to lean on an alliance with Iraq and Libya . . . From Syria's point of view, a balance is preferable at this stage. In the future, it is possible that Syria will try to bring about additional developments in order to realize the dream of greater Syria.

Allon was more explicit; he argued that once the Syrians were deployed in Lebanon, they would reach an understanding with the PLO and the 'radicals'. 'If the Syrians enter, they will stay'.[57] He added however, that the 'Syrians are already there' (meaning in Lebanon), but it is 'good that we are here and they are there'.[58] The last phrase is significant in revealing the extent of Israeli reluctance to become militarily involved in Lebanese affairs. The Israeli decision-makers preferred to react to the evolving situation rather than to formulate policy on the basis of concern about a possible future development — Syria turning against the Christians — which in any case was not certain.

The Syrian behaviour in Lebanon in April–May and the Israeli perception of the existence of a limited commonality of interests between Israel and Syria in regard to Lebanon, somewhat lowered Israeli concern about future Syrian incursions. In addition, Israel and the United States maintained their system of consultations about future developments. A sense of uncertainty persisted, however, among Israeli decision-makers about American intentions and the exact nature of American–Syrian understandings.

By deploying its forces inside Lebanon, Syria also affected the perceptions of all the external actors — Israel, the Arab states and the United States — about the balance of interests in Lebanon. Its move served as an important signal to the other Arab states and had further significance in the Middle Eastern regional sub-system. In the context of the Israeli–Egyptian Sinai II agreement and its subsequent increased isolation, Syria signalled its ability to continue to manoeuvre successfully in the regional system. Paradoxically, it did this with the acquiescence of Israel, its feared opponent. Moreover, it did it while at the same time deepening its relations with its erstwhile opponent, Jordan. The Syrian–Jordanian association developed against the background of feelings of isolation on both sides resulting from the Sinai II agreement. This new association also affected the Syrian posture in Lebanon; Jordan would benefit if Syria were further to weaken the power of the PLO, Jordan's main foe.

The period between the initial Syrian drive into Lebanon in April and late May was characterised by continued Syrian efforts to stabilise the situation while increasing its influence in Lebanon. By that time Syria had already decided that Sarkis should be the new President, and had secured the backing of the Christian leadership. The opponents of the *status quo* rejected the Syrian choice and now realised that Syria was in fact turning completely against them. The PLO tried in vain to mediate between Syria, the National Front and Kamal Junblatt. After Sarkis was elected on 8 May, the National Front and its affiliates initiated a new round of violence. By that time a few Syrian and mainly Saiqa forces were fighting against the various National Front militias, and the Syrian–Christian coalition had become a working alliance.

The Syrian efforts to stabilise the situation failed and the fighting continued intermittently. Against this background, the dilemmas facing the Syrian leadership were unchanged — only the stakes had risen. Syria committed itself to the success of the newly elected President Sarkis and to the continued ascendancy of the Christians. Its efforts to woo the National Front and the PLO failed, and even the limited deployment of Syrian forces did not convince the opposition forces to change their minds. Asad therefore had to initiate a radical turn in policy while taking Israeli reactions into account; the latter was accomplished through the good offices of Washington.

The inherent ambiguity concerning Israeli tolerance thresholds and possible American reactions to Syrian behaviour prompted Syria to try and reduce the uncertainty. This attempt went beyond the contacts with Washington and Israel's public formulations. Perhaps the most intriguing effort in this context was the activity of King Hussein. In April, the King visited Washington and discussed there possible Syrian moves in Lebanon. The United States indicated that it was opposed to a massive Syrian intervention.[59] This, however, did not preclude a more limited Syrian intervention. Hussein also raised the issue in his direct contacts with Israel.[60] One such contact was made at a meeting in London, on his return from Washington. At that meeting Hussein elaborated on shared Syrian, Jordanian and Israeli interests in Lebanon, which were to smash the PLO finally and totally.[61] There may have been other occasions on which Hussein communicated these messages directly to Israel.[62]

Hussein's initiative seems to have had two objectives: first, to assist the Syrians in their attempts to clarify Israeli tolerance thresholds in regard to Lebanon; and second, his own interests in demonstrating to Israel that his new alliance with Syria was not aimed against Israel, but rather could serve shared interests. (In any case, the Israeli decision-makers appreciated that Hussein's alliance with Syria was limited and that it involved no military implications).[63] Be that is it may, the Hussein initiative culminated in an Israeli assurance to Syria, via the King, that Israel trusted Hussein and would follow events with an 'open mind'.[64]

In the meantime the Civil War continued and the constitutional reform that had been agreed upon by the Syrians, the Maronite leadership and some other elements of the *status quo* was now completely rejected by the more radical anti-*status quo* coalition. Thus, the need to intervene militarily was increased in order to pre-empt a complete breakdown of the Lebanese state.

In late May, President Faranjiyya and President-elect Sarkis extended a request to Asad to intervene.

Most importantly, however, when Syria decided in late May to extend its military intervention, it did so based on the assessment that its action would not trigger an Israeli military reaction. It should be stressed, however, that Syria was not completely sure of the Israeli reaction. Deep suspicion and great ambiguity about Israeli (and American) behaviour persisted. Moreover, the Syrians never formally clarified the understandings reached between them and Israel through the good offices of the United States. Syrian military moves, therefore, had to be limited and cautiously executed.

The initial Syrian action was to enter Lebanon from the north with a force of about 2,000 men and about 60 tanks, and to occupy areas near Tripoli. A larger force, comprising about 4,000 men with 100 tanks, penetrated along the main Damascus–Beirut highway, and quickly advanced through the Beqa, imposing control over large areas around the highway. In a few days, the Syrians began pushing towards the south and southwest. Their southernmost line of advance was, however, clearly delineated; at no point did they cross a line running roughly from Rashiya in the east, through Jezzin in the centre, and west to Sidon on the coast. As noted earlier, Israel had communicated this line to Damascus via Washington.[65] Syria, however, probably relying on its communications to Washington in which it gave its own interpretation of what should be the limitations on the use of military force, went in some respects beyond Israel's 'red lines'. The size of the forces intervening in fact exceeded those specified by Israel, and tanks were involved in the fighting. Syria probably assumed (and correctly so) that these excesses would be tolerated by Israel because it was fighting a common enemy — the PLO and the Muslim militias.

The indirect understandings between Israel and Syria, the fact that Syria directed its military effort against the PLO and its allies, and the American backing for the Syrian intervention, all dictated a tone of restraint and caution on the part of Israel. An example of that caution was the reference in the Israeli daily *Ha'aretz*, to a comment at the previous day's Cabinet meeting: 'The opinion was expressed that for the time being there is no reason to deviate from the policy of non-intervention. The Syrian forces are not approaching the Israeli border, and in their present location they do not constitute a security threat'.[66] Israel, however, maintained its basic deterrence posture. The Israeli Government had not ruled out an Israeli reaction 'if Syrian intervention increases'.[67]

The Syrian forces clashed with the Muslim and PLO militias in several places, and their advance was slow and difficult. Nevertheless, they succeeded in forcing their way towards West Beirut and Sidon. They established themselves in parts of the Beqa and created a Syrian-controlled military zone there. By mid-June, they had imposed a semi-siege of West Beirut and of Tripoli. The difficulties which they encountered and their limited success surprised the American administration, which had expected a more forceful Syrian push, and only gradually became accustomed to the slow and cautious Syrian strategy.

On 9 June the Arab Foreign Ministers convened in Cairo and decided to call for an immediate cease-fire and the establishment of a small inter-Arab force to be sent to Lebanon to replace the Syrian forces. This force was to be responsible for internal security in Lebanon and would remain there only as long as required by the Lebanese President. The Foreign Ministers also decided to form a special committee to act on behalf of the Arab League in its efforts to end the hostilities in Lebanon.

Although small units comprising Sudanese, Saudi and Libyan forces did arrive in Lebanon following these resolutions, their actual impact and that of the Arab countries in general on developments in Lebanon was very limited, and the Syrians remained the main external actor. The front supporting the *status quo* continued to back the Syrian move. On 30 June, President Faranjiyya told the Secretary-General of the Arab League that the latter had no right or authority to discuss relations between Lebanon and Syria.

The focus of fighting at the time was in Beirut; the Palestinian quarter of Tel-Za'atar and the neighbouring areas came under heavy attacks from Christian militias, and the Syrians gave these militias some support. Fighting also continued in Tripoli, parts of the Beqa and other parts of Beirut. The Syrian forces applied pressure, but were careful to limit their actions to certain parts of Lebanon.

As part of their effort to secure a wider consensus to back their role in Lebanon, the Syrian leadership met with a PLO delega-tion in Damascus and by late July had reached a further agree-ment with them. This came to naught, however, and in the light of the limited success of the Syrian forces, the Syrian military effort was expanded.

The Syrian intervention was closely followed in Israel. Peres, in another public statement, indicated three criteria for the assessment of Syrian activity: first, the side against which they were operating; second, whether the size of the Syrian forces deployed demonstrated that their purpose was to effect a cease-fire or to control the whole of Lebanon; and finally, whether the Syrian intervention extended to south Lebanon. In order to maintain the basic Israeli posture of deterrence, he added that Israel was following developments closely and was aware that changes might occur.[68] Allon emphasised the last two points: the geographical 'red line' and the basic Israeli deterrence posture.[69]

The tone of caution adopted by the Cabinet reflected a broad domestic consensus. Thus, Menachem Begin, leader of the Likud opposition, stated on 6 June that the Likud did not and would not encourage Israeli military action in Lebanon.[70]

This Israeli caution and 'acceptance' of the Syrian action had several consequences, all of them to Israel's advantage. To begin with, Israel saved itself a large-scale military action to help the Christians, or to halt the Syrian intervention. Secondly, the *status quo* in Lebanon had been secured and the PLO–Muslim coalition had suffered a heavy blow. Furthermore, Israeli relations with the United States were not strained. Within the Middle East, the Syrian action led to further deterioration in inter-Arab relations. Finally, an important precedent in Israeli–Syrian relations had been established whereby the two sides recognised that they had sets of coincidental interests and also demonstrated their ability to reach indirect and tacit agreements for the limitation of their military behaviour.

By this time, Israeli decision-makers were becoming increasingly aware of the direct military advantages contained in the evolving Syrian deployment in Lebanon. Syrian forces there were deeply involved in costly and difficult policing operations. Moreover, these forces had to be deducted from those which Syria could direct against Israel on their main front — the Golan Heights.

During the summer of 1976, the Syrian units kept up their pressure on the anti-*status quo* elements and on 29 August reinforcements were sent into Lebanon. On 28 September, together with the Christian forces, they launched an offensive against the Palestinian forces east of Beirut and succeeded in clearing the areas around the Beirut-Damascus highway. On 12 October, they attacked again along the Beirut-Damascus highway and in the region east of Sidon, and made significant gains in both areas.

Increased Syrian pressure on the Palestinians, and the threat to other Arab states involved in Syria's securing an exclusive role for itself in Lebanon, eventually brought about intensified activity on the part of the other leading Arab states. A compromise was worked out in which Syria attained most of its objectives. The Riyadh conference and the Cairo Arab summit, both in October, gave legitimisation to the Syrian operations in Lebanon under the guise of the Arab Deterrent Forces (ADF), of which the Syrians comprised by far the largest element. Following the establishment of the ADF, Syrian units moved into Beirut and imposed control on most of northern and central Lebanon. These swift moves involved pushing PLO units from the areas now under Syrian control down into south Lebanon.

From the Israeli point of view, these developments constituted a potential threat. Not only could the border area again become a focus of terrorist activity (after more than a year of relative calm), but the Syrians were approaching the 'red line' in the Sidon area. Israel therefore issued a strong deterrent warning directed at both the Syrians and the PLO. Warnings were also sent via Washington. Finally, Israel transferred reinforcements to the border area, and this provided an additional tacit signal. During the tense days of late November, when Syrian forces were active close to the 'red line', Israel continued its warnings, while publicly conceding that the Syrian deployment was not an offensive one and that the Syrians were deployed in what appeared to be policing operations.

Syria responded in a conciliatory manner to the Israeli warnings. It turned to Washington and stressed that it was not opposed to the Israeli 'Good Fence' policy, and that it did oppose PLO raids on northern Israel. Furthermore, it declared its intention of disarming the PLO. This was a remarkable situation: the Syrians were apparently seeking a new understanding with Israel whereby they would be allowed to be deployed in the south, and to destroy the PLO there. Against the background of these communications, Kissinger attempted, in late November, to persuade Israel to accept the idea of Syrian deployment in South Lebanon in order to disarm the PLO. Israel insisted that it would welcome a move by President Sarkis (who was the titular head of the ADF) to disarm the PLO, but that it would reject Syrian deployment in South Lebanon. One of the ideas put forward by Israel was that a special Christian-Shi'i force under the overall command of President Sarkis should be formed with the task of policing the south. Kissinger pointed out, however, that in fact only the Syrians were capable of effectively pacifying the south and disarming the PLO.

In view of Israel's opposition, Washington again consulted with both Syria and Sarkis and raised the possibility of forming a local policing force in the south under Sarkis' control. Sarkis, however, rejected the plan as unfeasible. In the meantime, the situation in the south deteriorated further as PLO units continued to move into the area. In view of this, Washington fully endorsed the Syrian position and, in accordance with the Asad–Sarkis plan, proposed an ADF (namely Syrian) deployment in Tyre and around Nabatiyya, with the caveat that the size of the units should be small.

Israel therefore faced a major dilemma which was also to recur later: to accept Syrian deployment in the south as a pacifying measure but that would allow the south to be turned into a Syrian military base. Israeli suspicions of long-term Syrian intentions persisted, however, and Israel decided to maintain its opposition to Kissinger's ideas.[71]

NOTES

1. For accounts of this policy see, in the first place, Adeed Dawisha, *Syria and the Lebanese Crisis*; Itamar Rabinovich, *The War for Lebanon 1970–1983* and Itamar Rabinovich and Hanna Zamir, *War and Crisis in Lebanon 1975–1981* (in Hebrew). For general accounts of domestic political and foreign policy developments in Syria: see Patrick Seale, *The Struggle for Syria: A Study of Post-War Arab Politics 1945–1958*; Itamar Rabinovich, *Syria under the Ba'th 1963–66 The Army–Party Symbiosis*; Moshe Ma'oz, *Syria under Hafiz al-Asad: New Domestic and Foreign Policies*; Nikolaos Van Dam, *The Struggle for Power in Syria*. My analysis is based partly on these accounts, partly on interviews with Israeli and American officials and ex-officials who put forward their interpretations of Syrian policy, and finally on my inferences from the communications conducted between Damascus, Washington and Jerusalem. My conclusions may, of course, differ from the various interpretations.

2. A paradoxical demonstration of the Syrian claim was the absence of a Syrian ambassador in Beirut. The Syrians considered Lebanon part of Syria and hence there was no need for diplomatic relations between them.

3. Nikolaos Van Dam in his book *The Struggle for Power in Syria* stresses that the Alawite officers completely controlled the armed forces. Moreover, whereas officers from other religious communities, and primarily the Sunnis, came from different regions and thus were divided because of their varied regional backgrounds, most of the Alawites came from the Latakiya region.

4. Within the armed forces the Alawites co-operated with officers from other religious and regional minorities, but undermined attempts to organise these officers as important contenders in the struggle for power. Druze, Ismaili and Hawrani factions were eliminated in succession. See Van Dam, *The Struggle for Power in Syria*.

5. Interestingly enough, Christian officers hold important positions in the Syrian armed forces, albeit mainly in the technical services. They have never tried to organise themselves on a sectarian basis. See Van Dam, *The Struggle for Power in Syria*, p. 102. In his famous speech of 20 July 1976 Asad repeatedly emphasised the importance of having co-operative relations between Muslims and Christians in the Arab countries. For the text see *Foreign Broadcasts Information Service* (FBIS), 20 July 1976. The text is also reproduced in Rabinovich, *The War for Lebanon*.

6. Dawisha, *Syria and the Lebanese Crisis*, pp. 70–71 and 100–102. See also the valuable analysis in Moshe Ma'oz, 'Hafiz al-Asad: A Political Profile'.

7. A similar conclusion (without identifying the two contending approaches in Damascus) though stated differently, was reached by Rabinovich, *The War for Lebanon*.

8. These ideas received their ideological formulation in the political cum cultural movement of the 'Hebrews' nicknamed derogatorily as the 'Cananites'. (The latter term was eventually accepted by the movement, although always with some reservation.) The movement, the ideology of which was articulated by Yonatan Ratosh and Adaya Horon, had some intellectual appeal in Israel in the 1940s and 1950s. It identified itself as anti-Zionist or at least non-Zionist. The movement could perhaps better be characterised as post-Zionist. Its ideas also circulated in other groups, and in any case echoed some strong undercurrents operating in Israeli intellectual milieux.

9. Ben Gurion, *Diary*.

10. *Ibid.*, p. 454.

11. For the exchange of views between Ben Gurion and Sharet, see Moshe Sharet, *Yoman Ishi* (Personal Diary) (in Hebrew) *Ma'ariv*, 1978. All the material relevant to Lebanon has been assembled in a special publication edited by Ya'acov Sharet, published in 1983. It includes excerpts from the Diary, for the following dates: 25, 26, 27, 28 February 1954; 16 and 28 May 1955; 17 June 1955. It also includes letters from Ben Gurion to Sharet on 27 February 1954 and the latter's response on 18 March 1954.

12. See Ya'acov Sharet's collection, pp. 10–11.

13. *Ibid.*, pp. 12–15.

14. Moshe Dayan, *Avnei Derech* (in Hebrew), p. 255.

15. Interview with retired Israeli officials.

16. The following account is based on *1,000 Hayamim* (Hebrew), Israel Defence Ministry Publishing House, 1971.

17. There were attempts to reach a new accommodation with Jordan, but they were placed low on Jerusalem's list of priorities. The interesting and promising 'Jericho Plan', for example, was neglected because it appeared to interfere with the more important objective of changing the pattern of conflict with Egypt.

18. Dawisha, *Syria and the Lebanese Crisis*, pp. 87–8.

19. *Ibid.*, pp. 92–3; Jeffrey White, *National Security Policy Decisionmaking in Israel*, p. 167.

20. Allon personal account (referring to meeting of Foreign and Defence Committee 3 June 1975).

21. Allon personal account. For an excellent detailed account of specific Israeli moves see White, *National Security Policy Decisionmaking*. The quotation is taken from interview with Allon in *Kol Yisrael*, 20 September 1975, quoted in White, p. 171.

22. *Newsweek*, 20 October 1975, p. 44.

23. Interview in *Kol Yisrael*, 31 October 1975.

24. *Kol Yisrael*, reported in *Davar*, 15 October 1975.

25. *Kol Yisrael*, 19 November 1975.

26. Report in *Yedioth Ahronot*, 24 October 1975.

27. *Ha'aretz*, 2 November 1975.

28. Dawisha, *Syria and the Lebanese Crisis*, p. 94.

29. Rabin had been Chief of Staff; Allon was a high-ranking general during the War of Independence and was considered a leading strategic authority; Peres was Director General of the Defence Ministry, and Galili was former head of the Haganah.

30. *Ma'ariv*, 8 January 1976.

31. *Ha'aretz*, 12 January 1976, report of Rabin's interview on German television.

32. See White, *National Security Policy Decisionmaking*, pp. 183–4.

33. Interview with Asad in *Events* (London), 1 October 1976, pp. 25–6, quoted in Dawisha, *Syria and the Lebanese Crisis*, p. 180.

34. See White, *National Security Decisionmaking*, p. 181. Also Rabinovich, *The War for Lebanon*, pp. 97–101.

35. Peres, *Kol Yisrael*, 20 January 1976; White, *National Security Policy Decisionmaking*, p. 181.

36. Gur, *Al Hamishmar*, 21 January 1976.

37. Rabin, *Pinkas Sherut*, pp. 493–9.

38. *Ibid.*, p. 494.

39. *Davar*, 22 January 1976, p. 1.

40. Allon personal account (referring to Foreign and Defence Committee 3 June 1975).

41. Interview with a top Israeli decision-maker.

42. Schiff and Yaari, *Milchemet Sholal*.

43. Interview with a top Israeli decision-maker.

44. A high-level Kat'aib delegation, led by Joseph Abu Halil, arrived in Israel around 10–11 April 1976.

45. Allon personal account.

46. A view expressed by Allon on several occasions.

47. Interview with a leading decision-maker referring to meeting of the Foreign and Defence Committee of the Knesset on 10 September 1976.

48. Interview with a top Israeli decision-maker (referring to Foreign and Defence Committee 11 May 1976).

49. See for example *Yedioth Ahronot*, 12 March 1976.

50. Apparently there were several definitions of this critically important line. It is clear that óne definition communicated in late March was that mentioned here. On the other hand, one ex-official interviewed pointed out that the only definition of a geographical line was the one running from Rashiya through Jezzin to Sidon. That this was indeed the line ultimately agreed upon is clear. It was formulated according to Rabin in June. An analysis of Israeli positions suggests that this ultimate line had been communicated to Washington before the Syrian invasion of 31 May.

51. The above account of Israeli–American communications is based on an interview with a top Israeli decision-maker. Israeli–American contacts had usually been conducted directly by Kissinger himself or under his direct supervision through the Israeli embassy in Washington to Israeli Foreign Minister Allon, and sometimes through meetings of Rabin or Allon with the American Ambassador to Israel.

52. Based on Allon personal account.

53. See, for example, Zeev Schiff, *Ha'aretz*, 14 April 1976. Also Asher Ben Natan, political adviser to the Minister of Defence, was quoted in *Ha'aretz* of 31 March 1976: 'Israel will not intervene in Lebanon as long as the Syrian presence there is "camouflaged", but Israel will take steps if that presence becomes official'.

54. Interview in *Ma'ariv*, 14 April 1976.

55. *Ibid*.

56. Interview in *Ha'aretz*, 30 April 1976.

57. Allon personal account referring to Foreign and Defence Committee, 6 April 1976.

58. *Ibid*.

59. *Kol Yisrael*, 3 April 1976 and an interview with a top Israeli decision-maker.

60. Interview with Gideon Raphael, and other oblique references.

61. *Ibid*.

62. For references to Hussein's initiative, see Allon personal account referring to consultations on Lebanon held on 13 April 1976.

63. Interview with retired Israeli top official.

64. Interview with Gideon Raphael then Israeli Ambassador to Britain.

65. Rabin, *Pinkas Sherut*, p. 503; interview with top Israeli decision-maker.

66. *Ha'aretz*, 2 June 1976, p. 1, article by Mati Golan.

67. *Ibid*.

68. *Kol Yisrael*, 2 June 1976.

69. *Ibid*.

70. *Kol Yisrael*, 6 June 1976.

71. According to Allon's personal account.

3

From War to Crisis: Israel and Syria in Lebanon 1977–81

By the end of 1976, the Lebanese Civil War had come to an end with Syria established as the dominant external power in Lebanon. Syria's influence was severely constrained, however, by a series of Lebanese and regional factors. In the first place, the relative order that was established with the Syrian invasion failed to create sufficiently solid foundations for a national consensus. Rather, all that emerged was the *de facto* legitimisation of a certain limited political division of the country. The Christian zone, comprising East Beirut and the northern part of Mount Lebanon, crystallised into a semi-independent canton. Similarly, albeit on a smaller and less significant scale, a semi-independent Druze canton emerged in the Shuf mountains. The Syrian army was not deployed in either of these areas. More ominously, two additional semi-independent areas gradually developed in the south of the country. Close to the Israeli border, several Christian villages formed an independent militia aided and backed by Israel. For the most part, the PLO controlled the areas bordering on the northern boundary of this enclave. The Syrians established direct rule in a large crescent-shaped area extending from Tripoli in the north-west, through the Beqa in the east and south-east. A Syrian brigade was also deployed in West Beirut. Parts of the country such as the area from the Zaharani and along the coast to Beirut, while under PLO influence, were not firmly controlled by any group.

President Sarkis' regime tried in vain to overcome these divisions. The country operated in a loosely disorganised way, with the central government largely irrelevant. Such a situation threatened the breakdown of law and order. Nevertheless, order was maintained in some areas, primarily in the Christian and Druze semi-cantons, and to a certain extent in the regions under Syrian control. On the other hand, in West Beirut and other areas in which the PLO had established control, limited anarchy existed with different militias fighting each other, while the Palestinian organisations imposed their brutal rule over the local, mostly Shi'i, community. It should also be noted that the fragmentation of the political system did not preclude economic development. In fact, Lebanon very quickly began a process of economic rehabilitation, and within a short period had entered a period of considerable economic prosperity.

SYRIA'S POSTURE

In the first half of 1977 Syria emerged from the isolation in which it had found itself in the mid-1970s. The Riyadh and Cairo conferences ostensibly healed the cleavage in Egyptian–Syrian relations caused by the Sinai II agreement. Syrian relations with Egypt and also with Saudi Arabia improved considerably, and there was at least ostensible revival of the more relaxed relations which had characterised the period leading to the 1973 war.[1] Sadat and Asad met several times, and on the face of it, appeared to consolidate their alliance. Indeed, as had happened several times previously, they also created a formal joint political and military leadership (which in fact had no real substance), and General Gamassy was appointed Commander of the Egyptian and Syrian fronts.

In contrast, the more radical Arab states, in particular Iraq, Libya, Algeria and South Yemen, failed to establish a united front, and were engaged in their immediate conflicts and problems. Other countries, such as Jordan, Sudan, North Yemen and the Gulf states, adhered to the grouping of Egypt, Syria and Saudi Arabia.

Thus, Syria could feel relatively comfortable within the Arab context. It believed it had tied Egypt to a general Arab approach to the Palestine problem, thus precluding a repetition of the independent (and therefore dangerous for Syrian interests) Egyptian move in signing the Sinai II agreement. Against this background, it felt relatively free to deepen its involvement and influence in Lebanon.

The Nabatiyya encounter

One of the areas which remained completely outside the Syrian zone of influence was south Lebanon. Here two developments appeared to be threatening Syrian influence and control: the emergence of a local Christian militia which defended several villages and received aid from Israel and, more importantly, the increased power of the PLO. Syria was, however, unable to move south because of the Israeli deterrence posture.

In January 1977 it apparently decided to ignore the Israeli deterrence threats by moving a small unit southward. This decision was motivated by a desire to impose control over all groups in the area, but mainly the PLO. In this sense, Syria was simply continuing its policy of 1976, and may have hoped that Israel would therefore tolerate its action. The Syrian move could be construed as not necessarily threatening Israeli security interests, and Damascus might even have assumed that Israel would perceive it as ultimately serving Israeli security interests. Furthermore, Syria was sending only a small force. Thus, in the light of the political context and the small size of the force involved, the Syrians hoped that Israel would not reject their move.

Syrian considerations might also be assessed within the context of the increased PLO activities against Israel, beginning late in 1976. Escalation of the tensions along the southern border carried the threat of an Israeli reaction. Furthermore, Israeli backing for the Christian militia in the south might serve as a precedent for Israeli activity throughout the whole of southern Lebanon. Syria's continued fear of uncontrolled escalation leading to Israeli military intervention, and to the further division of Lebanon, drove home the absolute need to try and impose control in the south. The Syrian dilemma was that movement of Syrian forces south of the 'red line' was liable to trigger precisely the Israeli military intervention which they sought to avoid.

Israeli decision-makers were forced to confront once more, as in November 1976 when the idea of a Syrian move into the south was first raised, the trade-off between immediate current security and long-term basic security. It was understood that Syrian deployment along the border would probably diminish the threat of PLO activity. Indeed, one might add that, in view of Syria's cautious and controlled behaviour in the Golan

Heights, Syrian deployment could have completely precluded terrorism from the north. On the other hand, Syria might use its deployment in the south as an additional springboard for a conventional attack on Israel. Israel eventually decided to oppose the Syrian move very strongly.

Israeli reactions

A new Administration came into office in the United States in January. During the Nabatiyya crisis in January 1977 Israel was still unclear about the policies of the Carter Administration. Moreover, Israeli leaders were generally concerned about developments in the Arab world and their impact on Lebanon. During much of 1976 the Sinai II agreement was correctly seen as a divisive force in the Arab world, but by the end of the year things appeared less certain, with the apparent *rapprochement* between Egypt and Syria. Against this background it was unclear what the long-range effects of the Syrian deployment would be. Admittedly, the Syrian involvement in Lebanon was still seen as serving some Israeli interests, but Israel had to follow developments carefully.[2] Indeed, Peres stated in January 1977 that the situation in Lebanon remained unstable and volatile, while Gur voiced Israeli uncertainty about Syrian intentions.[3]

The Syrian decision to send troops to Nabatiyya, the central inland town between the Litani and the Zaharani, should also be seen within the context of a decision made by the four-nation Arab Committee supervising the ADF activities. The committee, in agreement with President Sarkis, decided on the collection of all heavy weapons held by the various militias. This policy met with only very limited success, however. On 20 January the ADF was authorised to confiscate these weapons. The Syrian force which moved into Nabatiyya was under orders to confiscate the heavy weapons there and, in fact, to impose Syrian authority in the area.

The Syrians, who were aware of Israel's rejection of plans for Syrian deployment south of the 'red line', chose to try and probe the Israeli tolerance threshold. They probably calculated that a limited move, ostensibly endorsed by President Sarkis and with the implicit intention of imposing control over areas in which the PLO operated, would not necessarily meet with strong Israeli opposition. Thus, a limited probe in an ambiguous context appeared to constitute a sufficiently low-key action to be acceptable to Israel. Furthermore, the Syrian regime was probably confident of American goodwill towards the move. Indeed Israeli decision-makers suspected that the move was co-ordinated with American officials below the level of the Secretary of State and his immediate advisers. Thus, on 23 January 1977, a small Syrian force entered the Nabatiyya area.

The Israeli reaction was firm but cautious. Israel referred to the 'red line' and warned Syria, but did not threaten immediate military action. It did, however, turn immediately to Washington and requested that the Israeli position be communicated with firmness. In its initial reaction, Israel made it clear that it was aware that the size of the Syrian forces deployed was very limited. This seemed to imply that the Israeli response was flexible. At the same time, Israel viewed the Syrian move as a test of its 'specific deterrence' posture in Lebanon.[4] It refrained from issuing a direct ultimatum to Syria and preferred to use the Jerusalem–Washington–Damascus channel to indicate that the Syrian move violated the Israeli tolerance threshold and that the Syrian forces should be withdrawn.

This cautious Israeli reaction and the decision not to resort immediately to a direct ultimatum were apparently influenced by several factors. Important considerations were the size of the Syrian contingent, and the ambiguity of their mission. Not only would the Syrians most probably act against the PLO but there was also the possibility that Syrian control of the Nabatiyya area could be useful for the Christians, as it would enable direct contact between the Christians in the south and those in the Beirut area. In any case, at that stage they constituted no threat of any kind to Israel. Furthermore, there was awareness of the American position which only a short time before had favoured such a Syrian move and which certainly would not view with favour any consequent military escalation. Finally, Israel was also aware of the more crucial diplomatic issues that it had to confront in the near future: a new American Administration, the possibility of a renewal of the Geneva Conference and, within that context, its future relationship with Egypt.

On the other hand, as the days passed, it appeared that the credibility of Israeli deterrence was being tested in two ways. First, it was feared that limited and ambiguous moves, if not deterred, might be followed by other military moves which would ultimately erode the whole Israeli posture on south Lebanon. Secondly, it was felt that Israel's deterrence credibility might be adversely affected.[5] Thus, Israel gradually raised the level of its communications and signals to Syria, which were relayed via Washington as well as in public statements. Thus, for example, Allon stated on 26 January:[6]

> The Syrians generally act with care . . . The attempt to take control of Nabatiyya and to approach the Litani brings them dangerously near to deviating from the parameters acceptable to us. Israel has the moral right and the operational power to insure its security interests along the border with Lebanon.

In what eventually became a standard signalling procedure, Israel finally resorted to its third and strongest channel: military moves. On 30 January, press reports suggested that the military and civilian population in the area of the Israeli border had been placed 'on alert'.[7] As the Nabatiyya semi-crisis deepened, the Israeli Cabinet reaffirmed its concern at its meeting on 30 January. Several points arose from the Cabinet's deliberations. First, Israel indicated to the US that it was not opposed to the presence of Lebanese army units in the south. Second, it hinted that there would be strong opposition to any unilateral moves undertaken without prior Israeli agreement. Third, while the Syrian deployment in Nabatiyya did not pose an immediate danger to Israel, it created a precedent for further deployment of Syrian forces in the area.[8]

When the Washington channel failed to produce immediate results, Israel stepped up its verbal warnings and also toughened its position by demanding, through Washington, that there be a time limit for a positive Syrian response. It still waited for reactions from Syria via Washington, however. Indeed, the first positive news came on 2 February, when Syria and Lebanon declared that the unit in Nabatiyya was under the authority of President Sarkis. Syrian prestige therefore ceased to be directly involved in the matter. A decision to withdraw the force could now be presented as a Lebanese decision.

No further signals were forthcoming from Damascus, and on 6 February the Israeli Cabinet apparently decided to raise the level of implicit military threats. Among the various moves which followed that decision, Allon summoned the Deputy Chief of Mission of the US embassy and communicated to him the gravity with which his government viewed the situation. Simultaneously the Israeli Ambassador in Washington met

Secretary of State Vance and was reportedly assured that the US would attempt to speed up matters.

In one of its communications with Washington Israel warned that it reserved the right to take military action in south Lebanon. This warning raised the level of threat, but was accompanied by a rider to the effect that an Israeli military action need not necessarily lead to a direct clash with the Syrian forces. Israel could move forces into south Lebanon, without encroaching on the Syrian deployment in Nabatiyya.

The US counselled caution and this acted as an important restraining factor. Moreover, Secretary Vance was scheduled to visit the Middle East. The initiation of military action would have been a major embarrassment for the new Secretary of State — a consideration which was significant in Israeli calculations.

By 10 February there had been a considerable improvement in the situation. Syria agreed to a phased withdrawal from Nabatiyya. Philip Habib, the American official in charge of the negotiations, worked out the details of an agreement with Syria and Israel (through Ambassador Dinitz in Washington). On 11 February Rabin announced that an agreement had been reached, and on 14 February the withdrawal from Nabatiyya was completed. Thus, after two weeks of tension during which the Israeli deterrence threshold was tested, the Syrian probe proved futile. The deterrence process had proved significantly successful.

DEVELOPMENTS IN LEBANON DURING 1977

Throughout 1977 the Syrians persisted in their attempt to impose control over Lebanon while not allowing any change in the balance of forces, thus ensuring that no group obtained an exclusively predominant position. This policy began to concern the Maronites, however. They had welcomed Syrian intervention in the hope that Syria would completely crush the PLO–Muslim coalition and thus open the way for a Christian return to power, even if that power were somewhat curtailed. Events were to disappoint and disillusion them. The Syrians renewed their contacts with the PLO and appeared reluctant to withdraw from Lebanon. Moreover, the more relaxed Syrian relations with the Muslims and the PLO convinced part of the Maronite community that the Syrians might one day turn against them. Things appeared even more threatening when the Syrian position changed once again in late 1977.

The breakdown of the American effort to revive the Geneva process eventually led to a major turnabout in the Egyptian position and to Sadat's decision to pursue an independent political initiative; hence his Jerusalem visit in November 1977 and the consequent breakdown in Egyptian–Syrian relations. Indeed, Sadat was all along doubtful as to the possible success of the Geneva process and was ready for a separate Egyptian move.[9]

The Egyptian move shocked Syria. It was again left isolated. Its semi-alliance with Egypt proved to be of no benefit and its relationship with Iraq did not improve. In the meantime, Jordan preferred to make no decision and to await the emergence of a general Arab consensus. These developments also affected Syrian behaviour in Lebanon. In the first place, Syria hoped to receive Sarkis' backing for its position. However, Sarkis, like Hussein, was hesitant even though he was dependent on Syrian power. Indeed, several important Christian and Muslim leaders voiced their backing for Sadat's initiative. Only the PLO gave full support to Syria's strong rejection of Cairo's move. These developments explain the emergent limited understanding between Syria and the PLO in Lebanon in late 1977-early 1978.

Christian disappointment with the Syrian role also resulted from the heavy-handed way in which the Syrian forces treated the Lebanese in general, especially since the Christians felt superior to the Syrians in terms of education and general outlook. The majority of the Christians were opposed to a breach with Syria, however. Among the Kataib, it was Bashir Jumayyil who began to argue in 1977 that the Lebanese should turn against Syria. But even within the Kataib the majority continued to endorse the Syrian role. By late 1977, however, Camille Chamoun also came to the conclusion that Syria had begun to play an anti-Christian role in Lebanon. A consensus thus began to emerge between Kamil and Bashir, even though they remained divided in terms of their organisations. Between them, they controlled the majority of the Christian militias.[10] Eventually, clashes between the Christian militias and the Syrian army began — the first initiated by Chamoun's militia on 7 February 1978, in the Fayadiyya barracks in Beirut.

Bashir Jumayyil, for his part, encouraged by Israeli deliveries of arms, was ready to initiate a dangerous move against Syria. However, before becoming too heavily involved in such a confrontation, he turned against that part of the Christian front which continued to orient itself towards Syria. Beginning in May 1978, armed clashes began between the Phalangists and ex-President Faranjiyya's militia. On 13 June the Phalangists killed Faranjiyya's son, Tony, along with his family and body guards. The rift between the Jumayyil family and Faranjiyya became critical. Syria moved in to aid its protégé, Faranjiyya, and to demonstrate its ability to control events in Lebanon. It appears that this move also took place against the background of continued Phalange and Chamounist militia attacks against the Syrians. Heavy Syrian shelling of the Christian quarters in Beirut ensued in June and July, and continued in some fashion until October. The Syrian action involved heavy shelling of parts of East Beirut and primarily of the Ashrafiyya quarter. Significantly, however, Syria refrained from trying to conquer East Beirut.

Israeli reactions

When the Begin Government came to power in May 1977, one of the first areas which came under scrutiny was the Israeli policy on Lebanon. This was divided into two sub-sets: developments in the south, and the Israeli–Syrian–Christian complex. On both questions Begin pronounced his conviction that the policy pursued by the Rabin Government represented the optimal strategy.[11]

However, in July 1978, this policy was tested in Beirut. The Christians appealed to Isreal for help. As mentioned in Chapter 2, Israel had formulated an ambiguous posture which could have been interpreted by actors other than the Christians as that, in the case of a threat to the existence of the Maronite community, Israel might move to their aid. Simultaneously, it signalled to the Christians that they could not expect such assistance, or at least that Israeli aid was not guaranteed. By the nature of things, the ambiguity of the Israeli posture was also related to the series of events that might have led to the threats to the Christians. Consequently, when Bashir Jumayyil turned to Begin and asked for Israeli intervention, many in the Israeli leadership pointed out that the Christians had provoked the heavy-handed Syrian reaction, and that Israel should not help them.

Israel therefore decided on a middle-of-the-road reaction:

refraining from actual military intervention, while signalling its willingness to delineate more clearly another 'red line' — defence of the Christians against a major Syrian onslaught. Thus, on 6 July 1978, two Israeli fighters flew over Beirut breaking the sound barrier. This demonstration of force was accompanied by armoured concentrations on the Golan Heights. The Israeli signal succeeded and Syria stopped its bombardment. Encouraged by this, the Phalangists renewed their activities against the Syrian forces. In reaction, Syria struck in the north and occupied a northern part of the Maronite 'canton', but refrained from an attempt to take over the Maronite zone completely. This time Israel refused to intervene. The Christian militias were prepared for the time being to reach an accommodation with Syria, and this was facilitated by Arab and international intervention. At the Bayt al-Din conference 15–17 October 1978, an agreement was reached which included arrangements for a cease-fire and which renewed the Arab mandate for the ADF, thus reconfirming the principles laid down at the earlier Cairo and Riyadh conferences.

1977–81: THE DEVELOPMENT OF THE CHRISTIAN ENCLAVE IN THE SOUTH

Beginning in May–June 1976, several Christian villages in south Lebanon, mostly near the Israeli border, came under pressure from units of the Lebanese Arab Army (LAA) commanded by Lieutenant Hatib and certain Palestinian units. The villages resisted the pressure and turned to Israel for aid and supplies. Israel began the policy of the 'Good Fence' whereby Lebanese villagers received medical aid and supplies. Eventually, Lebanese workers were allowed to cross into Israel. More importantly, Israel began supplying the villages with arms and ammunition. In the meantime Major Sa'd Haddad, a regular officer of the Lebanese army, was sent with the blessing of part of the Christian community (the Chamounists) with instructions to organise the defences of the south. Haddad received the support of Israel and eventually, with Israeli backing and generous aid, organised the defences of the Christian villages in the zone. His militia, armed by Israel, fought off LAA and PLO pressure, and by March 1977 went on the offensive in an attempt to take control of several important villages in order to widen the

69

security zone of villages under his control. The offensive was initially successful but the Palestinian units launched a counter-offensive, forcing the Christian militia to retreat. The PLO militia recaptured the town of Khiam, and brought increased pressure to bear on Marjayun and Qlaia. Israel extended some artillery aid to the Christians, but its support was insufficient.

As pointed out earlier, the Lebanon question and Syrian involvement there had always been perceived by Israel as a lower priority than the Israeli–American context and the process of possible political accommodation with Egypt. The settlement of the Civil War by means of Syrian intervention, and the final restatement of the geographical 'red line' during the Nabatiyya episode, made the Lebanese set of problems less urgent for Israel. It was now clear, however, that the situation in south Lebanon, while not of major political-strategic importance was likely to become a permanent source of irritation to Israel and would demand its continued attention. Moreover, the persistent low-level violence there allowed for local military activity which — if unchecked and uncontrolled — could set in process developments of greater import. Indeed, the Israeli Northern Command sometimes developed its own initiatives and became the centre for ideas concerning a radical and activist solution to the problem of south Lebanon and to the Lebanese question in general.

When the south Lebanese Christians were beaten back in early April 1977, Israel began to take the situation more seriously and considered counter-measures. It also suspected Syrian encouragement of PLO activity. Israeli reactions were cautious, partly because the issue was perceived as not constituting a great threat to Israeli security, and partly because of the domestic political problems that arose with the resignation of Prime Minister Rabin. Also, the United States strongly advised caution. Israel used the Washington channel to restrict Palestinian activity and to mobilise Syrian restraint of the PLO. Allon delineated four principles which were to govern Israeli reactions:[12]

> Israel will not tolerate the penetration of Syrian or pan-Arab forces south of their existing positions. Second, Israel will under no circumstances agree to terrorist activity whether by firing of shells and Katyusha rockets across the border or infiltration of forces into our territory. Third, Israel will not accept or tolerate activity against the Lebanese villages which

are close to our border and considered by it to be friendly. We, as Jews, will not stand for massacres. This will not be tolerated. Finally, no interference with the humanitarian activity of the open gates of the 'Good Fence' will be tolerated.

The United States made an effort to resolve the threatening development through its contacts with Syria. By mid-April, the Palestinian military activity had subsided.

However, the security vacuum created in south Lebanon 'invited' Palestinian activity. Syrian forces were not allowed into the south by the Israeli deterrence threshold; the Lebanese Government was unable to extend its authority into the south, and the local Shi'i population was incapable of resisting PLO movement there. This was a formula for future local escalations of the conflict.

The Litani Operation

The Litani Operation was the culmination of a process of local escalation in south Lebanon coupled with terrorist actions by the PLO inside Israel. In retrospect, it appears that the Litani Operation was not a sign of a new strategy or a major departure from previous perceptions. Hence, in order to evaluate its roots and its significance, we have to look into developments in south Lebanon throughout the summer of 1977 and the following winter.

Once Israel decided to back Sa'ad Haddad's militia and to protect the Christian villages, it became necessary for the Israeli Defence Force to increase its activity in the border area. As PLO strength in the south increased, the ability of the Christian militia to defend the Christian villages diminished and direct Israeli activity became necessary. Israeli incursions into south Lebanon were therefore inevitable.

When the Likud Government came to power in May 1977, there was no significant change in the general Israeli strategy. Although the new Defence Minister, Ezer Weitzman, was less patient with Palestinian activity, he was nevertheless not keen on a real change in strategy.[13] Nor did Begin direct any major change in policy and strategy in regard to Haddad's area, or to the general situation in south Lebanon.[14]

During the summer of 1977, Syria was trying to control and limit the activities of the PLO in Lebanon in general and in the south in particular. Within the context of these activities the PLO was forced to sign the Shtura Agreement on 24 July 1977, which stipulated that Palestinian forces should withdraw from the area bordering Israel, elements of the Lebanese Army should be sent to the south, and south Lebanon should be declared a demilitarised zone.[15] The agreement did not come into force, however, and the clashes between the PLO and the Christians in the south continued.

Late that summer, Israel became more concerned because of the clear increase in the size of PLO forces in the south. It also rejected the idea of sending Lebanese army units into the south (an idea backed by the United States and Syria). This would have meant the closure of the 'Good Fence' and the end of the close relations with Haddad's militia. This left, in fact, only one option open: to increase the military backing to the Christians, allowing them to conduct large-scale military operations. It should be noted that the Israeli reasoning was in a sense a logical continuation of the strategy devised and implemented by the Rabin Government, which rejected the idea of a Syrian deployment in the south and encouraged the activity of Haddad. It is true that the Lebanese army was not the Syrian army. However, it was doubtful whether the Lebanese army would have been capable of imposing its will on the PLO. Furthermore, the Lebanese army was seen at the time as being under Syrian control.

Needless to say, Israel was concerned not only with the pressure applied on the Christian villages in the south, but also with the possibility of renewed Palestinian actions against northern Israel.[16] Aiding the Christian militia appeared to be the most effective means of limiting the activities of the PLO.

In the second half of September, Israel provided support to the Christian offensive against the town of Khiam. Israeli armour took part in the operation and occupied positions in south Lebanon. In response, the Palestinians began rocket attacks on Israel.

While the fighting continued, Israel also sent deterrent signals to Syria. The United States was active in trying to calm the situation and to pre-empt further escalation. Under US pressure, the Israeli forces withdrew and a cease-fire was declared. This was not a formal cease-fire but a series of 'understandings' and tacit agreements between Israel, Lebanon, the Palestinians, Syria and Haddad, all attained through the good offices of the United States. The objectives of the Israeli action were to strengthen the hand of the Christians, and if possible, to achieve the evacuation of the PLO from the south. The second object-ive, however, was difficult to fulfil. Israel was thus left with two options, as stated at the time by an Israeli observer:[17]

> The basic approach adopted by the present Defense Minister
> . . . sees the goal as the removal of the terrorists from our
> northern border. This objective can be achieved either by
> helping to form a strip of strong and viable Christian settle-
> ments in southern Lebanon or by independent Israeli military
> activity in the field. Israel has so far chosen the first option.

It might be that, once Israeli involvement began and the United States tried to negotiate a cease-fire, Israel decided to try and use the situation for an overall settlement of the situation in south Lebanon.[18] However, the initial Israeli decision and its later policy on south Lebanon, tend to suggest that such an objective was not prominent in Israeli calculations.

The cease-fire collapsed because of the inherent tension between the Palestinians and the Christians in the south. The Palestinians increased their presence in the south and also moved in heavy weapons, to increase the pressure on the Christians. Israel extended artillery support to the Christians but avoided intervening with ground units. In November a process of direct escalation between Israel and the Palestinians developed. In retaliation for Palestinian rocket attacks on northern Israel (which might in turn have been retaliation for Israeli artillery shelling), Israel launched a series of air strikes.

November was the month of Sadat's visit to Jerusalem and this major development absorbed the attention of both Israel and the Palestinians. The remainder of 1977 and early 1978 was characterised by relative calm along the border.

Certain developments in south Lebanon caused concern for Israel, primarily the deployment of some Saiqa units (under Syrian control) in positions close to the Christian enclaves. More ominous was the deployment of elements of the more extreme Palestinian organisations in the Beaufort Crusader castle — a position dominating some of the Christian villages, which enabled them to harass these villages. The pressure in Israel to

73

relieve the Christians increased and some kind of military operation seemed to be on the cards.

On 11 March 1978, a group of Palestinians landed on the Israeli coast. After murdering an American tourist, they hijacked a bus full of civilian passengers and drove to the suburbs of Tel-Aviv where they were stopped by Israeli security forces. In the ensuing battle thirty-five Israelis, most of them civilians, were killed and seventy-one wounded.

This murderous operation sent a wave of outrage throughout Israel. Since the first half of the 1950s, when the strategy of retaliation was formulated and implemented, Israelis have been conditioned to avenge terrorist attacks on Israeli targets, especially civilian ones. The salience of revenge in Israel is such that an operation is expected to be almost automatic. Moreover, the Israeli retaliation is usually designed to cause more damage and pain to the Arab side than was caused to Israel. This pattern is even more clear when the number of Israeli casualties from an Arab terrorist attack is high.

Immediately following the 11 March terrorist action, consultations on both the military and the political level about an Israeli military action in south Lebanon began. They extended over three days, from 11 to 14 March, when the decision to invade south Lebanon was finally taken.

Throughout the decision-making phase, the plan of operations was to attack south Lebanon, with the objective of causing as many casualties as possible to PLO units, destroying their infrastructure and establishing control over certain important dominating positions within a 10 km strip from the international border. There was some confusion, however, as to the political and strategic rationale and objectives of the planned operation.

The basic motivation was to punish the Palestinian organisations.[19] An additional line of argument was to affect the ability of the organisations to operate from Lebanon. There was also the objective of deterring future terrorist activity. However, the plan ultimately responded to the Israeli need to create some kind of security zone along the border within which the Haddad militia could extend its control — obviously with continued Israeli military help. Such a security zone would alleviate the threat to the Israeli settlements in the north *and* would also resolve the problem of the Christians.

In retrospect, it seems quite clear that throughout the consultations, some important questions remained unanswered:

What was the political objective of the operation? What was the strategic objective or objectives, i.e. deterrence against future Palestinian operations and if so, what type of operations? Was there to be imposition of permanent Israeli military control over parts of the area to be taken? What areas should be taken? For how long, if at all, and in which parts of the area to be taken should Israeli units establish a permanent presence? What was to be the role of Major Haddad's militia following the operation? Most importantly, what kind of political order was to be established in south Lebanon, and with what actors would it be negotiated: Syria, the almost non-existent Lebanese government, or the PLO?

Consequently, there were also voices within the defence establishment recommending a more limited 'surgical type' operation rather than a massive penetration into Lebanon. Those voices were apparently raised by only a minority, since the pressure to retaliate was enormous. The rationale for the operation and its size had in fact to be formulated in a rather *ex post* manner. The basic decision to retaliate on a massive scale had never really been in any doubt.

It seems that possible Syrian reactions *were* considered. Throughout the operation Israel was careful not to provoke Syria into a military confrontation. The initial decision to penetrate to a depth of only ten kilometres was probably also related to the ambiguous relationship with the Syrians. According to the established 'red line' Syria was 'allowed' to operate north of the Zaharani but was not to move south of it. Also, the area south of the Litani had always been considered an area in which Israel could undertake small-scale military operations. However, the intended push into Lebanon was of a different character and as such Syria's reactions had to be taken into account. It seems, then, that the Syrian deterrent posture played a part in the initial decision to limit the Israeli military action geographically.

Israel had also to take into consideration the effects of the operation on the United States and Egypt. Public statements by the Carter Administration prior to the operation indicated that Washington was concerned about possible heavy civilian casualties and the disruption of the peace process. Israel could therefore assume that, provided the operation was limited and Cairo's response moderate, it would not meet with strong American opposition. As for the Egyptian reaction, Israeli decision-makers assumed that an operation in Lebanon could be decoupled from the negotiations with Egypt.[20] However, in order to increase mutual confidence, Weitzman passed on to Egypt at the start of the operation a message stating, 'Our forces began a limited operation along the Lebanese border in order to remove the terrorist bases from the area. I hope that this limited action will not disrupt the talks between our two states.'[21]

In view of all these considerations, the final plan of operations called for an Israeli push along the 100 km of border to a depth of about 10 km, the destruction of Palestinian bases there, and the creation of a *cordon sanitaire* in the area.[22]

When the operation began on 14 March 1978, at 23.15 GMT, the Israeli political context and objectives were not clear to the military and political leadership. As is usual in such circumstances, military events tend to dictate political and strategic developments. Military-tactical factors gain in importance and decision-makers tend to cling to them when making decisions on future behaviour.

The first stage of the operation code-named 'Even Hachochma' (the wisdom stone) was completed by 15 March. Opposition to the action was very limited; most of the Palestinian guerrillas withdrew in the face of the superior Israeli forces, and did not even participate in the fighting. According to various estimates there had been about 5,000 armed Palestinian guerrillas in south Lebanon, but their exact distribution was not known. Even if all of them were concentrated near the international border, they would not have been a match for the Israeli forces. Apart from the ground thrust, Israeli air and naval units attacked many Palestinian bases throughout Lebanon.

As noted, the initial plan called for the seizure of a series of dominant positions in south Lebanon, thus relieving the pressure on the Christian enclave. But even in the early stages, this plan was superseded by a second one, namely to link the various dominant positions into a coherent strip, about ten kilometres in width, along the international border. Such an expansion was dictated by the weakness of the opposition, and by the logic of the topographical situation. Thus, on the recommendation of the military command in the field, the Israeli units moved to control this strip.

Simultaneously with the launching of the operation, Israel notified the US about the operation, stressing that it was not planning to stay in Lebanon. In that communication, as well as in public statements, Israel declared that its objective was to reach a solution to the problem of south Lebanon. Once that was achieved, Israeli forces would withdraw. Israel also stated that it wanted negotiations to begin promptly. Thus, although the initial objective of the operation was to exact vengeance and to strengthen the position of the Christians, wider politico-strategic objectives were added. The operation began to assume the character of an exercise in 'compellance', that is, the use of military force to create new political facts. This, as we shall see, was not to be achieved, however.

The initial US reaction was perceived by Israeli decision-makers as indicating that the US was ready to acquiesce in the operation. But, in fact, the US was increasingly concerned about Israeli plans for south Lebanon. With no prior political preparation or co-ordination between Israel and the US, Washington was not sure of Israel's real intentions there. Furthermore, it was not clear what kind of 'solution' to the situation Israel was interested in and by means of what procedures. The US was also concerned about the Egyptian–Israeli peace process which had begun only a few months before and which still seemed extremely vulnerable to negative regional developments. Sadat's position in the Arab world might be adversely affected if it appeared that he did not react strongly to an Israeli attack on the Palestinians and to a full-scale Israeli invasion of an Arab country. Secondly, the US was probably concerned about Israeli–Syrian relations. The set of understandings, both tacit and explicit, reached between Israel and Syria, in which the US was partly related as a go-between, was liable to crumble under the pressure of the Israeli invasion. Moreover, the US was interested in expanding its influence in Syria, in order to bring it into the orbit of American influence and the process of peace negotiations. The Israeli invasion seemed adversely to affect American prospects on these issues as well.[23]

It is possible that had Israel co-ordinated its military activities with the United States beforehand, or at least proposed a realistic and feasible plan for south Lebanon of which the operation was a part, the US might have co-operated in the implementation of the political aspect of that plan. There was no consultation with Washington, however, nor was there a broad political plan.

In its absence, the US did not co-ordinate its activities with moves by Israel, but sought to glean some advantage from a quick political move to obtain the withdrawal of Israeli forces from south Lebanon. When the Lebanese Government began preparations to request a Security Council resolution demanding an immediate Israeli withdrawal, the United States took the initiative, and proposed a draft resolution which eventually became Security Council Resolution 425, thus creating UNIFIL.

The possibility of such an American initiative should have forced Israeli decision-makers to search for some political plan as an alternative or supplement to the initiative. Instead, however, as before, the Israeli response was in the military realm. A decision was taken to push on to the Litani river. The logic of this move was that, should the Security Council decide to send UN observers or forces to south Lebanon, their area of control would extend to the Litani river, thus creating an even wider buffer zone between Israel and the Palestinian guerrillas. In addition, Lebanese villages beyond the 10 km strip had begun to surrender and this almost 'invited' the Israeli forces to move ahead. Finally, it became evident that Syria would not intervene in the fighting.[24] The decision to expand the operation was taken on 18 March by Begin, Weitzman and Gur. The advance was implemented and completed, the following day.

The advance was executed with almost no military clashes. One village after another surrendered without opposition. Most of the Palestinian guerrillas had already fled, and there were only sporadic exchanges of fire. The Israeli forces, however, decided not to take the town of Tyre and its immediate environs where there was a large concentration of Palestinian refugee camps. It was felt that an attempt to conquer Tyre would involve many civilian and Israeli casualties and might deteriorate into a bloody battle with counterproductive international results.

On 20 March therefore Israel decided to accept Security Council Resolution 425 and to withdraw from south Lebanon. It insisted, however, that UNIFIL be more than a token force and that it be deployed throughout the area south of the Litani. The actual Israeli withdrawal was conducted in three phases and completed only on 13 June. UNIFIL, in fact, never achieved control over Tyre and was unable to control even the Christian strip which by then extended along the whole border to a depth of approximately 10 kms. It proved partly useful, however, as a screen against Palestinian infiltration into Israel proper, but as later events were to prove, it was incapable of halting Palestinian shelling of the Christian enclave or of northern Israel.

Throughout the operations, Israel was careful to signal to Syria that the battle was not directed at it, that the objectives of the operation were limited, and that there was no need for it to intervene. This set of signals indicated Israeli concern to maintain the 'red line' and to avoid a military confrontation. Israeli caution in this respect dovetailed with the deterrence threshold established between Israel and Syria during 1976 and 1977, and with the regional and Lebanese political contexts. This latter point requires brief elucidation.

In pure deterrence terms, Israel did not radically transgress the understandings which existed between the two countries. It had always maintained that south Lebanon was an area of vital importance for its security. Moreover, the possibility of an Israeli military action in south Lebanon had always been taken seriously by American, Syrian and Lebanese decision-makers. Israel had always emphasised that it would consider a *Syrian* move south of the Zaharani as unacceptable, and indeed had acted accordingly during the Nabatiyya episode. On the other hand, the Israeli penetration deep into Lebanese territory did put the Syrians in a difficult political and perceptual position. In the eyes of the Arab world the Syrian military presence in Lebanon was legitimised by the Riyadh and Cairo conferences, but its role also meant the defence of Lebanese territory against Israeli invasion. Furthermore, the Syrian presence was sanctioned by the invitation of the Lebanese President. The Israeli invasion did not have such legitimisation. Finally, the invasion took place precisely when relations between Syria and the PLO were in the process of improvement. The Syrian reluctance to aid the PLO in its time of need must have signalled to that organisation that Syria was not a reliable patron.

Syria was also constrained by other factors. Although the Israeli invasion strained the set of deterrence understandings, it was not a clear violation of them. Syria was not forced to respond within the framework of the deterrence understandings but it had to be sensitive primarily to the politico-strategic context. The decision of whether to react or not remained primarily a question to be decided in the light of three variables: first, the military balance between Israel and Syria and whether Syria could mount a viable and efficient military response to the Israeli action; secondly, how the invasion affected Syria's relationships with various factions in Lebanon; and finally, what was to be the shape of the ultimate Israeli deployment in south Lebanon. In the event, Syria was spared any need to respond because within a few days Israel was forced (or rather helped) out of Lebanon by US pressure and the Security Council decision.

In order to justify its behaviour before the Arab world, Syria pointed out that one of the Israeli objectives was in fact to trigger off a military confrontation with Syria. Syrian spokesmen insisted that Syria would choose the time and place for a war with Israel. Syria also used the Israeli operation as an additional instrument in its propaganda confrontation with Egypt. It contended that Israel had invaded Lebanon with the blessing of Egypt. This was, of course, a distortion of the truth. Israel had in fact notified Egypt about the campaign once it had begun, and also continued sending messages concerning the development of the operation.[25] This was remarkable in itself; indeed, Israel was surprised that Egypt was ready to accept these messages. Israel maintained links with its erstwhile arch-enemy, Egypt, while conducting military operations against the Palestinians. It could not be said, however, that this amounted to Egyptian–Israeli collusion.

Nevertheless, the nature of Syrian–Egyptian relations was such that Syria had some reason to blame Egypt. Since President Sadat's visit to Jerusalem in November 1977, the two countries had been on a collision course. Syria could not hope that Egypt would stand by it in the event of a military confrontation with Israel. Syria's military vulnerability was thus increased enormously. Hence, its readiness to respond militarily to Israel in ambiguous situations diminished considerably. Furthermore, given Syria's weakened military posture, Israel felt less constrained in reacting militarily to PLO provocations. The latter point must, however, be qualified. The process of accommodation with Egypt placed Israel in a sensitive position. It was anxious to maintain the momentum of the peace process, and a major military action was liable to hamper that process.

It can be said, then, that the Litani Operation clarified the deterrence thresholds of both Israel and Syria in south Lebanon. The Israeli 'red line' (established in 1976) against Syrian deployment south of the Zaharani did not necessarily involve a legitimisation of Israeli military operations up to the Litani. But following the operation, it became clear that Syria was prepared to tolerate Israeli operations in that area. What the Syrian reaction would be were Israel to advance further north across the Litani and through to the Zaharani remained unclear (this particular point was clarified in 1982).

The moderate Syrian reaction, the total tranquillity along the Israeli–Syrian cease-fire border on the Golan Heights, and the generally encouraging experience accumulated during the period 1976–7 about possible tacit co-ordination between Israel and Syria in regard to developments in Lebanon, led some Israeli decision-makers to the conclusion that the best solution to the festering problem of south Lebanon lay in an agreement between Israel and Syria in which Syrian forces would be deployed in south Lebanon in exchange for a Syrian undertaking not to allow Palestinian activity from there against Israel. Gur was one of the leading proponents of this view.[26] However, the animosity towards Syria and the suspicions about its long-range intentions were sufficient to eliminate Gur's plan.

The deployment of UNIFIL in south Lebanon created a new situation with both benefits and costs for Israel. On the positive side, the PLO military units were not allowed to be redeployed south of the Litani (except for the Tyre enclave). The infrastructure of the Palestinian organisations south of the Litani had been destroyed by Israel, and no opportunity was allowed for it to be repaired. Furthermore, UNIFIL had become an additional obstacle to the penetration of Palestinian units into Israel. There were numerous attempts by such units to cross the UNIFIL-held territory on their way to the international border, and on many occasions the UNIFIL units were able to stop these attempts. Needless to say, UNIFIL activity in halting these penetrations was not uniform. A lot depended on the performance of the different units and on the readiness of officers and soldiers to become involved in skirmishes with Palestinian guerrilla groups. However, it can safely be said that the UNIFIL units served as an additional barrier against Arab infiltration into Israel.

There were, however, also some negative outcomes from the Israeli point of view. To begin with, the presence of UNIFIL made Israeli military penetration through south Lebanon more difficult politically. Palestinian terrorists might skirmish with UNIFIL units. Israel could not afford such actions. In order to strike at Palestinian guerrillas, Israel had to operate either from the air or from the east outflanking the UNIFIL-held area. This, of course, imposed certain constraints on Israeli operations. Furthermore, many soldiers in the UNIFIL troops were meeting Palestinians for the first time and learning about their cause and their sufferings. PLO propagandists were very active in trying to spread PLO ideas among the UNIFIL units. Indeed, not only were these soldiers influenced by PLO propaganda, but they communicated it in various ways to their respective homelands. Finally, the occasional clashes between UNIFIL units and Israeli soldiers only intensified this trend of opinion in UNIFIL.

The Litani Operation was conducted by Israeli forces equipped with heavy armour and a lot of fire power. The Israeli High Command was anxious to keep down casualties as much as possible and therefore relied on applying intense fire power whenever there was any resistance. As a result considerable damage was caused to civilian property along the routes of the Israeli advance. In some places a mass civilian migration ensued. Those fleeing were primarily Shi'i civilians who, along with the Christians, had been the main victims of the war in the south. They had suffered enormously from the Palestinian organisations that had controlled the area until the Litani Operation, and also from Israeli retaliatory actions. Tens of thousands fled their homes, much property was destroyed, and there were many casualties.

However, within a relatively short time after the Litani Operation, the Shi'is began to return to their homes. Some of those who lived within the narrow strip along the international border, which now became completely dominated by Major Haddad's militia, even joined forces with Haddad. In the rest of the area south of the Litani, the Shi'is enjoyed the protection of UNIFIL.

In summary, the Israeli operation failed in its attempt to destroy the Palestinian organisations in the south since most of the Palestinian guerrillas fled northwards and built up an elaborate infrastructure north of the Litani. It also failed in its attempt to impose a new political order in the south. In deterrence terms *vis-à-vis* Syria, the operation and its outcome further clarified Israeli and Syrian deterrence thresholds but did not clarify the deterrence situation as regards the area between the Litani and the Zaharani. The main positive outcomes lay in the creation of an additional buffer against Palestinian terrorism and in the strengthening of the Christian enclave. Finally, it demonstrated the level of accommodation reached between Israel and Egypt. The latter achievement remained, of course, a function of the overall political relationship between the two countries.

The 1979 air clashes

The Syrian posture

From the beginning of Sadat's peace initiative, Syria had become increasingly aware of its complete strategic vulnerability *vis-à-vis* Israel. Its attempts to mobilise other Arab countries in the formation of a meaningful bloc came to nought. Syria was still hoping that the peace initiative would fail, but when the Camp David accords were signed in September 1978, the weakness of its position was painfully exposed. This time, however, it found some ostensible Arab solidarity. On 1 October, Iraq called for a summit meeting (the ninth of its kind) aimed at forming an Arab association which would force Egypt to change its posture. In addition, Syria and Iraq overnight transformed their hostile and bitter relationship, and formed a new alliance. The leaders of the two countries met in Baghdad on 24 October and signed an agreement of co-operation and co-ordination. As is usual in the Arab world on such occasions, committees were formed to prepare for far-reaching co-operation. Thus, for example, one committee was instructed to prepare a draft for a defence pact which would serve as the basis for full military unification between the two countries.

The Ninth Arab Summit demonstrated the divisions in the Arab world.[27] For a short time the summit succeeded in overcoming these differences, but it failed in its attempt to force Egypt to abandon its search for peace with Israel. Egypt was threatened with sanctions if it continued this policy, but it rejected the threat. From the point of view of Syria, another disturbing development was the gradual cautious dialogue which evolved between Jordan and Egypt after the summit.

In the follow-up to the summit, at the conference of Arab Foreign and Finance Ministers held in late March 1979, several decisions were taken regarding sanctions against Egypt. At that conference, as well as during the summit, Iraq took up a middle-of-the-road position on the question of such sanctions, between the moderate Arab countries led by Saudi Arabia, and the extreme stands taken by Libya, Syria and the PLO. By mid-1979, the movement for pressure against Egypt had run its course, and was non-existent for all practical purposes. In the six months from October 1978, when expectations of unity between Syria and Iraq were running high, to the summer of 1979, relations between the two countries began to deteriorate and to return to their original animosity. By August 1979, the relationship had entered an extremely cool period.

While Syria was searching for alternatives to the role that Egypt played in the front against Israel, and was feeling increasingly vulnerable, the Asad regime also encountered growing internal difficulties. Opposition from fundamentalist Muslim organisations led by the Muslim Brotherhood was again mounting and reached its climax in the autumn of 1979.

Developments in the Arab world made Syria more cautious, if anything, about the danger of a military confrontation with Israel. It was still suffering from the criticism that it had done nothing to help the PLO during the Litani Operation. In addition, it had continually to weigh up its relationship with the PLO and to assess the costs and benefits involved in improved relations. On the one hand, the Camp David accords and the Israeli–Egyptian peace treaty signed in March 1979 should have made relations between Syria and the PLO closer than before. On the other hand, Syria probably viewed the improvement of relations between the PLO and Jordan with suspicion. Moreover, it continued to be concerned about the PLO's relative independence and also the influence exerted on the organisation by other Arab countries (primarily Iraq). This ambivalence characterised Syrian attitudes towards the PLO all along. Finally, Syria would not allow itself to be drawn into a confrontation with Israel, at a time not of its own choosing.

Given all these conflicting factors, Syria would probably have preferred to avoid a confrontation with Israel unless forced into it by the dynamics of the Israeli–Syrian relationship or by events inside Lebanon. These forces were to evolve during 1979.

The Israeli posture

The appointment of General Eitan as Chief of Staff of the IDF in April 1978 signalled the beginning of a gradual departure from the previous Israeli strategy and tactics in regard to Lebanon. Apart from being extremely 'hawkish' in his general outlook, General Eitan had been chief of the Northern Command until 1977, and tended to focus his attention on the possibility and desirability of a military confrontation with Syria. He also approached the Palestinian problem in a straightforward military way, disregarding the complex politico-strategic issues involved. It is little wonder, then, that he was influential in convincing Defence Minister Weitzman of the desirability of initiating a change in Israeli strategy in regard to PLO deployment in south Lebanon. Indeed, he found similar enthusiasm for such a change in the person of his successor as chief of the Northern Command, General Bengal, who was able to facilitate the evolvement of such a policy.

The new strategy abandoned the responsive pattern that had characterised previous Israeli strategy. Instead, it aimed at initiating a continuous campaign of harassment of the Palestinian forces, on the ground, in the air and from the sea. The objective was not response and deterrence, but rather destruction of the opponent or, at least, putting him completely on the defensive, thus preventing him from conducting terrorist operations against Israel. The campaign involved massive air strikes on Palestinian bases. On the ground, large-scale commando-type raids were conducted against the same objectives, increasing many times over the collateral damage to the Palestinian and Lebanese civilian populations. Following the Litani Operation, the Palestinian organisations had concentrated on building their bases and infrastructures north of the Litani (with the exception of the Tyre enclave); the Israeli offensive therefore moved north of the area targeted before the Litani Operation. The area between the Litani and the Zaharani now became the central focus of Israeli attacks, and the Israeli air offensive extended far north to include the Sidon area as well.

As recounted in Chapter 2, Israel had, by late March 1976, drawn up a general guideline concerning aerial activity in Lebanon. It was formulated as a deterrence threat to Syria and consisted of a ban on Syrian activity in Lebanese airspace. Other rules of the game were not spelled out but past experience was the determining factor. Israeli aircraft had operated over Lebanon for years. There were two types of Israeli air activity: bombing strikes at Palestinian bases in south Lebanon up to the Litani river, and surveillance and intelligence-gathering flights over the whole of Lebanon, including the Beqa valley along the Israel–Syrian border. The intelligence gathered referred to both Palestinian activity in Lebanon and — in the case of flights along the eastern edge of the Beqa — Syrian military activity in Syria. Indeed, Israeli intelligence flights have been conducted over Syria itself from time to time.[28] This situation was a function of Israel's obvious air superiority. Thus, the Israeli 'red line' of 1976 corresponded in fact to a situation that was already in existence. Because of the Syrian need to obtain Israeli acquiescence in their invasion of Lebanon, they did not challenge this 'red line'. Indeed, the Israeli threat in that respect was so strong and credible, that Syria refrained from violating it[29] even when it modified the system of 'red lines' in other respects, for example, by increasing the size of its ground forces in Lebanon and by introducing weapons systems on the ground which infringed the Israeli 'red lines'. From 1976 to 1979, the Israeli air strikes conformed to the pattern previously established. Israel had struck primarily in areas in the southern parts of the country. The situation was modified by the Israeli campaign against the Palestinian organisations in 1979.

The Syrian decision to react was some time in coming. It is likely that it was reached in the light of several factors. The main stimulus was probably that the extent and intensity of the Israeli air activity exceeded the geographical limits that had been accepted up to then, and indeed sometimes even included bombing missions quite close to Syrian units. Secondly, there was the need to emphasise Syrian commitment to the Palestinian cause, both in terms of the relationship with the PLO and in the Arab world. This was doubly important in view of the total lack of Syrian activity during the Litani Operation which had brought many critical comments from various quarters. Finally, the Syrians may have suspected that the Israeli ground and air campaign was a prelude to more far-reaching Israeli military plans in regard to Lebanon.

The initial Syrian decision was to try and restore the previous pattern of air activity. To this end Syrian interceptors on several occasions during Israeli air strikes or intelligence missions flew in attack configuration close to the Israeli aircraft. They did not actually try to intercept the Israeli fighters, but they flew in such a way as to create concern about their intentions. This was a major break with past practice. In the first place, the Syrian Air Force was now operating in the skies over Lebanon. Secondly, they flew in combat formation close to the Israeli aircraft, and there was no doubt that they wanted to signal a certain message.

The Syrian air activity was indeed perceived by Israel as a message but the contents of the message were initially misunderstood. The Israeli military leadership was convinced at the time that Syria was not interested in a military confrontation with Israel. The Syrian activity was therefore interpreted not as a stage in tacit bargaining but rather as a hollow propaganda exercise intended for Palestinian, Lebanese and, most importantly, domestic Syrian and general Arab consumption.

However, when the Syrians persisted in their operations and even tried to intercept Israeli aircraft, Israel changed its perceptions of the Syrian objectives. It became clear that Syria was signalling its intention to bring about a basic change in the pattern of Israeli air activity. This intention was reinforced when Israeli air surveillance detected the introduction into Lebanon of Syrian radar for air defence units (although no air defence weapons had been introduced). It was clear that Israel must formulate a response to the Syrian activity.

Israel made the following calculations. In the first place, it was not interested in a full-scale military confrontation with Syria. In that respect the first Likud Government did not differ from the previous regime. A war with Syria would make no sense politically and would be costly. Moreover, the United States would view such a confrontation with great displeasure and the operation was liable to threaten the evolving peace with Egypt. At the same time, however, Israel was not ready to withdraw under Syrian air pressure. Finally, Israel was interested in maintaining the instrument of air bombardment against the Palestinians. It therefore decided to exhibit a forceful, yet controlled response to the Syrian attempts. On 27 June 1979, there was an air encounter in which five Syrian Mig 21 fighters were shot down. The 'air bargaining' continued with the Syrians resuming their flights sporadically, while Israeli aircraft tried to avoid such encounters. On one occasion, however, a limited encounter developed and one Syrian Mig was shot down. Simultaneously, the scope of the Israeli air strikes diminished somewhat. In September, however, Israeli air activity was again expanded with heavy attacks on Palestinian camps in the Sidon area, well north of the Zaharani and not far from the southern entrances to Beirut. There was another Syrian interception attempt on this mission. The Israeli response was swift. In an encounter soon afterwards, on 24 September four Syrian planes were brought down. Fears increased that a general confrontation between the two countries was imminent. Both sides were in fact careful to ensure that no such thing occurred. As a result of this deterrence dialogue, Israel had reemphasised its obvious air superiority. Within a few months ten Syrian Mig 21s had been shot down. At the same time, it appeared that Syria was ready to go to great lengths to counter what it considered to be a change in the Israeli pattern of air activity. The Syrian response was an exercise in deterrence aimed at putting pressure on Israel to refrain from a certain kind of military activity. Syria also applied pressure on the PLO to scale down its activity. Moreover, it signalled its lack of interest in a major confrontation with Israel.[30]

Israel correctly perceived the Syrian signal and ultimately decided to modify the pattern of its military behaviour. The use of the air instrument against the PLO diminished after the September encounter. Simultaneously, however, Israel signalled its readiness to defend its aircraft in Lebanese air space. In this respect there was a return to the *status quo ante*. However, the Israeli–Syrian encounters did result in a change in the pattern of air behaviour in the skies over Lebanon. The Israeli air force continued its activity over Lebanon but refrained from air strikes north of the Zaharani, and in general became more selective in its activity. A precedent was also created for the use of the Syrian air force in Lebanon. Indeed, Syrian combat aircraft have since operated over Lebanon. The Syrians have refrained, however, from flying over the southern part of the country and also from the use of their air force for strike missions inside Lebanon.

In retrospect, the events of 1979 were an exercise in 'specific deterrence' on the part of Syria against Israel, which ultimately proved to be partly successful. Syria was ready to go to great lengths and to suffer defeats in the air encounters but insisted in signalling its intentions. It became clear that these air encounters contained the potential for escalation, but this was a development that both sides acted to avoid. However, it was Israel which was deterred from a certain mode of military activity, and it was Syria which not only succeeded in this act of deterrence but also created a new 'rule of engagement' by which Syrian aircraft were 'allowed' to operate in parts of Lebanon, albeit under considerable constraints. From September 1979 until early 1981, the two sides were careful to avoid new air confrontations. Syrian aircraft at times flew close to Israeli planes (but never in south Lebanon) but refrained from intervening in their activity. On the whole, the Israeli aircraft remained the masters of the Lebanese skies but under newly accepted limitations. The Syrian air force was 'allowed' to fly there, but not on combat missions.

The tacit bargaining of 1979 was remarkable in one other important respect. During 1976, and in the formulation of the famous 'red lines', the most important channel of communications between Israel and Syria was Washington. Tacit deterrence threats and tacit bargaining were used extensively but were in the last analysis dependent on the understandings made through indirect (American) diplomatic channels. In 1979, on the other hand, the evidence suggests that the bargaining was entirely tacit but was carried out by 'moves in the field'. In this sense, the case seems to follow the classical pattern of tacit bargaining. It should also be noted that there was an initial Israeli misperception of Syrian intentions, that is, the notion that Syria would not press ahead with its air activity. Once the real Syrian bargaining position had been grasped, Israel reacted toughly by the initiation of air battles. Later Israel half accepted the Syrian 'demands' and scaled down its activity. Through all this, Israel also 'accepted' a new definition of the rules of air engagement in Lebanon.

It should be added that the United States was deeply concerned about the evolving situation and was very active in trying to restrain the military activity. Washington was unhappy about the extent of the Israeli offensive against the PLO in south Lebanon and communicated its displeasure on many occasions. US policy was not in opposition to *any* Israeli activity, but was rather an insistence that the military response be proportional to the Palestinian provocation. The American intervention was apparently an important factor in the Israeli decision in the early autumn of 1979 to refrain from continued widespread military activity in Lebanon.[30] Israel's decision to reduce its activity was linked, however, to a warning that, if Palestinian activity continued, Israel would use its power in a tough manner and on a large scale.[31]

Finally, the Israeli campaign did indeed force the Palestinian organisations to change their strategy. Beginning in late 1979 they scaled down their infiltration into Israel and instead began a process of entrenchment in south Lebanon. Instead of guerrilla-type operations, which constituted a nuisance for Israel, they began building up their long-range potential by the deployment of Katyusha rocket launchers and artillery. In addition, the headquarters of the organisations which had been in the Tyre area were pulled back. In this sense, the Israeli activity appears to have been successful.

The Zahle encounter

From the middle of 1979 Syria faced increasing difficulties in three different areas: within the context of inter-Arab state relations; on the domestic front where violent oppositions continued to ferment; and finally, in Lebanon, where, as will be described below, opposition to it mounted. Syria's weakening position in Lebanon enabled even President Sarkis to adopt an independent position. He demanded that the problem of south Lebanon, including both the Palestinian presence and the Israeli retaliation, be discussed at the forthcoming tenth Arab summit. His initiative displeased the Syrians, as it was a demonstration of independence and was close to the position of the Lebanese Front. Moreover, placing Lebanese problems on the agenda of the Arab summit would enable other Arab countries and especially Iraq to reopen the whole subject of the Syrian presence in Lebanon.

At the summit itself, which convened in October in Tunis, Syria and the PLO co-operated in mobilising opposition to Sarkis' initiative. After long deliberations the summit set aside the Lebanese demands. Lebanese displeasure was somewhat alleviated by handsome promises of financial support. The summit again demonstrated the deep splits within the Arab world and its inability to devise plans for joint political effort on any issue, including Lebanon. One semi-operational decision was to create a 'follow-up' committee to supervise the implementation of various undertakings in regard to south Lebanon.[32]

The difficulties faced by Asad both in the Arab world and at home would not have been sufficient to force a change in the Syrian posture in Lebanon. But combined with Syria's continued inability to impose its will in Lebanon, they obliged Damascus to search for ways to diminish the Syrian presence, and so reduce the costs involved in staying there. In January 1980, Syria announced a plan for a limited withdrawal from the Beirut area. Some Syrian units were to remain in Beirut, thereby maintaining influence over developments in the political centre of Lebanon, but most of the Syrian forces were to be deployed in the Beqa valley. Interestingly enough, the Syrian decision, rather than evoking a sigh of relief from the different political groupings in Lebanon, in fact raised the concern of many groups. Both Christians and Muslims feared that the complete withdrawal of Syria from Beirut might bring a renewal of the Civil War. Paradoxically therefore, the Syrian announcement strengthened Syria's position in Lebanon.

While the Syrians were involved in attempts to defend their

flanks both in the Arab world and in Lebanon, events inside Lebanon reinforced two political forces. Less important in terms of the country's political system was the continued entrench- ment of the PLO and the consolidation of its control over various parts of the country. The more important development concerned the emergence of the Phalangists as the central power in the Maronite community. On 7 July 1980, after two years of competition with the Chamounists, the Kataib, under the ener- getic and ambitious leadership of the young Bashir Jumayyil, destroyed the military power of the Chamounist militia in one violent confrontation. Surprisingly, the old leader of the National Liberals, Chamoun, accepted the outcome of the bloody encounter, the Kataib became the dominant power in the Lebanese Front, and Bashir Jumayyil emerged as a candidate for leadership of the community and possibly of Lebanon as a whole. Competition for the position of President (elections were to be held between 23 July and 23 September, 1982) had by then already begun.

The Lebanese Front redefined its political goals: the first and more ambitious goal was the maintenance of a unified Lebanon, in which the Maronite community would continue to play the central role and which the other communities would accept as being a special case in the Arab world. If that formula was not acceptable the alternative was to be either partition or 'cantoni- sation', that is, a loose confederation of semi-independent cantons divided along ethnic and religious lines.[33]

Recognising its generally weakened position, Syria tried to renew its dialogue with the Lebanese Front. As had occurred several times in the past (and as we shall see, was to occur again), Syria hoped now to establish a close relationship with the Christians in Lebanon. However, the Christian leadership made demands which were unacceptable from the Syrian point of view, and in the summer of 1980 the negotiations broke down. While the Lebanese Front made great strides, the National Front disintegrated. The Sunni elite lost their power, and the various militias connected with the Front proved no match for the Christians or the Palestinians. Another development to emerge at this stage, and which was to assume great significance later, was the initiation of steps towards organisation of the Shi'is. The power of the Shi'is was, however, not fully exposed until after the 1982 War.

The stengthening of the Lebanese Front and its deepening

relations with Israel raised hopes of a complete redrawing of the Lebanese political map. By December 1980, the Lebanese Front was ready to challenge Syria. This decision was most probably taken on the assumption that Israel would back the Phalangists in case of a serious confrontation with Syria. There have even been suggestions that they received promises to that effect from General Eitan when he visited Junieh in December 1980.[34] It is significant that, in October 1978, Israel promised the Maronites that it would use its air force should the Syrian air force attack the Christians. Israel repeated that undertaking during the Zahle encounter.[35] The promise was made orally but Begin felt committed by it.

By the time the Phalanges were ready to challenge Syria, the latter had already recovered somewhat from its feelings of complete vulnerability. In October 1980, it had signed a Friendship and Co-operation agreement with the Soviet Union. Furthermore, it now found some solace in its closer relations with Libya (though, of course, the announcement of unity between the two countries remained a hollow one) and Algeria. Finally, the war between Iraq and Iran allowed it some breathing space since the attention of Iraq, the traditional enemy, was diverted to Iran. Apparently, most important was the fact that, by mid-1980, Arab disunity had grown to such dimensions that Syria's isolation ceased to be a special case.

The newly emergent association between Iraq and Jordan, and the news of the possibility of Jordan opening negotiations with Israel and joining the peace process, while leaving Syria out in the cold, prompted Damascus to show its hand. When the Eleventh Arab Summit met in Amman between 25 and 27 November 1980, Syria and its allies — Libya and Algeria — refused to participate. Moreover, as a demonstration of compellance, Syria deployed an armoured division on the Syrian–Jordanian border in an attempt to affect the summit deliberations. Under heavy Syrian pressure, Lebanon also decided not to participate.

In defiance of the Syrian pressure, the summit agreed to look again into the financing of the ADF in Lebanon. Indeed, during 1981 Saudi Arabia and Kuwait decided not to extend their annual financial support to the ADF because they claimed it had in fact become a Syrian force.[36] Whether or not they actually implemented that decision is not clear. Their reluctance to strain relations with Syria was evident in the attempts at previous summits to assuage Syrian displeasure. After the summit King

Hussein criticised the Syrian position and strengthened his relations with Iraq. Syria reacted ferociously and Haddam even warned that next time the Syrian army would invade Jordan and bring about the collapse of the Hashemite regime.[37]

The Christian challenge to the Syrians took place at a point of great strategic significance for Syria. Zahle, a predominantly Christian town, is situated on the Beirut–Damascus road, which is an essential link between Syria and its units in the Beirut area. Moreover, it lies on the western slopes of the Beqa, which is again an essential strategic area for Syria. Finally, the Syrians probably suspected that a Christian move to control the Zahle area would serve as the prelude to an attempt to create a bridge from Zahle due south, connecting with Israel and the Christian enclave along the southern border. This encirclement would isolate most of central and southern Lebanon from the Syrian forces.

A unit of the Phalanges was deployed in Zahle (where Phalangists had never been deployed before) and, in addition, the Christians began building a new road, north of the Beirut–Damascus road, to link Zahle with the heart of the Maronite enclave north-east of Beirut. The Phalanges were most probably hoping that their activity would trigger off a Syrian reaction, and that this would provoke Israel into a military move against Syria. Events came to a head when a Phalange unit ambushed a Syrian unit near Zahle, killing several Syrian soldiers. The Syrian reaction was brutal and massive. Zahle was heavily shelled and Syrian units attacked an important Maronite position on Mount Senin, north-west of Zahle. The Syrians now threatened the very heart of the Maronite 'canton'. The strong Syrian reaction signalled its determination to hold on to its positions and influence in Lebanon. An even greater escalation of the conflict was threatened if the Maronites did not lower the scale of their activity. Two additional issues were apparently prominent in Syrian calculations. The presidential elections were one year away, and the Syrians, well aware of the intentions of Camille Chamoun and Bashir Jumayyil, who were both possible candidates for the Presidency, wanted to register their determination to force the election of one of their Maronite allies. A strong military reaction would also demonstrate that they were deeply suspicious of the growing relations between Israel and the Phalanges. If provoked, they would react strongly. Indeed, one observer has suggested that Syria expected some escalation of

the conflict with Israel and even relished it.[38] This point is difficult to prove or disprove. It appears that the Syrians would have
preferred to avoid a confrontation, but that they were ready to
react forcefully if faced with a major challenge.

They were also probably aware of the possibility that Israel
would use its airforce in case of an escalation. In order to deter
such a development they prepared ground emplacements near
Zahle, suitable for the deployment of SAM missiles. They did
not, however, actually deploy the weapons. The Syrian signal
was clear: they were not ready to violate the unwritten agreement of 1976 according to which they were to refrain from introducing SAM missiles into Lebanon. But they signalled to Israel
that if Israel violated *its* side of the agreement, that is, directly
attacked Syrian units in Lebanon, then Syria would react even to
the extent of violating the 'red line' concerning the deployment
of SAMs.

Indeed, the possibility that Syria would introduce SAMs into
Lebanon as part of a process of escalation was recognised in
Israel. It was discussed in September 1979 within the context of
the air battles,[39] and again during the deliberations about an
Israeli reaction to Syrian moves during the Zahle encounter.[40]

The tough Syrian reaction placed Israel in a difficult position.
Not only were the Christians in Zahle under increasing pressure,
but the Syrians also appeared to be threatening the Christian
'canton' itself. In retrospect, and on the basis of Syrian
behaviour both before this action and after the 1982 War, it
appears clear that the Syrians were never willing or ready to
destroy the Christian community in Lebanon.[41] Rather, they preferred to reach agreement with them and to impose their will in
Lebanon in co-operation with, rather than against, them. However, the attack on the important Christian position — the
'French Room' on Mount Senin — led to Christian accusations
that the Syrians planned the destruction of the Christian
enclave. The Israeli Government was put under increasing pressure from Bashir Jumayyil and Camille Chamoun to save the
Christian community. Within the government, however, there
was deep disagreement about the role which Israel should play.
While there was some general Israeli commitment to the
Maronites, which had deepened in the wake of Begin's promises
of 1978 and 1980, members of the Cabinet and the heads of both
the Mossad and AMAN pointed out that the Zahle affair was
probably started by the Christians as a deliberate provocation

designed to draw Israel into war with Syria. They added that, in any case, such a war was not in Israel's interests.

Two developments seem to have forced Israel's hand. The first was the alleged use of Syrian attack helicopters against Christian positions on Mount Senin. The second was the news of a compromise agreement between Syria and the Christians, which had almost been signed and which included Christian consessions. The use of attack helicopters could have been interpreted as a violation of the 1976 agreement about the non-use of Syrian aircraft in Lebanon. The possibility of an agreement with Syria would clearly affect the Israeli–Maronite connection.

Israel therefore decided to react in a limited way, and against precisely the instrument that had violated the 'red line'. Israeli fighters attacked and destroyed two Syrian helicopters near Zahle. It later became clear that these were cargo helicopters carrying soldiers. In reaction Syria introduced SAMs into the prepared emplacements and thus violated another 'red line'. Israel now faced a new strategic and political situation which required yet another major decision.

The few SAMs which had been deployed did not serve as a direct strategic threat to Israel. Indeed, just a few kilometers to the east, across the border inside Syria, there had for some time been several SAM batteries. Hence, the new deployment, although extending the range covered by Syrian air defence, made little difference in terms of Syrian intercept potential. More important was the wider strategic consideration — the SAM deployment violated a deterrence threshold. It therefore affected the credibility of the deterrer (Israel) and theoretically might serve as a precedent for further Syrian violations. Similarly, since it threatened the credibility of other Israeli undertakings to the Maronites, the latter might stop relying on their relationship with Israel.

The Israeli dilemma was acute. To strike at the SAM sites might lead to another undesired and needless confrontation with Syria. To back down might lead to a loss of credibility. After a brief period of soul-searching, Begin opted for an air strike against the SAM deployment to be carried out on 30 April. Weather conditions forced Israel to postpone the implementation of that decision. Meanwhile, the United States, gravely concerned about the international implications of an Israeli strike, and concerned that Soviet reaction might lead to a crisis between the superpowers, applied pressure on Begin. As Israel itself was concerned about the possibility of an undesired escalation, the American intervention was not perceived as necessarily adversely affecting Israeli interests. Israel consented and cancelled the air strike.

The United States proposed to mediate between the two regional powers. Philip Habib, who already had experience in Lebanese affairs, was dispatched to the Middle East with the mission of achieving the removal of the SAM batteries. He shuttled between Jerusalem and Damascus but failed to accomplish this task.

The deterrence 'dialogue' in the Zahle affair

What were the actual deterrence thresholds (the 'red lines') violated in the Zahle encounter? There were in fact two such thresholds. The first, a less explicit one, concerned the general political and strategic situation in Lebanon and the trilateral relationship between Israel, Syria and the Christian community. This threshold dates back to 1976 when the initial set of understandings between Israel and Syria was secured, on the basis, among other things, of mutual recognition of coincidental interests in the defence of the Maronites and the denial of military success to the anti-*status quo* forces and the PLO. Within the context of that recognition, Syria was 'allowed' to invade the country and impose its will there, but the special connection between Israel and the Maronites was recognised. The level of commitment to the Maronites was in fact more limited than that signalled by Israel to Syria. Nevertheless, an ambiguous situation emerged in which Syria sensed that Israel might react forcefully to a Syrian attempt to crush the Maronite community completely (not that Syria planned to do so). This Syrian perception probably deepened when Israel sent deterrent signals during the 1978 confrontation in Beirut. The actual strengthening of relations between Israel and the Maronites in the wake of that encounter, of which the Syrians were clearly aware, could only have lessened the ambiguity clouding the Israeli commitment. However, the bombing of Zahle and the Syrian advance on Mount Senin were a far cry from an attempt to destroy the Maronite community. An Israeli reaction was therefore not necessarily required by the logic of deterrence.

In another respect Syrian behaviour in Lebanon during the

period 1977–81 did transgress the initial tacit understanding formed in 1976. Syria tried to impose its will and to establish a more durable connection with Lebanon. In that sense, and in contrast to its half-hearted and always ambivalent backing of the PLO, it overstepped the initial understandings. To be sure, this development had received the backing of the United States and also reflected vital Syrian interests in Lebanon. Nevertheless, it served as legitimate grounds for Israeli apprehensions. In retrospect, however, it appears almost inevitable bearing in mind that Syria is favoured in the balance of interests between itself and Israel in Lebanon.

The other type of deterrence understanding concerned the more specific 'red lines'. The use of attack helicopters in ground attacks against the Christian militia on Mount Senin was another example of the Syrian tactic of operating with an element of ambiguity. While attack helicopters could be described as aircraft, they could also be viewed as a ground weapon system. The Israeli reaction was therefore only partly 'legitimate' in terms of the understandings between the two countries.

A broader question, and one which has had direct relevance to the deterrence question, was the background to the confrontation around Zahle. The Phalange operation was intended to provoke an escalation of the conflict between Israel and Syria. In other words, the mechanism of deterrence, which was designed to increase strategic stability, was, on the contrary, used to destabilise relations between the two countries. The dilemma faced by Israel extended beyond issues of deterrence and credibility. It revolved around the question of whether Israel should allow itself to be drawn into a confrontation which, at least at that time, it did not desire. Indeed, when Begin had committed Israel to help the Christians in 1978 and again in 1980, he had also added that 'the Israeli government saw no reason for changing its earlier decision not to be drawn into war with Syria except on the basis of its own considerations'. He qualified that reservation by adding 'This does not contradict the statement that the security and survival of the Christians and the preservation of a non-hostile Lebanon are vital to Israel's security'.[42]

Israeli–PLO confrontation

Following the Israeli campaign against the PLO in south

Lebanon in 1979, the PLO changed its strategy and concentrated on building an extensive civilian and military infrastructure. A PLO mini-state emerged north of the Litani and for some way along the coast north of the Zaharani. The PLO invested great efforts and financial resources in creating bases and various facilities. Most importantly, it began a gradual transformation from a guerrilla force into a semi-regular army. The level of guerrilla activity against Israel diminished considerably. Much emphasis was placed on the build-up of concentrations of artillery and Ketyusha rocket launchers. This concentration was partly the result of the aforesaid transformation, but was mainly aimed at two other interrelated objectives. First, deterrence of a direct Israeli attack on, or at least massive harassment of the Palestinian bases; the thrust of the PLO deterrence effort was implied in the threat to harass northern Israeli settlements. Secondly, the deterrence threat created an option for the use of such harassment as an instrument of terror. The second use was, of course, in line with previous PLO activity from across the border, but the concentration of artillery exceeded previous levels.

Indeed, notwithstanding pronouncements to the contrary, the PLO leaders, as a result of the development of an elaborate civilian and military network of bases and facilities and of a growing material welfare, lost part of their revolutionary zeal. There developed a body of vested interests in the maintenance of the semi-autonomous mini-state, and as a result the level of activity against Israel significantly decreased. Most military activity was directed against Haddad's enclave, or in self-defence against Israeli attacks. Infiltration into Israel was made much more difficult because of the various Israeli security measures in south Lebanon and along the Israeli–Lebanese border. Artillery shelling became very sporadic. During the Zahle encounter, PLO activity against Israel diminished below even the usual level due to the fear that Israel might take advantage of the situation in order to attack the PLO in south Lebanon.

On the Israeli side there was dissatisfaction with the way in which the Zahle encounter ended. Habib's mission failed, a compromise agreement in which most of the Syrian conditions were met was reached between Syria and the Maronite leadership, Syrian forces remained on Mount Senin, and Syrian SAMs remained inside Lebanon. Israel was looking for some 'compensation'. The obvious target was the Palestinian bases. Thus, on

28 May 1981, Begin approved Eitan's proposal to renew the campaign against the PLO. It should be added that both Eitan and Bengal (and indeed, the whole of the Northern Command) by now formed an active lobby pressing for a large-scale campaign against both Syria and the PLO.[43]

The escalation in the south began with air strikes in different places in south Lebanon and north to Damur on the coast. One of the targets was a Libyan air defence unit armed with SAM-9 missiles near Damur. The Israeli strikes continued until 3 June. The Palestinian organisations, fearful of escalation, reacted only with artillery shelling against the Christian enclave in the south.

The second round of the campaign opened six weeks later. Following an artillery exchange between Haddad's militia and the Palestinians, Israel immediately swung into a massive air attack. Palestinian bases in the south and all along the coast up to Tripoli in the north were bombed and strafed. Among the targets were the PLO headquarters in Beirut, and this attack involved the death and injury of many civilians. The reaction of the Palestinian artillery was controlled and limited. Some Israeli settlements were shelled but no casualties were suffered. The Israeli air offensive continued for five days, by which time the Palestinian organisations had reached a major strategic decision — to react with heavy shelling of Israeli settlements.

The Palestinian artillery reaction continued for twelve days, during which period the Israeli air strikes and heavy artillery bombing continued. However, the Israeli air force found it difficult to locate the thinly spread Palestinian artillery pieces. Very conscious of the plight of the inhabitants of the northern settlements, Israel faced a problem. The obvious way to destroy the Palestinian positions would have been to undertake a ground operation, but that was liable to involve undesired escalation of the conflict, possibly with Syria. Moreover, the United States was very unhappy about the Israeli air offensive which appeared to be unjustified and out of all proportion. American reactions were also tense because of the recent Israeli strike on the Iraqi nuclear reactor at Oziraq. In summary, Begin realised that a process of de-escalation was required. Philip Habib was commissioned to obtain a cease-fire. This was indeed accomplished very quickly through Saudi mediation. Israel refused to agree on a cease-fire with the PLO, an organisation it did not recognise. Habib's mission was therefore to secure an ostensible cease-fire between Israel and Lebanon. In fact, however, the agreement was between Israel and the PLO.

Expectations and manoeuvring

The armistice reached between Syria and the Lebanese Front following the Zahle episode did not change in any fundamental way the existing tensions between these two actors. Under the leadership of Bashir Jumayyil and Camille Chamoun, large segments of the Maronite community remained dissatisfied with the continued anarchy in Lebanon and with the presence of Syria and the PLO. The ever increasing support extended by Israel to the Phalange militia in the form of arms, military instruction and training convinced Bashir Jumayyil that with the help of Israel he might be able to achieve his twin objectives: to push Syria and the PLO out of the country and to reimpose Maronite dominance. His own personal ambition was to become the President of the new Lebanon. While aware of the existence of other communities, he was apparently confident that, after long years of bloodshed and anarchy, members of the other communities would accept his leadership in the hope that this would restore law and order to the country. In fact, however, he failed to create meaningful contacts with the leaders of the other communities. In any case, he probably envisaged that the new Lebanon would work out a new formula in which the other communities would also find a secure place. Indeed, his caution during the 1982 War, and his reluctance to become deeply involved in it, demonstrated his desire to reach a working relationship with the other communities.

However, Bashir's bloody past and his image (partly justified) of recklessness and extremism, made national *rapprochement* under his leadership a very questionable proposition. Nevertheless, during the second half of 1981 and early 1982 the Lebanese Front and its core military arm, the Phalanges, continued to increase their power and influence. The Christian 'canton' became the most orderly part of Lebanon.

The meetings between Bashir Jumayyil and his lieutenants with Israeli military and Mossad representatives intensified during this period. Jumayyil worked hard to convince Israel of the need to launch a military operation which would force Syria and the Palestinians out of Lebanon and create a context within which he could emerge as the only credible candidate for the presidency. It is therefore clear why he was worried that, if and when Israel did decide to attack, it might implement only a limited plan and abstain from reaching Beirut or from fighting Syria.[44]

While Bashir Jumayyil, with the backing of Camille Chamoun, was actively preparing the ground for a major reshuffle of the political factors in Lebanon, other Christian leaders maintained reservations about his ambitious plan. Even within his own family and the Kataib party, Bashir was to encounter doubts. It is not even clear, for example, where his father, Pierre Jumayyil, stood on the issue. It has been suggested that Bashir's brother, Amin Jumayyil, tried to maintain the close relationship with Syria which the Kataib had developed in 1976 and after. Other Christian leaders were also not committed to Bashir's tactics and his political objectives. However, because of the strong aid and backing he received from Israel, and the strength and determination he began to demonstrate, Bashir succeeded in mobilising the support of large segments, albeit not all, of the Maronite community. It must be added that Bashir himself was aware that, even following the hoped-for political change, Syria would continue to play a major role, and that the Maronites would have to continue to cultivate relations with Damascus. Indeed, according to one source he even indicated this to his Israeli interlocutors during the many meetings which took place before the outbreak of the war.[45]

His activity was also facilitated by the continued anarchy which reigned in West Beirut and other parts of the country, by the widespread disenchantment with the role of Syria, and by the deep animosity felt by then by almost all the communities in Lebanon, whether Christian, Muslim or Druze, in regard to the behaviour and role of the Palestinian organisations. The situation thus appeared to be ripe for a radical political change.

An important step towards the implementation of the Israeli military operation occurred in January 1982, when the Israeli Defence Minister, Ariel Sharon, made a clandestine visit to Junieh and East Beirut. During that visit, the Christian hosts, primarily Bashir Jumayyil, and the guests, Sharon and other members of the Israeli defence and intelligence community, worked out the broad politico-strategic principles for the ensuing operation. According to one version of these meetings,[46] the hosts were careful not to commit themselves to participating actively in the military operation, or at least remained ambiguous about their commitment. The Israeli guests were nevertheless confident of the undoubted ability of the Israeli forces to implement any military plan in regard to Lebanon, even if it included a major military confrontation with Syria. Thus, the political parameters for a military operation appeared to have been clarified. Neither Sharon nor Eitan, who pressed for the operation, bothered to consider the extent of Jumail's support within the Maronite community and in Lebanon in general. Moreover, they did not occupy themselves with a deeper analysis of the Byzantine pattern of inter-community relations in Lebanon or of the Machiavellian political behaviour adhered to by all parties in Lebanon.

Indeed, during the tense months of the winter and spring of 1982, Jumayyil and his advisers were also considering other options. In April and May they renewed the dialogue with Syria. No understanding was reached, but this episode underlines the lack of complete commitment by the Phalanges to the Israeli 'connection'.[47]

Developments inside Lebanon, and primarily the date of the coming elections for the presidency, forced the internal actors and Israel to reach major decisions. As we shall see in the next chapter, by December 1981 the chief Israeli decision-maker had already made up his mind on the necessity for a major operation in Lebanon.

NOTES

1. This time, however, the three countries were not preparing for war. Egypt, at least, was trying to further the Geneva Conference initiative.
2. See the analysis in J. White, *National Security Policy Decision-making in Israel.*
3. Peres on *IDF Radio*, 4 January 1977 and Gur on *IDF Radio*, 16 January 1977 (both quoted in White, *National Security Policy Decision-making*, p. 296).
4. For a fuller discussion of 'specific deterrence' in this context see Chapter 6.
5. Allon personal account, referring to his presentation at the Foreign and Defence Committee, 30 January 1977.
6. For the negotiations with Washington, I refer to an interview with a leading Israeli decision-maker. The quotation is taken from Allon's

interview in *Yediot Ahronot*, 28 January 1977 (Weekend supplement, p. 1).

7. *UPI*, 29 January 1977.

8. *IDF Radio*, 1 January 1977 and *Israel Government Press Office*, 30 January 1977 (an official communique was published following the Israeli Cabinet meeting of 30 January).

9. On this see William Quandt, *Camp David*.

10. On the developments within the Christian views in this period see, for example, Zeev Schiff and Ehud Ya'ari, *Milchemet Shollal*, (Hebrew), pp. 56–8. According to this source, already in late 1977 Bashir Jumayyil was trying to convince Israel that it should intervene militarily and advance on Beirut.

11. This statement was given in the Foreign and Defence Committee. Taken from interview with a leading Israeli decision-maker.

12. Interviewed on Israeli Television, 12 April 1977.

13. Author's interview with an Israeli decision-maker.

14. *Ibid.* For a different interpretation see Jeffrey White, *Towards the Litani Campaign: An Assessment of the Begin Government's Policy in Lebanon and the March 1978 Incursion*, pp. 13–14. White argues that it was a high-level Israeli decision to move into a new offensive posture in regard to southern Lebanon.

15. See 'Lebanon: Again the Cairo Agreement', *Middle East Intelligence Survey*, 16–31 July 1977. Other sources did not mention the demilitarisation of the south. Itamar Rabinovich and Hanna Zamir, *War and Crisis in Lebanon 1975–81* (Hebrew).

16. See, for example, interview with Gur on *Galei Zahal*, 3 September 1977.

17. *Kol Yisrael*, 27 September 1977 quoted in White, *Towards the Litani Operation*, p. 39, fn. 82.

18. This is indeed White's interpretation, see *ibid.* pp. 22–4.

19. This was apparent from various pronouncements. See for example Begin's address to the Knesset on 3 March 1978.

20. Indeed Egypt did not publicly warn Israel against retaliation.

21. Ezer Weitzman, *The Battle for Peace* (in Hebrew), p. 254.

22. *Ibid.*, p. 253. Other sources, however, state that it was not clear at the time of planning whether a security zone under Israeli–Christian control was stated as a clear objective.

23. For a useful analysis of the American–Israeli interactions following the operation see White, *Towards the Litani Operation*. See also Cyrus Vance, *Hard Choices*.

24. On 18 March 1978 Asad made a speech in which he stated that Syria would 'not be dragged into a risky position'. (Quoted in White, *Towards the Litani Operation*, fn. 97). Gur also referred to the tacit understanding between Israel and Syria which had developed (author's interview with Gur). He also mentioned that the Israeli decision to push to the Litani was helped by the total lack of Syrian intervention during the first phase of the operation, *Jerusalem Post*, 31 March 1978, p. 1.

25. These contacts were initially conducted through the Israeli military mission in Cairo. During the operation, the communication channel was between General Gazit, head of Israeli military intelligence, and General Gamassi, the Egyptian War Minister.

26. Indeed, Weitzman also endorsed that view. See, for example, *ibid.*, p. 256. For further details see *Koteret Rashit*, 14 May 1986.

27. For a useful elaboration of these developments in the Arab world and of the Arab summit meetings see Avraham Sella, *Achdut Betoch Perud* (Unity in Division) (in Hebrew).

28. For this point see, for example, Ze'ev Schiff, *Ha'aretz*, 11 October 1979.

29. Syrian aircraft did fly on rare occasions in the northern parts of Lebanon, in the area of Tripoli. These were probably air surveillance missions.

30. See, for example, *Ha'aretz*, 28 June 1979 referring to communications by Syrian officials emphasising that Syria was not interested in being 'dragged' into a war with Israel.

31. See, for example, Ze'ev Schiff, *Ha'aretz*, 28 September 1979.

32. Sella, *Achdut Betoch Perud*, p. 196.

33. Rabinovich, *The War for Lebanon*, pp. 114–15.

34. Schiff and Ya'ari, *Milchemet Shollal*, p. 24. Eitan denied these allegations, *ibid.*

35. See Rabinovich, *The War for Lebanon*, p. 166; Schiff and Ya'ari, *Milchemet Shollal*, p. 68. The Israeli promise was revealed by Begin during the Knesset meeting of 3 June 1981.

36. On the summit see Sella, *Achdut Betoch Perud*, pp. 220–3.

37. *Ibid.*, p. 237.

38. Rabinovich, *The War for Lebanon*, p. 116.

39. See, for example, Schiff, *Ha'aretz*, October 1979.

40. See Schiff and Ya'ari, *Milchemet Shollal*, p. 68.

41. In fact, a report by an Israeli liaison officer who was dispatched to the Zahle area on a fact-finding mission stated clearly that there was no danger of annihilation of the Christians in Zahle. The Israeli Cabinet, however, never saw that report. See Shiffer, *Kadur Sheleg* (Snow Ball) (in Hebrew), p. 41.

42. See *Divrei Haknesset*, 3 June 1981, quoted in Rabinovich, *The War for Lebanon*, p. 166.

43. See Schiff and Ya'ari, *Milchemet Shollal*, p. 27.

44. For a detailed account of the Israeli contacts with Bashir Jumayyil during that period see *ibid.* For an account of the developments in Lebanon throughout this period see Karim Bakradouni, *La Paix Maniqnée.*

45. Interview with a high-ranking Israeli official.

46. Schiff and Ya'ari, *Milchemet Shollal.*

47. See Rabinovich, *The War for Lebanon*, p. 124.

4

The 1982 War

ISRAEL'S WAR OBJECTIVES[1]

Identifying and analysing the Israeli war objectives is a difficult task. In the first place, it appears that different decision-makers may have had different objectives, or attached to them different priorities. Furthermore, the desire to avoid opposition in both the planning and operational stages of the war meant that only some of the objectives could be disclosed publicly. Israeli leaders had to contend with possible Syrian, American, Soviet, Arab and domestic negative reactions. Indeed, as will be argued below, the war was probably seen as part of a larger scheme that was to be implemented gradually. However, this scheme could not be revealed as it was the potential source of enormous domestic and external political opposition.

The objectives of the war were related to five different yet overlapping contexts: the immediate security of northern Israel; the general Palestinian issue encompassing the future of the West Bank, the role of the PLO and the future of Jordan; the Lebanese context; the Israeli–Syrian context; and the role of Israel in the Middle East state system.

In analysing the Israeli approach to the war, two complex issues need to be addressed: first, the power position of Israel in the Middle East; and second, the deliberate use of military power for the accomplishment of politico-strategic ends. The first will be dealt with extensively here, while the second will be only touched on within the context of overall Israeli policy *vis à vis* Syria both in this chapter and in Chapter 6.

By the second half of 1981, Israel was in a better security

position than ever before. This was due primarily to the peace agreement with Egypt, but also to the disarray in the Arab world. Since 1948 Egypt had been Israel's most dangerous opponent. Of the states bordering Israel, Egypt has the largest armed forces, and is the leading Arab country in many other respects. It participated in all the Arab–Israeli wars. The 1979 peace treaty led to a profound change in the relationship between the two states, and Egyptian foreign policy has increasingly reflected this new orientation. Indeed, it is apparent that Egyptian policy towards Israel had changed course even before Sadat's visit to Jerusalem in 1977. By the mid-1970s, Egypt had opted for a military build-up that, in comparison to its previous behaviour and the behaviour of other leading confrontation states, was markedly restrained. While pursuing a limited increase in some capabilities, Egypt essentially limited itself to the replenishment of losses incurred in 1973. This trend was already part of the process which ultimately led Egypt to the peace treaty. In addition, the Egyptian armed forces are currently converting from Soviet to Western weapon systems. This transformation will take another five years or more, during which time many problems will persist related to the integration of the different weapons systems. This obviously limits Egyptian preparedness for war. Furthermore, the demilitarisation of the Sinai renders problematic any Egyptian offensive against Israel.[2]

For a time, in the mid-1970s it was suggested that the 'Eastern Front', consisting of Syria, Jordan and Iraq, might develop into a major threat to Israel. However, it is doubtful whether this notion has ever possessed any great validity. With Egypt a nonparticipant, the 'Eastern Front' countries did not pose a critical threat for Israel. But even if the concern was at the time wellfounded, the 'Front' soon disintegrated with each country going its own way. Syria, the most likely candidate for the initiation of another round against Israel, was left isolated.

Among Israeli political and military decision-makers, many were aware of Israel's favourable security situation. Others were not. The former Chief of Staff General Eitan, for example, remained unconvinced as to the depth or likely duration of the new Israeli–Egyptian relationship, and has been deeply committed to the view that the first priority of all Arab leaders is, in the last analysis, to launch a total war against Israel.[3] The peace with Egypt, according to Eitan, only gives Israel a breathing-space during which military blows must be directed at other Arab forces.

The Palestinian context

There was, however, one factor — the PLO presence in Lebanon — which aroused the concern not only of alarmists such as Eitan, but also of others who perceived the balance of power as generally favourable. From late 1981 official Israeli spokesmen have tended to exaggerate the dangers inherent in the PLO presence there. These exaggerations continued during the war. Israeli leaders pointed out that the PLO was in the process of developing a conventional military capability,[4] and particularly emphasised the increased number of artillery pieces acquired by the PLO since 1981. It seems, however, that most Israeli military leaders, when referring to the increase in PLO military capabilities, were concerned about its potential ability to harass Israeli settlements in northern Israel, rather than its constituting a strategic threat to Israel. Moreover, it was assumed that if the PLO were to repeat its 1981 heavy bombardment of Israeli settlements, Israeli forces could move quickly to destroy the PLO infrastructure in south Lebanon and thus eliminate the cause of the nuisance. There was no objective military urgency in acting before the renewal of such activities.

It is much more likely that the leading Israeli decision-makers were concerned about another issue relating to the PLO; namely, their perception of the PLO as an effective political constraint against Israeli plans in the West Bank and Gaza.[5] The autonomy talks were at an impasse as Egypt and Israel failed to agree on the nature of the autonomy. Furthermore, it was difficult to elicit support for the talks among the Palestinian population in the West Bank.

Palestinian opposition in the West Bank is complex and varied. The most radical groups oppose any negotiations with Israel and cling to an extreme posture of total war. Yet already in the 1970s and early 1980s many in the West Bank, among them PLO adherents, were ready to accept some version of co-existence with Israel but were opposed to the Camp David process. Still others were probably ready to participate in the autonomy talks but were hesitant because of their deep suspicions as to the Israeli interpretation of autonomy and the Israeli policy of creeping annexation. It is possible that such groups would even have been ready to participate, were the annexation policy to change and were they convinced that the ultimate outcome of the negotiations would be a return to Arab sovereignty.

According to official Israeli thinking in 1982, the more moderate West Bankers were terrorised by the PLO. Only the destruction of the PLO could change their attitudes.[6] Crushing the PLO was therefore crucial to the resolution of the West Bank issue, and in particular in obtaining an agreement on autonomy.

There is little doubt that the real intentions of the Likud Government were to obtain the eventual annexation of the West Bank, in one form or another. An autonomy without real political substance was one way to secure that objective. Alternatively, if the autonomy talks were to fail altogether, the continuation of the *status quo*, coupled with the Israeli policy of settlement, would ultimately lead to a *de facto* annexation. The PLO was also seen as an obstacle in this second scenario. Complete destruction of the PLO, so it was argued, would undermine its power and international recognition and pave the way for the complete subordination of the West Bankers.[7] Finally, it may be that beyond these apparently rational calculations, there lies a deep-seated hatred of the PLO, which is perceived as Israel's arch-enemy.[8]

Israeli officials have argued that the Palestinians are not identical with the PLO, that the latter does not really represent them and that, were it not for the fact that they are terrorised by the PLO, many Palestinians would have been ready to come to terms with Israel. Furthermore, there was the notion that, by destroying the PLO, the very essence of Palestinianism would disappear; and that in a sense it was the PLO which finally created the notion of a Palestinian separate nationality. Once destroyed, the very idea of a Palestinian entity would fade away.

These Israeli perceptions and analyses of the PLO and its military and political power were a mix of contradictions, paradoxes and misperceptions. The first misperception was the claim that the PLO constituted a military threat to Israel. At most, as will be argued below, it comprised some nuisance value. Secondly, the political power of the PLO has always been paradoxical. PLO international prestige has increased (particularly in Western Europe) as it has diminished its military activity; indeed, PLO recognition was greatest when it suffered military defeats.[9] Furthermore, the influence of the PLO in the West

Bank was primarily due not to terror (although it did play some role) but rather to the widespread feeling of national identity and the perception among West Bankers that the PLO was their most genuine representative. This did not mean that they were not ready to acquiesce in a 'Jordanian' solution. It did mean, however, that in the Israeli policy of *de facto* annexation, the West Bankers saw the chances of a Jordanian solution as diminished and were more prepared to accept the PLO's extreme position. The Israeli policy did not encourage genuine Palestinian nationalists who probably would have accepted variants of a Jordanian–Palestinian solution to the West Bank.

A deeper paradox was contained in the perception of the future of the West Bank. By destroying the PLO in Lebanon, Israel was hoping to encourage groupings in the West Bank that would be ready to negotiate with Israel within the framework of the autonomy plan and which would eventually be ready to accept a *de facto* Israeli annexation. But no Palestinian leader in the West Bank was ready to accept such a solution as final. Even the leader of the 'Villages Association', Mustapha Dodin, who was initially seen by the Israeli Government as the proponent of such an approach, eventually came out in favour of the Reagan Plan.

Another ironic outcome of the war in Lebanon relates to the role of Jordan. In the eyes of West Bankers, the only acceptable alternative to a PLO solution is Jordan. By destroying the credibility of the PLO by the war in Lebanon, Israel in fact encouraged the strengthening of the pro-Jordanians in the West Bank. Indeed, as will be argued below, Israel 'succeeded' in strengthening the 'Jordanian option' throughout the Middle East and in the United States. But a 'Jordanian option' was the last thing that the Likud Government would have liked to see implemented, since such an option entails the return of the West Bank or most of it to Arab sovereignty.

However, it can be seen that these contradictions would have been resolved if, indeed, some decision-makers had intended to achieve more than the destruction of the PLO. One might speculate that among these decision-makers, who also strongly favoured the annexation of the West Bank, there were those who probably recognised that annexation would create grave demographic problems for Israel. The inclusion of another 1.2 million Palestinians in Israel (above and beyond the 600,000 Palestinians who are Israeli citizens) would have made the Palestinian population a third of the overall population of 'Greater Israel'. Given the much higher birth-rate among the Palestinians, such a minority would probably constitute almost half the population within a decade or so. Such a development would totally change the nature of the country. The same decision-makers would have probably liked to reverse these trends. Although academic works should usually avoid it, one is tempted to make speculative assumptions about leaders' intentions, if they correspond to the logic of the situation. Although this has not been stated by any of the decision makers involved, it could be speculated that the war in Lebanon was perceived by some of them as creating an option for a process which might lead to the transformation — the nature of which to be discussed below — of the relationship between Jordan, the West Bank and Israel.[10] This transformation might then bring about the emigration of many of the West Bank inhabitants to the eastern side of the Jordan river. The way would then be clear for the final annexation of the West Bank.

Such a possible ultimate objective also fits with another notion formulated by the then Defence Minister, Ariel Sharon. He maintained that Jordan is really the 'Palestinian state'.[11] The only obstacle to the transformation of Jordan into a Palestinian state is the existence of the Hashemite Dynasty. Once that dynasty and its Bedouin constituency had been removed, a Palestinian state would emerge. The PLO leadership and the various Palestinian elites could fulfil their political aspirations, and their anti-Israeli energy would subside. The emergence of a Palestinian state in Jordan depends on the violent removal of the kingdom. This end could perhaps have been secured by pushing the Palestinian refugees in Lebanon into Jordan, a task the Christian militias were eager to fulfil. In short, it is possible that the war in Lebanon was perceived as being part of a much larger scheme aimed at the complete transformation of the Palestinian problem. These plans were not seen as necessarily contradictory to the smaller plans, but possibly as alternatives, which could be accomplished *in toto* or in part. It was probably considered that each step was worthwhile in and of itself.

Once the war had begun, an additional rationale for the destruction of the PLO's presence in Lebanon (including Beirut) was suggested. This was the notion that the PLO had become a threat to Israel because it had attained the capability of completely destabilising the Israeli–Arab relationship. According to this idea, the PLO's main objective in the consolidation of its position in south Lebanon was to create an option to ignite an Israeli–Arab conflagration which would wreck any possibility of the emergence of a peaceful system between the two sides. The argument holds that, once the PLO had built up a considerable artillery contingent in Lebanon, together with some ability to defend itself initially against an Israeli attack, it would wait until a convenient opportunity had arisen in terms of inter-Arab relations, and then act to throw the area into war. In other words, the PLO had acquired the potential for igniting a 'catalytic' war.[12] The most appropriate situation might have been one in which Syria was considering the possibility of a war with Israel, in a period of renewed unity among the leading Arab countries. The PLO could then force the hand of Syria even if the latter still hesitated. The PLO would provoke Israel into action, inviting a Syrian response. The ensuing escalation would engulf other Arab countries. The PLO's position also expanded the organisation's international capabilities. A major war might lead to an international crisis, something both superpowers preferred to avoid. Since the PLO was the linch-pin of the situation, the United States would have a strong interest in pre-empting the deterioration of that situation by political means. The United States would have to accommodate the PLO with concessions, and these would most probably be in Israeli 'currency', extracted from Israel under American pressure.

This explanation has three main faults. First, Palestinian rhetoric apart, the leadership of the PLO increasingly appeared to orient itself towards building a secure base in Lebanon rather than endangering the emergent PLO 'mini-state' in the south through a major conflagration with Israel. A whole complex civilian and semi-governmental infrastructure was developed and there consequently arose a set of vested interests in its maintenance. Secondly, when one considers Israel's military moves during the war, and against the background of the ambitious objectives held by some Israeli decision-makers, it seems that Israel was not over concerned about the danger of escalation. On the contrary, the threat of instability was in fact sought by Israel.

The third fault of this explanation relates to the extent that Israeli–PLO relations could have influenced Syrian military action. The record since the beginning of the Civil War in Lebanon suggests that Syria is capable of staying clear of Israeli–Palestinian clashes. Until 1982, the Israel–Syrian relationship in Lebanon demonstrated a high level of Syrian indifference to Israeli–PLO confrontations.[13] The deterioration in the relationship was due not to Syrian actions or initiatives, but rather to Israeli military moves directed not at the PLO but at the Syrian forces. Although Syrian behaviour may have been affected by Israeli–PLO confrontations, the most effective factors in the explanation of Syrian behaviour *vis-à-vis* Israel were Syria's assessments of the military balance between itself and Israel, the level of its political grievances and, finally, its ability to mobilise other leading Arab countries for a war against Israel.

According to another explanation of the Israeli military initiative within the PLO–Palestinian–Lebanese context, the operation was the logical and inevitable conclusion of the strategy of retaliation that Israel had pursued in Lebanon since the late 1960s.[14] This explanation seems unsatisfactory in view of the pattern of Israeli activity up to 1981, and the extended and ambitious objectives set by Israel for the 1982 War. From 1979–80 the activity of the Palestinian organisations began to change from harassment to deterrence and defence. Israel had little reason to continue, let alone step up, her previous strategy. In fact, from July 1981 the PLO ceased activity altogether, recognising that violation of the cease-fire would have invited a strong Israeli response. Moreover, Israel could have annihilated the PLO militarily in the south in a small-scale operation. Israeli objectives went far beyond the context of the PLO and the Palestinian presence in Lebanon, however. Indeed, prior to the war, the Israeli policy had been specifically to *avoid* a military confrontation with Syria (with the *partial* exception of air battles in 1979). By 1982, this policy changed profoundly, and the change was related not to the dynamics of Israeli–PLO conflict interactions but rather to the redefinition of Israeli objectives in regard to Lebanon, Syria and possibly even Jordan.

The Lebanese context of Israeli objectives

By 1980, the Israeli commitment to the Christians in Lebanon had deepened beyond previous undertakings. Israel increasingly saw in them an ally which should be defended, but which could also be instrumental in furthering Israeli objectives in Lebanon. Simultaneously, there came a change in attitude about the Syrian role in Lebanon. As noted earlier, the school of thought which perceived the Syrian role in Lebanon as militarily convenient for Israeli security interests declined in importance within Israeli decision-making circles. In addition, the rise to power of the Phalange under the energetic and ruthless leadership of Bashir Jumayyil created the impression in Israel that a potential power centre had been formed in Lebanon which in time of crisis might be able to defeat the other militias.

In the Israeli internal debate in the various agencies concerned with Lebanon, there had been a variety of opinions about the Phalange and about Bashir personally. These differences cut across all the different organisations. The agency most heavily involved in actual contacts with the Phalangists (and before July 1980, with the other Christian militias as well) was the intelligence service, the Mossad. Such contacts usually create a sense of affinity and sometimes empathy. Hence, within the Mossad itself a group emerged which became increasingly committed to relations with the Phalangists, to the point that illusions were entertained about the latter's readiness to co-operate militarily with Israel upon request. Assessments of Phalange military capabilities were also incorrect.[15] There emerged the notion that once Israel acted militarily in Lebanon, crushing the Palestinians and neutralising the Syrians, the Phalange would be able to handle the anti-Israeli militias in Beirut and its environs and to gain control over the city.[16] It should be emphasised, however, that other members of the Mossad were not as deeply committed to the contacts with the Phalangists. While seeing them as useful allies that ought to benefit from Israeli assistance, their possible partnership in a large-scale military operation was negated. Indeed, the head of the Mossad, General Hofi, had a very instrumental and detached approach to relations with the Maronites in general and the Phalangists in particular. He shared the view that they should be helped and that Israel could gain some limited advantage from the relationship. On the other hand, he considered the Syrian role in Lebanon as not entirely counterproductive from the Israeli viewpoint. Furthermore, he was reserved about Israel's grand politico-strategic designs for Lebanon. Whether he communicated these assessments and with what firmness to the Prime Minister, to whom he was directly responsible and with whom he met regularly, is not entirely clear.[17]

In the military intelligence (AMAN), which commands tremendous power within the Israeli intelligence community, and which is also responsible for the preparation of the national strategic assessment, there existed a whole range of opinions about the relationship with the Maronites and the Phalange.[18] AMAN was not directly responsible for the contacts with the Christian militias, and as such did not develop the same level of empathy towards them. Moreover, it is clear that the head of AMAN, General Sagui, had great reservations about these contacts.[19] For some time, he completely opposed all contacts with them, and he was even doubtful as to the wisdom of developing a relationship with Major Haddad in the south.[20] Other elements within the military intelligence were more positively inclined towards both Haddad and the militias in the Christian enclave further north. Even among these groups, the emphasis was on the instrumental approach rather than considering them as 'strategic allies'. For example, the head of the research branch, General Y., considered at the time a 'pro-Phalangist', proposed the approach adopted by the Rabin Government of taking advantage of limited relations with both Haddad and the Phalange. This implied backing them with arms and with an Israeli guarantee against their destruction. However, he did not endorse the notion calling for the imposition of Phalange rule over Lebanon by means of a war directed at Syria and the Palestinians. It appears therefore that, all in all, most of the high-ranking officials in the intelligence agencies concerned with relations with the Phalange were rather reluctant about the possible contribution they could make to a large-scale Israeli military operation. Moreover, the directors of both the Mossad and AMAN had reservations about the planned war. General Sagui opposed the war plans during several preparatory meetings.[21]

Within the military itself, there existed three schools of thought. Many in the General Staff had deep hesitations concerning the war and any attempt to secure far-reaching objectives in Lebanon. However, the Chief of Staff, General Eitan, had favoured the war for some time. In the initial stages of his term of office, Eitan's main interest was in a campaign designed to break the backbone of the Syrian military machine, and he was less inclined to the close relationship with the Christian militias. He initially regarded Bashir Jumayyil with little respect. Later on, however, he turned the focus of his interest to the Palestinian presence in Lebanon, and to the role which the Phalangists might play in destroying the Palestinians' hold there. In Eitan's perception, the question of Lebanon became increasingly interwoven with the Palestinian problem. He consequently changed his view of Jumayyil and the Phalangists, whom he came to regard as reliable allies. Outside the General Staff, the most fervent supporters of a war were concentrated in the Northern Command. This tendency had begun while Eitan was responsible for the Northern Command, and continued under the leadership of General Bengal.[22] Among other high-ranking officers in the command there were those who saw a battle against the Syrians as the main priority, whereas others focused their attention mainly on the Palestinian issue. While differences between these two viewpoints did surface during the war, supporters of both approaches favoured a large-scale military operation. In September 1981, following the appointment of Sharon as Defence Minister, plans for both the large-scale operation code-named Oranim, as well as for more limited operations, were taken out of the files and updated.[23]

The aims of the war were, of course, essentially formulated by the Prime Minister, the Defence Minister and the Chief of Staff. The timing of operations was affected by the deepening relationship with the Phalange and the approaching Lebanese presidential elections due to be held initially in July 1982 (this date could be postponed until September). The main objective of the war was to obtain a basic change in the politico-strategic situation in Lebanon. This required the destruction or neutralisation of all the military elements which might inhibit the election of a President who was allied with Israel.

The plan assumed that the Phalange would play a part in the military operations, in particular in Beirut. Once the Syrians and the PLO had been defeated, it was assumed that the Phalangists would become the only military power in the country (apart from the Israeli army), and would be able to assert effective control. If Bashir Jumayyil became President, Lebanon would become the second Arab country ready to sign a peace treaty with Israel. Moreover, since Maronites and other Christians in Lebanon do not really feel 'Arab', the relationship between the two countries would be deeper and more multidimensional than the relations between Israel and Egypt. The Lebanese relationship would be based on a community of interests, as well as on ideological affinity; both countries reject the Pan-Arab notion of an exclusivist Arab Middle East.

Prime Minister Begin, who undoubtedly has wide political

vision and who was reared in the power politics of Eastern and Central Europe, was searching for a new realignment of forces in the 'heart' of the Middle East, and he referred to a new Cairo–Jerusalem–Beirut axis.[24] Realising full well the small size and essential vulnerability of Lebanon, Begin was probably hoping that the new Lebanon would be politically and strategically dependent on Israel. The emerging 'axis' would therefore not necessarily be an equilateral tripolar system. It would comprise two leading 'poles' — Israel and Egypt — with a third 'pole' Lebanon, linked primarily to one of the leading 'poles' — Israel.

The Israeli objectives in Lebanon required, however, a military campaign against both the PLO and related militias *and* against the Syrians. Only with the destruction of both these actors was the emergence of a 'new order' possible.

The Syrian context

By 1979–80, Israel's leading decision-makers had changed their perception of the Syrian role in Lebanon. They increasingly adopted the view that the Syrian presence was harmful to Israeli interests and that the Syrians should eventually be expelled. This viewpoint was underlined by the increased commitment to the Maronites and the readiness to become involved in the Zahle crisis. However, there remained doubt as to the wisdom of a full-scale military campaign against Syria. There was also concern about the implications of such a war for Israeli relations with the United States and Egypt, and about possible Soviet reactions.

The desire to conduct a military operation against Syria was related to three different issues. The first relates to the Lebanese situation as discussed above. Any attempt to install a new order in Lebanon would have to deal with the Syrians. The second issue was the strategic and military aspect. The Syrian army had grown considerably over recent years and Syria continued publicly to adopt an extreme anti-Israeli posture. Moreover, Syria was perceived as aligning itself totally with the PLO in Lebanon. It was argued that Syrian military power should be destroyed before it could be used against Israel. Shattering the Syrian forces would postpone Syria's war plans indefinitely. Alternatively, a war would reinforce the effect of Israel's deterrence against any Syrian-initiated war in the future.[25] This view was enthusiastically shared by the Northern Command and by the Chief of Staff (although, in Eitan's case, at the beginning of the war he preferred to emphasise the Palestinian issue). It is likely that other members of the Israeli decision-making group endorsed the same view.

It is possible to speculate on the existence of a third, rather enigmatic objective in Israel's pursuit of a war against Syria. A blow to Syria (inside Lebanon), might lead to far-reaching changes in Syria itself, including the breakdown of the regime and the disintegration of the state. This view seems to be based on assumptions as to the lack of Syrian political coherence, and was reinforced by the violent opposition to the regime deriving from the persistent and deep animosity of parts of the Sunni majority to the Alawi leadership. These ethnic and religious cleavages underpinned the notion that Syria might be on the brink of political collapse. A military blow could have ignited the explosive domestic situation. According to one version referred to by a foreign source, some Israeli planners envisaged the possible division of Syria, following the expected military defeat, into at least three different regions: a Druze area in the south, a Sunni area in Damascus and central Syria, and an Alawi region in the north-west.[26]

The future role of Israel in the Middle East

Two notions underlined at least the approach of Sharon to Israeli–Arab relations. First, Israel was militarily superior to the Arabs;[27] and second, military power could be used effectively and with few constraints, for the implementation of fundamental political objectives. The second notion was shared and spelled out further by Begin.[28] The time had come, they argued, to translate these two notions into hard political currency. The situation in the Arab world was uniquely suitable for such a development. Egypt had signed a peace treaty with Israel, Iraq was deeply involved in the war with Iran, and the rest of the Arab world appeared to be critically divided about almost everything. There appeared therefore to be a potential for collecting politico-strategic dividends. One could speculate that in Sharon's view (and possibly in Begin's as well) Israel could emerge as a hegemonical power in the 'heart' of the Middle East, with the Palestinian problem solved; Syria defeated and possibly disintegrating; Jordan undergoing a major and weakening transformation; and Iraq engaged continuously in the conflict with Iran. The only solid and stable military power would be Israel.

Such a development might also lead to the increased importance of Israel in the eyes of the United States, and Egypt would have to acquiesce in the new balance of power in the region. A final note must also be added. Despite the feelings of power and military superiority, some Israeli leaders (and certainly Begin) suffered from deep anxieties as to the maintenance of Israeli power in the future. Thus, the readiness to go to war, based essentially on Israeli strength, was paradoxically shored up by irrational fears of future doom.

ISRAELI DELIBERATIONS PRIOR TO WAR

From the very beginning, it appeared that the person to make the ultimate decision on going to war was the Prime Minister. Mr Begin, who enjoyed tremendous prestige in his party and in the country, had reached a position in which he was able to carry the government with him. But Begin probably needed beside him a decision-maker who would push him in the direction of war. This was the role of Sharon. Sharon, together with Eitan, prompted and encouraged Begin and ultimately won the Prime Minister to their views. It is still not clear, and probably never will be known, whether Begin would have decided on a war without Sharon's insistence. It seems probable, however, that the Defence Minister played a crucial part in the Prime Minister's eventual decision. Indeed, Eitan had proposed the basic plan for the war long before Sharon took office.

However, as will be described below, even the authoritative Begin encountered strong opposition within the Israeli Cabinet to the idea of military action. Only gradually did he overcome that opposition. It may also be added that Begin probably had his own hesitations during his deliberations on the issue which extended from the autumn of 1981 until the final decision in June 1982. Together with his associates he had to weigh the external (American, Soviet and Egyptian) constraints, and also try to secure a wide national consensus for the operation.

Decision-makers usually operate on the basis of their understanding of preceding events and experience. American reactions to Israel's actions since mid-1981, such as the attack on the Iraqi nuclear reactor at Osiraq, the Golan annexation and the 'Jerusalem Law' (passed in the Knesset on 30 July 1980, announcing the whole of Jerusalem as the capital of Israel), had been cautious and moderate.[29] In each of these cases the initial American reaction was negative but eventually faded away. American behaviour appeared to be falling into a pattern. Begin, encouraged by this apparent pattern and relying on the strong American animosity towards the PLO, seems to have concluded that Israel could rely on at least a few days of military operations uninhibited by the United States. On this point, his estimate proved to be over cautious. Begin also acted to mobilise American support for an Israeli-initiated military operation. General Sagui went to Washington in February with instructions to mobilise such support. Sharon was in Washington in May for the same purpose. Without necessarily seeking American approval, Begin's intention was to 'prepare the ground' in the US so that the Israeli action would come as no surprise.[30]

As for the Soviet reaction, the Israeli decision-makers concluded that the Soviet Union would not intervene so long as the war was limited to Lebanon itself.[31] It was thereby accepted that Soviet reactions would ultimately depend on the extent and intensity of the Israeli–Syrian military confrontation. This conclusion probably motivated Israeli caution during the first days of the war, and was also behind the continuous signals at that time, to all parties concerned, that Israel was not seeking to attack Syrian units in Lebanon.

Israel was also confident that the likely Egyptian reaction would also be moderate. This assessment was based on signals that it had allegedly received from Cairo to the effect that a limited Israeli operation in Lebanon would not necessarily aggravate Israeli–Egyptian relations. It might also be assumed that the Israeli leadership was ready to accept some deterioration in relations with Egypt resulting from the war.

In any case, all these reactions depended to a certain extent on the conditions attendant on the opening of hostilities. Since July 1981, when the cease-fire was reached, Israel had continued to insist that any PLO provocation would lead to an Israeli attack. In fact, it frequently redefined and lowered the level of the provocation.

Another problem was the approaching time for the final withdrawal from Sinai. Some decision-makers who were interested in the operation argued that it would be advisable to act before the final withdrawal took place. It was argued that until the withdrawal had taken place, Egypt would find it difficult to violate the agreement with Israel since its primary interest was to secure the last phase of the withdrawal.[32]

The decision process[33]

On 20 December 1981, the Israeli Government convened for its weekly meeting. This meeting was held in the aftermath of the Israeli decision to enact the 'Golan Law', which formally imposed a new regime on the Golan, a move that was very close to formal annexation. This law led to severe American and international criticism. However, instead of trying to placate world public opinion, the Israeli Cabinet was presented at that meeting with the formal proposal to launch a military operation in Lebanon. The plan which was presented by Sharon and Eitan was the 'Big Plan', and included the proposed penetration of Israeli forces through to the Beirut–Damascus highway, coupled with a landing north of Beirut at the main Christian port of Junieh, the encirclement of Beirut and linking up with the Phalangists in the eastern sector.

The Prime Minister called for adoption of the plan. However, some members of the Cabinet were opposed to it. These initial reactions surprised and annoyed the Prime Minister and he immediately decided to cancel the proposal.

By that time it was clear that Begin was convinced of the desirability of a large-scale military operation in Lebanon. Alternative plans for such an operation recurred time and again. However, when a plan for military action was raised in early January 1982, he hesitated, probably because of the opposition he had previously encountered in the Cabinet. Sharon and Eitan then reverted to another tactic, that is, to the idea of large-scale air bombardment of PLO concentrations. They rightly assumed that these bombings would provoke the PLO to retaliate militarily against northern Israel, as indeed had happened in 1981, and that this would serve as the desired pretext for the large-scale operation. However, when such proposals were raised in the Cabinet, several members were again in opposition. The Prime Minister therefore decided to refrain from action.

Nevertheless, the pressure was kept up for a military action. For example, in early March 1982, the Prime Minister convened a group of Ministers at his home. Sharon and Eitan again raised the idea of military action. They argued that such an operation prior to the final withdrawal from Sinai would serve as a test of the seriousness of ultimate Egyptian intentions. Once the final phase of withdrawal had taken place, Israel's freedom of action would be curtailed. Three Cabinet members — Foreign Minister Shamir, Ehrlich, the Deputy Prime Minister, and Burg, Minister of the Interior and Police — rejected this idea and maintained that it was a mistake to link the two issues. The possible link nevertheless played a role in other Cabinet discussions during the spring.

Sharon and Eitan turned to every possible pretext for a military action. On 25 March a hand grenade was thrown at an Israeli military car in the Gaza Strip. On the same day, leading members of the Cabinet were convened to discuss a proposal for retaliation by bombing PLO concentrations in Lebanon. Members of the Cabinet again suspected that the real objective of the exercise was to provoke the PLO into retaliation in order to provide a pretext. Seven members of the Cabinet opposed the proposal, which had the support of Begin and Sharon, and it was rejected.

On 3 April an Israeli diplomat was murdered in Paris. The idea of an air strike was again discussed but was postponed because of bad weather. Begin tried to mobilise the opposition Labour Party behind the idea of a war. He first mentioned it in a meeting with Peres (and other associates) on 16 February 1982. Peres voiced his opposition to the 'Big Plan', while not necessarily opposing a limited controlled operation against the PLO. Begin came back to the issue in a more extensive way in a meeting on 6 April, in which he and a team of Cabinet members met with the leadership of the Labour Party. At this meeting he first revealed to the Labour leaders the reason for the postponement of the air strike in April. Sharon then went ahead and pointed out that if the air strike had led to a 'strategic reaction' (apparently meaning Palestinian shelling) then Israel would have attacked along three routes: the coastal road, the central region and the eastern sector. He added (one might say sanctimoniously) that the Israeli forces would seek to avoid a confrontation with the Syrians, but he assumed that the Syrians would fight. According to Sharon, the Israeli objectives were to be the following:

(i) The destruction of the Palestinian organisations and their infrastructure in Lebanon and their expulsion from that country.
(ii) The formation of a new regime in Lebanon by the Christians and the Lebanese army.

(iii) Intervention by the Syrians might lead to their expulsion from Lebanon. Sharon added that the penetration through to and north of Beirut, and to the Beirut–Damascus road, would take 48 hours.

The Labour leaders responded that they were in favour of a strike on the Palestinian organisations but that they were opposed to the other two objectives.

On 9 April, amid mobilisation of some Israeli units and American efforts to dissuade Israel from an attack, the Cabinet was convened for an informal meeting. Eleven members were in favour of a proposal to launch an air strike. Five opposed it. The Prime Minister suggested that a committee comprised of six ministers should have the ultimate discretion as to when to launch the air strike. The committee, comprising the Prime Minister, Sharon, Shamir, Burg, Erlich and Shostak, the Minister of Health, met several times, and it became clear that some of its members were in fact opposed to the whole idea of an air strike. A variety of reasons led to a succession of cancellations of the proposed operation. Finally, following the death of an officer killed by a land mine inside south Lebanon, a limited air strike was carried out. The PLO, aware of the dangers involved in a reaction, remained quiet and refrained from opening fire. On 9 May the Israeli air force again attacked PLO concentrations in Lebanon. This time the PLO reacted with a scattered and totally ineffective shelling. About 100 shells fell in different areas in northern Israel but nobody was hurt and damage to property was negligible. The impression was that the ineffectiveness was intentional. The apparent objective of the bombardment was to serve as a signal, but not to escalate the conflict. It might even be speculated that the shelling was conducted not by the Fath militia but by other Palestinian organisations belonging to the PLO but in opposition to Fath and its leader (and leader of the PLO), Arafat.

The light shelling by the PLO underlined the effective deterrence posture established by Israel and underlined the seriousness with which the PLO leadership related to the various indications that Israel was searching for a pretext to attack Lebanon. It also demonstrated the ability of the PLO Central leadership to impose control over their rank and file, an ability which was later demonstrated during the war itself.

Begin did, however, try to use the shelling as a pretext for an

Israeli operation. He sought to react immediately and again presented a proposal for a general military operation. During a Cabinet meeting on 10 May it was proposed to launch a retaliatory strike against the PLO. Members of the Cabinet again opposed the idea. A vote was taken in which the Cabinet was locked at seven-all. Following this meeting, the Prime Minister heard from various members of the coalition, and certainly from the opposition, their reservations about a major military operation. He decided to moderate his position. He informed Sharon and Eitan that he had decided not to propose a large-scale operation for a while and on 16 May he informed the Cabinet that it was not called upon to make any decision about the operation. However, he added that were any Israeli or even Jewish target either inside or outside the country to be the casualty of terrorist actions, Israel would act.

But while members of the Cabinet assumed that even in such a case the war would be only on a limited scale and would not be directed against Syria, the Defence Minister and Chief of Staff directed the General Staff to prepare for war, with the objective of taking Beirut, which would probably involve a war with Syria as well. This was the prevalent view at a meeting of the High Command on 13 May.[34]

The war decision

In early June the long-awaited pretext finally presented itself. Terrorists acting on behalf of the Abu Nidal organisation tried to assassinate the Israeli Ambassador to London, Shlomo Argov. Begin immediately convened the Cabinet. The meeting took place on Friday morning, 4 June 1982. Sharon did not participate in the deliberations because he was absent at the time on a secret visit to Romania. Under Begin's sponsorship, Eitan proposed air strikes against both Beirut and south Lebanon. The scale of the proposed bombing was such that it was quite unlikely that the PLO, or at least elements within it, would refrain from some form of retaliation. The irony of the situation was that the Abu Nidal organisation was not a part of the PLO, and indeed was one of its most deadly foes. It had in fact tried to assassinate Yasser Arafat and other leaders of the PLO. The Abu Nidal action, sponsored by the Iraqi intelligence agencies, was apparently designed to bring about precisely what eventually took place, that is, an Israeli military operation culminating in an Israeli–Syrian confrontation. Thus Iraq, the leading enemy of Syria in the Arab world, would secure its Syrian flank.

The proposal to bomb targets in Lebanon met with some uneasiness in the Cabinet. Some members felt that strikes against Beirut would lead to escalation of the conflict and to the war which they opposed. When the scale of the bombing was somewhat reduced, the plan was unanimously approved by the Cabinet. It was clear, however, that the probability of an escalation to war had risen significantly. Hence it was decided to empower the Prime Minister and the Foreign Minister to mobilise reserves in case of need. When Sharon returned that same evening, this discretionary power reverted to him.

The Cabinet also resolved that, if the PLO were to retaliate, the Israeli air force would strike at the sources of fire. Activation of ground units would require Cabinet approval. However, at the end of the Friday meeting, Begin convened another Cabinet meeting for the Saturday evening. This step, coupled with the beginning of mobilisation on the Friday evening, amply demonstrated that he was confident that the ground operation would ultimately take place.[35]

In the army itself the plans for a military operation moved into top gear. In the Northern Command there was a feeling of certainty; the plan for operation *Oranim* would now be realised.[36]

On Friday afternoon, 4 June, the Israeli air force struck at targets in Beirut and south Lebanon. As expected, the Palestinian organisations retaliated with artillery salvos at sectors of northern Israel. It must be added that, whether deliberately or inadvertently, the shelling was very scattered and ineffectual. Only one Israeli civilian was killed and damage to property was negligible. But this was the provocation needed. When the Cabinet met on the evening of 5 June Begin proposed a military operation. Sharon and Eitan presented the Cabinet with what came to be known as the 'Small Plan', that is, an Israeli operation in south Lebanon only, with no advance to the Beirut area. Moreover, the plan envisaged no major move against the Syrians in the eastern sector. The plan's main principles were:

(i) An Israeli advance along three main routes: in the western sector, in the direction of Sidon; in the central sector, towards the Zaharani; and in the Eastern sector towards the town of Hasbaia;

(ii) Israel would do its utmost to avoid a confrontation with the Syrians;

(iii) The extent of the operation would be up to 40 km from the Israeli border, in order to eliminate the possibility of artillery attacks on Israeli settlements;[37]

(iv) The duration of the operation would be about 24–48 hours.

During the Cabinet deliberations, it was emphasised that Israel would do its utmost not to engage the Syrians, and that Beirut and its environs were not among the objectives of the operation. Some Cabinet members felt uneasy about even the limited operation. Moreover, they suspected that it would serve as a prelude to the 'Big Plan'. In the vote on the issue three members of the Cabinet registered their reluctance to accept the plan. One of the opponents of the plan, Burg, suggested that the air bombardment be continued for a while, and that another meeting of the Cabinet be convened before a ground attack was launched. In a vote on his proposal, he was the lone voice in favour. A vote was then taken on the main proposal. Erlich and Berman abstained, while all others were in favour.

The mobilisation and concentration of forces led to grave concern in Washington. On the night of 5–6 June Ambassador Lewis implored Israel not to start hostilities. A similar message from President Reagan arrived at 6 a.m. on 6 June. Israel decided to go ahead with the operation, however.

The official version of the Cabinet's decision was announced on the Sunday morning as follows:

(i) The IDF is instructed to place the civilian population of the Galilee beyond the range of the fire of the terrorists who are concentrated, they, their headquarters and their bases in Lebanon.

(ii) The name of the operation is Peace for Galilee.

(iii) During the operation the Syrian army will not be attacked unless it attacks our forces.

(iv) Israel aspires to the signing of a peace treaty with an independent Lebanon, while preserving its territorial integrity.

In response to the urgent message from President Reagan calling for moderation and the avoidance of military action, Begin sent a letter in which he justified the decision to go to war on the grounds that for the previous 72 hours the north of Israel had been exposed to a terrorist campaign. He added that the Israeli forces had been ordered 'to push the terrorists north to a distance of 40 km' and insisted that Israel had no territorial ambitions in Lebanon. He also pointed out that Israel hoped to sign a peace treaty with a 'free and independent Lebanon'.[38]

Israeli ground forces entered Lebanon at 11 a.m. on 6 June. It is a purely speculative point, but it is highly probable that Israel would have launched the military operation even had the PLO shelling not taken place. The leaders who pressed for a military operation were so powerful in the Cabinet, and the frustrations in the army resulting from several previous mobilisations and cancellations so intense, that an operation was very likely in any case.

It seems clear that Sharon and Eitan were eager to implement the 'Big Plan'. Indeed, the 'Big Plan' guided many Israeli moves. On the other hand, the evidence clearly suggests that some military actions conducive to the more effective and immediate application of the 'Big Plan' were either cancelled or briefly postponed. This was done in order not to present the Cabinet and the public at large with a picture totally contradictory to the strategy decided upon. Four such military decisions were: that Israeli forces were not landed in Junieh north of Beirut;[39] that heliborne operations near the Beirut–Damascus highway did not take place; that the main Israeli attack in the eastern sector, towards the main Syrian deployment, was postponed until the fourth day of the war; and fourth, that the central column which moved in the direction of the Beirut–Damascus road, was halted for a few hours until a decision was taken at a high level. These restrictions did not hamper the overall advance in the western sector whose objective was Beirut and linking up with the Christian militia. They meant only a brief postponement of the strike at the Syrian forces, which was to come when the Prime Minister became convinced that the 'Big Plan' was feasible.

Indeed, the real puzzle is to determine the Prime Minister's objectives in the execution of the war. Several factors suggest that he was in favour of the 'Big Plan' at the time when the war was initiated. In asserting this, it is important from the outset to understand Begin's basic approach to international relations and to history. His intellectual outlook and political approach were formulated in the Central and Eastern Europe of the 1930s and

1940s and against the background of European history. The accepted view and practice in those parts of Europe at that time was the Clausewitzian view that the accomplishment of political objectives, whether in defence of the *status quo* or revisionist, by the actual use of force (in contrast to the threat of its use) was legitimate and justified. Begin internalised this outlook while perhaps being unaware of its practical limitations, so well understood by some of the Europeans themselves. This rather primitive (because of its lack of awareness of practical constraints) version of power politics also coloured his assessment of the ability of military force to create a new Lebanon at peace with Israel. Account must also be taken of the fact that, in December 1981, Begin had become a proponent of the 'Big Plan' and had actively tried to convince the Cabinet to adopt it. Two separate versions of the 'Big Plan' existed and apparently Begin endorsed both. First, there was the move on Beirut and the linking up with the Christians. As to that, the very formulation of the Cabinet decision to go to war, which was carefully phrased by Begin, makes it clear that Beirut was the objective. The decision referred to the destruction of the 'terrorists . . . headquarters and bases in Lebanon'. The main headquarters of the various PLO organisations were in Beirut.

As for a military move against Syria, which was the second variant of the 'Big Plan', Begin probably realised that the only way to create the conditions conducive to the creation of a new regime in Lebanon depended on the expulsion of Syria from Lebanon. Furthermore, he was clearly aware that Sharon had repeatedly noted in meetings with the Labour leadership the high probability that the Syrians would intervene in the planned operation. Finally, Begin's reference to the idea of the creation of the Cairo–Jerusalem–Beirut axis indicated the broad framework in which he viewed the war.

Begin's hesitations in the early stages of the war seem to have derived from his concern over possible external reactions, and his desire to mobilise the Labour opposition behind the operation. In this way it is possible to understand his restrained letter to President Reagan in which he emphasised that Israel was seeking to operate within a range of 40 km only, and his repeated public assurances that Israel was not seeking a military confrontation with Syria. In this respect, by waiting a few days before fully implementing the move against Syria, Begin demonstrated caution and good judgement.

In pursuit of his attempts to mobilise opposition support for the operation, he and Sharon met the Labour leadership — Peres, Rabin and Bas-Lev — one hour after the entry of the ground forces into Lebanon. Sharon explained that the advance would be to the line of Sidon–Lake Qarun, which would take the Galilee out of the range of PLO artillery, that there was no intention to strike at the Syrians, and that the advance would approach no closer than 4 km from their deployment. He noted that Israel was hoping that the Syrians would retreat, but he once again added significantly that in his assessment the Syrians would enter into a military confrontation. The Labour leaders, as in previous meetings, emphasised that the objective should only be the removal of PLO artillery from within the range of Israeli settlements and that Israel's actions should not exceed a limited operation. Begin assured them that this was in fact the objective of the operation. However, his later decisions clearly indicate that in that meeting he did not divulge his overall objectives. Were the Labour leaders taken in by that presentation? In attempting to answer this question it must be borne in mind that they were all astute leaders with tremendous experience in security affairs. Moreover, they maintained many contacts in the army and undoubtedly received informal information about military plans. Three answers are possible: they believed Begin but suspected Sharon — knowing his *modus operandi*; they did not believe the whole presentation but were ready to go along with it as it covered their public flank; and finally, they did not believe the presentation, but in political terms it was impossible for them to base their public reaction on the assumption that the Prime Minister was deliberately lying to them. In the event, two days later they endorsed the government's resolution in the *Knesset* referring to the advance to 40 km.

Meanwhile Begin waited to see the external reactions. The American reaction was quite moderate. Indeed, Reagan and Haig in particular, reached a decision to use the new developments in order to implement the American objective of re-creating a strong and sovereign Lebanon. The initial Soviet reaction was also quite mild. These cautious reactions created a context within which Begin decided that the 'Big Plan' was in fact politically feasible. By the evening of the first day of the fighting he was ready to allow a flanking operation in the western and central sectors, which was intended to bring the

Israeli forces to the Beirut–Damascus road. More important was the decision taken on the fourth day of the fighting to launch an offensive in the eastern sector against the main body of the Syrian forces.

THE MILITARY ACTIONS

The military moves of June 1982 have already been discussed elsewhere.[40] Although this aspect of the war requires further analysis, such a task lies beyond the scope of this book. They will, however, be treated here very briefly as indicators of the politico-strategic objectives of Israel and Syria.

The order of battle and deployment of forces

PLO deployment

At the time of the war, the Palestinian organisations were in the midst of a process of transformation from a guerrilla force into a semi-regular army. This process corresponded with their successful attempt to create a mini-state in parts of south Lebanon. It was also due to the ongoing Israeli offensive (until the cease-fire of 1981) against the Palestinian positions. This offensive forced them to concentrate on their own defence and to harden their deployment.

The Palestinians, who were divided into eight different organisations, the largest of which was Fath, were deployed in several concentrations, and numbered altogether between 13,000 and 15,000 men. It is probable, however, that some of these were in fact part-time militias and not part of the organised brigades and batallions. About half were deployed in southern Lebanon from Sidon due south and east. The headquarters of all the organisations and the other half of their men were located in Beirut itself.

The Palestinian organisations' contingency plans, in the event of major Israeli attack, apparently called for a halting operation followed by a retreat in an organised fashion towards Beirut and its vicinity. It was assumed that the advancing Israeli forces would suffer many casualties in the advance northwards.

The deployment of the Syrian forces

The Syrian regime used its military power in Lebanon for the imposition of its political and strategic objectives. Indeed, since their intervention in 1976, the Syrians had carefully tailored their military power to selected political ends. Syrian units had to fulfil two objectives. First, to police the country so as to enable Syria to achieve its political aims in Lebanon. The fulfilment of this task required the maintenance of pressure on all factions to desist from renewing the Civil War. A relatively quiet Lebanon was the precondition for the possible imposition of a President and Government convenient to Damascus. Second, the Syrian forces were required to defend the western flank of Syria, and primarily the Damascus area, from an Israeli outflanking military drive through southern Lebanon and the Beqa valley. This deployment could also serve as a deterrent against an Israeli overall attack on central or north Lebanon.

It is most improbable that the Syrian deployment was intended for an attack on Israel. Not only did the size of the Syrian forces and the way in which they were deployed preclude such an action, but even with a considerable increase in the size of its forces in Lebanon, it is unlikely that Syria would have used Lebanon as a springboard for an attack on Israel. The terrain in south Lebanon, as the Israeli forces discovered to their cost, favours the defence more than any other geographical area around Israel. The inferiority of the Syrian forces (even in conjunction with Iraq and Jordan) in comparison with the Israeli forces has been so clear that only by a major concentration of forces in an area where the defence did not enjoy a significant advantage, could Syria hope to secure a limited success. Furthermore, the main objective of Syria has not been to attack northern Israel but to seek the liberation of the Golan Heights. The Golan Heights also happens to be an area where defence does not have the same geographical advantage as in southern Lebanon and northern Israel. If we add to this Syria's tremendous investment in the development of its fortifications in the Golan, and the fact that an Israeli thrust in the Golan threatens Damascus directly, it can be assumed clear that in Syrian planning the Golan Heights was considered the main front for both offensive and defensive operations; south and east Lebanon remained secondary fronts for primarily defensive operations.

Syrian deployment in Lebanon was oriented to securing these objectives. Of its overall order of battle Syria usually deployed less than a quarter of its forces in Lebanon. In times of need, there had been an increase in that capability. Of the six armoured and mechanised divisions possessed by Syria in June 1982, only one mechanised division was usually deployed in Lebanon. At other times, one or two additional mechanised or armoured brigades were also deployed. When the military threat appeared less urgent, or when there was a need for training, the deployment pattern would change. Instead of a divisional structure, the Syrians would deploy three or four independent armoured and mechanised brigades plus several commando battalions. Sometimes the pattern differed: they would take a brigade from one of the six divisions and deploy it in addition to two or three of their above-mentioned independent brigades.

Just prior to the war, the Syrian deployment in Lebanon comprised the following: two armoured brigades, two mechanised infantry brigades, several commando battalions, and two small infantry brigades of the Palestine Liberation Army (PLA), which served with Syrian officers and which were under full Syrian control. These forces, under the command of General Adib Ismail, held positions in two defensive strips: the forward belt, with only light forces (and in the case of an Israeli attack, it would have in front of it the PLO positions), and the second main belt. In order to further their political aims, the Syrians relied on a large concentration of forces in Beirut itself and in its immediate vicinity.

The Israeli order of battle and missions

The Israeli 'Big Plan' called for the expulsion of Syrian forces from Lebanon, and for the destruction of the PLO deployment and presence. The accomplishment of these aims would open the way for the establishment of a new Lebanese government dependent on Israel, hopefully under the Presidency of Bashir Jumayyil, the leader of the Phalanges.

However, conscious of the political limitations imposed by the reluctance of the Israeli Cabinet immediately to endorse such an ambitious plan, the Prime Minister, who in any case apparently wanted first to measure international reactions, endorsed a cautious approach and initially ordered a more limited action. The military leaders responsible for the operation had therefore to design a plan which would eventually lead to the same military and political objectives envisaged for the 'Big Plan', but which would do it in a somewhat more gradual way. The Cabinet-endorsed 'Small Plan' was aimed ostensibly at attaining an Israeli advance of about 40–45 km into Lebanon, primarily in the western and central sectors. This perimeter 'allowed' only targets which were short of both Beirut and the crucial Beirut–Damascus road. Beirut lay about 30–35 km north of the furthest point on that circular perimeter. However, the 'Small Plan' in fact allowed for the option of the 'Big Plan'. It was clear to all commanders that the military objectives were more ambitious than those declared. Indeed, the landing of Force B in the Awali early in the war exceeded the 40 km perimeter.

The 'Small Plan' precluded the ambitious idea of landing troops in Junieh and of attacking the Beirut area from the north. It also dictated a slower move against the Syrians in the Beqa valley, and precluded the possibility of landing heliborne troops in strategic positions on the Beirut–Damascus highway. However, short of these restrictions, other Israeli military moves in the first two days were free from almost all political constraints.

The forces deployed for the operation were quite sizeable, and indicate that a military confrontation with Syria was planned from the outset. The suppression of the PLO alone would have required no more than 1–2 divisions at the outside. According to Richard Gabriel, altogether six divisions or divisional structures were earmarked for the operation. In addition, there were two independent task forces below the division level. It should be noted, however, that not all of these formations acted with their full complement. In some cases only one or two tank brigades operated in a tank division. In other cases all the brigades in a division were mobilised, but many units within the brigades as well as in the division were not moved up to the front. Thus, the actual forces engaged in battle were limited.

The nature of the terrain and the large built-up areas demanded that infantry units play an important role in the operation. Following the tradition of flexibility in the Israeli army, the divisions sent into battle often had less than their usual order of battle in terms of tank brigades, but incorporated paratroop and infantry units which were not normally attached to them. Moreover, units were moved from one division to another according to need.

Of the six divisional structures, four were designated for the western and central sectors. Two divisions plus the two task forces were designated for the eastern sectors. This allocation of forces seems to reflect a balanced division of effort. The two divisions operating in the western sector had as their objective the destruction of the PLO and the linking up with the Christian militias in the Beirut area. The two divisions in the central sector were to help in the initial objective of the encirclement and destruction of the PLO. They were also responsible for cutting off the Syrian forces from the PLO and the Beirut area. These objectives secured, the way would be open for the establishment of a new regime in Lebanon linked to and dependent on Israel.

The largest formation was assigned to the eastern sector. This reflected Israel's recognition that in terms of actual fighting the most formidable opponent would be the Syrian units in the Beqa. Moreover, it was assumed that once the Beirut area and the central sectors had been conquered, the Syrian forces in the Beqa would in any case be facing the threat of an encirclement from the west, and the routing of their forces in the Beqa would thus be easier. Even though the forces in the central sector were deployed with the option of creating pressure on the Syrian forces, it seems nevertheless that the overall forces earmarked for the western and central sectors were excessive. The emphasis on the western and central sector reflected the priorities of the Chief of Staff, who by the beginning of the war had changed his position on the relative importance of the two main military objectives. Eitan, who had been the leading supporter of a decisive campaign against the Syrians, became more inclined towards the notion of a Beirut-first approach. His new position seems to have derived from his increasing involvement over the years in contacts with the Phalangists, and partly from the importance he attached to the destruction of the PLO. His priorities were probably also affected by the general concern in the defence and military establishments that the Cabinet might intervene and change the scope of the war. Hence, it was most important to complete the task in the western sector as quickly as possible.

Military operations

The Israeli forces operating in the western and central sectors quickly overcame Palestinian resistance in southern Lebanon and created an option to move towards Beirut. Indeed, by the morning of 9 June, the fourth day of operations, one of the divisions operating in the western sector was given the green light to advance towards Beirut and to link up with the Christians inside East Beirut. Needless to say, this was clearly the real operational target of the forces in this sector from the very beginning.

Up to then, the Israeli forces in the western sector had operated in areas in which no Syrian forces had been deployed. However, the Israeli option to move on Beirut forced Syria to choose between a battle for Beirut or abandoning the area, and thus undermining its political influence there. Syria decided to signal its resolve to defend its political position in Lebanon, and if Israel chose to continue its advance, to fight. Thus, a Syrian mechanized brigade took up defensive positions south of Beirut. The continuation of the Israeli advance led to an immediate encounter with Syrian units.

A separate earlier advance by an Israeli formation in the central sector involved an even higher likelihood of direct contact with the Syrians. This formation moved in the direction of the Beirut–Damascus highway, thus threatening to cut off both the Beirut area *and* the central sector from the main Syrian concentration in the Beqa. Furthermore, having achieved its mission, this formation would be able to engage in an outflanking operation due east, thus threatening the entire Syrian deployment in the Beqa. A Syrian military response was virtually an inevitable outcome of the advance of the Israeli formation. Indeed, by 8 June, an Israeli–Syrian military battle had already taken place in the region of Jezzin. The overall mission of the said Israeli formation was confirmed by the Israeli Cabinet on the evening of 6 June. The Cabinet might have been hoping that the Syrians would withdraw from the Beqa as a result of the threatened outflanking operation.

Thus, the Israeli move in the central sector was an exercise in coercive diplomacy *vis-à-vis* Syria. By the same token it was a major escalatory step in the sense that it threatened to destroy the whole Syrian politico-strategic position in Lebanon.

Begin's caution and the absence of Cabinet approval limited the fighting in the eastern sector in the first three days to the breaking up of the PLO military presence in the forward area known as Fathland. However, military entanglement with the Syrians was developing in the meantime. As already mentioned, on 8 June, a major battle in the Jezzin area had already taken place.

All this time, Defence Minister Sharon continued to press

upon the Cabinet the need to attack the Syrian deployment in the Beqa proper. He raised the issue on 8 June but was turned down. The following day he returned to the same subject, arguing that during the previous night the Syrians had introduced many new SAM batteries into the Beqa, infringing the ability of the Israeli air force to attack targets throughout Lebanon. This was clearly a pretext intended to mobilise Cabinet support for the operation. Sharon proposed a full-scale air and ground attack against the Syrians. The Cabinet conceded the point and in vague language accepted Sharon's proposal in general but specified only the attack on the SAM sites. Thus while the Cabinet decision referred specifically only to the air strikes, authorisation had been extended obliquely for the ground operation as well. Bearing in mind Begin's authority in the Cabinet and his famous obsession with detail and the nuances of formal textual definitions, it seems highly likely that the decision to attack the Syrian forces on the ground carried his full backing.

A diplomatic interlude

While the war raged, Begin repeatedly stressed that Israel was not planning to attack Syria, unless Syria intervened in the fighting. On 8 June he met the American mediator Habib and asked him to communicate to President Asad the following points:

(i) Israel did not wish to fight Syria, and would not attack Syrian forces unless attacked first.
(ii) Syrian forces that had advanced beyond Syrian lines in the Beqa as of the beginning of the war, should withdraw.
(iii) The Palestinian fighters deployed inside the Syrian perimeter, should withdraw to a line 40 km distant from the Israeli border.

Habib left for Syria but before he had even met Asad, Israel had struck at the Syrian SAM batteries. The Israeli message sounded somewhat hollow after Israel had already attacked the Jezzin deployment and the SAM sites. As a result of the Israeli actions, Asad was left in a very difficult position. Moreover, he had not as yet extended any military support to the PLO. He was certainly unable to reduce his units in the southern Beqa as Israel had demanded. Nevertheless, in his response to Habib, Asad persisted in his attempt to limit the imminent escalation. He noted the following points:

(i) Syria did not desire a military confrontation with Israel.

(ii) Syrian units that had moved beyond the 5 June limit of deployment would retreat.

(iii) Syria could not make any decision about PLO deployment. This issue lay in the hands of the Lebanese Government and the PLO.

(iv) The key to future developments was in the hands of the United States.

(v) Israeli forces should also retreat to a line extending 40 km north of the Israeli border.

In his response, Asad in fact demonstrated his readiness to acquiesce in the destruction of the PLO and in a very deep extension of Israeli forces into Lebanon. He also signalled his readiness to accept American mediation. Simultaneously, Syria began to move reinforcements to the Beqa signalling its determination to defend its position there. However, this entire diplomatic interlude was superfluous, preceded as it was by the Israeli decision to strike at the Syrian forces in the Beqa.

The Israeli–Syrian confrontation in the eastern sector

The Israeli air force operated in the skies over Lebanon before the actual ground battle was joined, when it attacked PLO targets in Beirut and south Lebanon, beginning on Friday, 4 June. Once the war had begun, the air force increased its activities, attacking targets in both the western and central sectors, and destroying PLO units and infrastructure. It also gave continued air coverage to the advancing units. From a quite early stage in the fighting, Syrian aircraft conducted some combat flights in the same areas where the Israeli planes operated. This led to several air clashes in which Syrian planes were shot down.

The attack on the Syrian SAM sites began at 2 p.m. on 9 June and continued for approximately two hours. It was an extremely sophisticated operation conducted with perfect precision.[41] In total, some 17 of 19 SAM 2, 3, and 6 batteries were destroyed. Two more batteries were destroyed the following day. The Syrian air force went into the air soon after the attack began. The air battle continued throughout the afternoon and was renewed the next day. Altogether, in these air battles some 90 Syrian MIG 23s and 21s were downed. No Israeli aircraft was hit either by the SAMs or by the Syrian interceptors.

By the end of the operation, the Syrian air defence systems and air force had suffered a devastating defeat. One might speculate that this development, coupled with the mild Arab and other international reactions to the Israeli operation, convinced Prime Minister Begin that a ground strike at the Syrian forces would not hinder the expected Israeli political achievements, and the appropriate directives were issued.

By the time the Israeli attack began on the morning of 10 June, the Syrians had already reinforced their deployment in the Beqa. In addition to the two to three tank and mechanised brigades usually deployed there and in the Jezzin area, they moved in a full tank division. In addition, during 10 June and the following night, they began moving an additional armoured division to positions controlling the Beirut–Damascus highway.

The Israeli military advance aimed at dislodging the Syrian forces from the Beqa up to the critical Beirut–Damascus highway. Once Israel achieved control of this highway, so went the Israeli reasoning, the ability of Syria to influence political developments in Beirut and central Lebanon would be extremely limited. The Israeli advance met strong Syrian resistance and consequently was slower than expected. In any event, the cease-fire imposed on Israel by noon, 11 June, pre-empted the accomplishment of its objective.

The Israeli decision to abide by the cease-fire in the eastern sector was due primarily to American demands to stop the fighting. This requires a brief discussion. Israel had demonstrated several times during the war that it was ready and able to defy similar American demands when it considered that important Israeli interests were served by a continuance of the fighting. But at this early stage of the war, the American reaction was not yet clear and Israel was anxious to mobilise American support for its war aims. In any case, the Israeli leaders were not ready to run the risk of major disagreements with the United States, especially when it was perceived that the attainment of the political objective of the war — the establishment of a new pro-Israeli regime in Beirut — was possible without necessarily continuing the fighting in the Beqa. Even the Defence Minister who was probably interested in ultimately pushing the Syrians out of Lebanon altogether, was seemingly hesitant at the time to conclude the battle immediately. In Sharon's scheme of things, one phase was to follow another.

The cease-fire of Friday 11 June was adhered to in the eastern and central sectors, but had no effect in the western sector. The fighting around Beirut continued until Israel had encircled the city and linked up with the Christian militia. This the United States apparently did not oppose.

The battle for Beirut

By Monday 14 June, Israel had implemented many of the initial military objectives of the 'Big Plan', and had now created the option for the complete destruction of the PLO headquarters and infrastructure in Beirut itself. It had also temporarily neutralised the Syrians. Hence, any new regime in Lebanon would have to consider carefully the Israeli position and demands. Moreover, because of its close relations with part of the Maronite community, Israel could ostensibly rely on a strong grouping inside Lebanon which appeared to favour such a relationship with Israel *per se*.

It was on this basis that Israel publicly reformulated its war objectives, to correspond more closely to the original aims of the leading decision-makers. It insisted that:[42]

(i) All foreign armies (including the PLO) withdraw from Lebanon.
(ii) A new Lebanese Government be formed.
(iii) The new government sign a peace treaty with Israel.

The implementation of these objectives appeared even at this early stage to be extremely difficult. The passage of time demonstrated even more clearly the illusions on which these objectives were based. It was immediately clear that their realisation would require much more fighting and in difficult conditions, including a battle for Beirut, and the very real chance of another major battle against the Syrians. Furthermore, the objective of clearing the whole of Lebanon of PLO units was likely to revert to low-level warfare, and as such would be difficult, relatively costly, and highly dependent on close co-operation with the local population.

Even if Israel were successful in all these military operations, only the first objective would be secure. The other two were basically political in nature and depended on subtle social and political processes which military force by itself would be unable directly to determine. By publicly formulating these objectives, and in trying to implement them, Israel acquired for itself a massive political-military burden. Their attainment was shrouded with so many uncertainties and possible costs that the chances of success were at best very debatable.

Israel had first to overcome the immediate problem of Beirut. It has been suggested that an understanding existed between Israel and the Phalanges, according to which once Israel had neutralised the PLO and the Syrians in Lebanon south of Beirut, the Phalanges would clear West Beirut itself (East Beirut being in Christian hands in any case). Other sources, however, have reported that Jumayyil gave no such undertaking.[43] Whatever the case, when the Israeli forces encircled West Beirut, the Phalanges declined to fight. The task of clearing Beirut of the Syrians and the PLO was left to Israel.

Here, of course, Israel encountered a problem of very substantial dimensions. Modern armies, and the Israeli army in particular, are best suited for mobile fighting in open spaces. Most Israeli fighting units are organised around armoured divisions; only a smaller part of the army is organised with first line infantry units. All this makes it extremely difficult for the Israeli army to involve itself in fighting in built-up areas. Moreover, such fighting requires a readiness to suffer heavy casualties. The expected battle in Beirut was even more ominous in that Beirut is a large and densely inhabited city with thousands of multi-storey buildings. The PLO fighters were mingled with a population of about half a million people. Heavy fighting in Beirut would therefore involve not just heavy casualties among the Israeli forces, but also many casualties among the civilian population which consisted largely of Lebanese, who did not necessarily sympathise with the PLO.

The Israeli military planners had apparently not prepared themselves for these difficulties. It seems that they had, as mentioned before, relied on the Phalanges to deal with West Beirut, or were hoping that the PLO would disintegrate once the Israeli forces arrived on the outskirts of the city. Neither eventuality happened. By the second week of the war, the main outline of the next phase of fighting had emerged: if Israel insisted on the ambitious objective of pushing the PLO and the Syrians from Beirut, it would have to engage its own military forces in a very difficult operation.

If indeed the military option was to be used, three strategies seemed open. First, an all-out attack on West Beirut. Such an operation threatened death or injury to hundreds of Israeli soldiers, among them members of elite units, and would also lead to the destruction of parts of Beirut, and to the death of many thousands of Lebanese civilians. A second possible strategy was to impose a strict siege on the city, involving the complete blocking of food, water and electricity deliveries, coupled with heavy shelling. A third strategy involved not completely conquering the city, but some kind of 'salami' tactics. There would be a gradual advance into the city, taking one neighbourhood after the other. The second and third strategies could be combined. Moreover, both could serve as the prelude to the first strategy.

It is not clear what the initial preferred strategy of the Israeli leadership was. The first strategy was rejected in the initial phase of the Israeli presence around Beirut. The Beirut issue was raised in the Cabinet meeting of 15 June. After a discussion the Cabinet ruled against an attack on West Beirut, but decided to aid the Phalanges in their own advance on the city. The 'aid' would comprise artillery shelling and *not* the use of the air force. Accordingly, Sharon contacted Bashir Jumayyil and informed the Cabinet that the Phalanges would attack West Beirut probably towards the end of June.

The Phalanges did not attack. Another proposal submitted to the Israeli Cabinet suggested that the Phalanges would attack first and that the Israeli army would follow after a few hours had elapsed. The Cabinet apparently rejected this proposal. Throughout the first phase until late June, the Cabinet maintained its rejection of the occupation of West Beirut. Sharon tended to favour a direct attack on the southern part of West Beirut, but the Cabinet remained divided on this idea. In view of Cabinet opposition, and given the rising opposition inside the army itself to a direct attack, the first strategy became more and more difficult to implement.[44] The Cabinet then decided to adopt the second strategy. Implementation of the third strategy began in early August, apparently without full Cabinet blessing.

In a war which was to a large extent primarily directed at political objectives and influenced by a complex mix of political factors, the siege of Beirut became perhaps the most 'political' of all the battles. It was political in three different ways. First, because of the military constraints on an attempt to take the whole city by a military operation, Israel decided to accept the US initiative in trying to obtain the evacuation of the PLO from Beirut through political mediation. The military operations had therefore to be one of the instruments to secure precisely that objective. The second political dimension of the siege related to the impact of the Israeli operations in Beirut on Israel's political standing in the international community. The continued bombardment of the city and the siege were closely reported by the large community of reporters there representing the international media. The television and the press in the United States and Western Europe gave extensive coverage to the horrifying effects of the Israeli bombardment and shelling of the civilian parts of Beirut. The third political aspect of the siege concerned the future of the political system inside Lebanon. On the one hand, the *status quo* forces were convinced that only the evacuation of the PLO and the Syrians from Beirut would clear the way for a renewal of their control in Lebanon. On the other hand, heavy shelling of parts of West Beirut threatened to bring counterproductive effects. The Maronites needed the co-operation of the Sunni Muslim leadership in West Beirut for the re-establishment of the *status quo ante*. But the bombing of parts of West Beirut raised the animosity of its population against the Israelis and their allies, the Maronites. Hence, many Maronites had a dual approach to the bombing: to a certain extent satisfaction, while remaining uneasy about its political consequences.

The main Israeli considerations remained focused on two aspects of the Beirut situation: the feasibility of a military operation and its costs in terms of casualties to Israel, and the possible reactions of the United States. When Begin visited Washington on 21–25 June, he apparently promised President Reagan not to conquer West Beirut. Israel found itself confronting a grave dilemma: to concede the objective of expelling the PLO from Beirut, or to rely on the siege strategy and hope that the political effort launched by the United States would obtain the withdrawal of the PLO.

Israel refused to relinquish its objective and instead opted for the long haul of the siege strategy. For six weeks the Israeli artillery and air force continued the bombing and shelling of Beirut up to the Corniche al-Mazra'a, and coupled it with the imposition of restrictions on the transfer of food, water and electricity to the town. Throughout the siege, Israel suffered political costs in terms of its international standing and probably also in terms of the emotions it aroused among the Lebanese living in West Beirut. The siege also led to a tremendous increase in the salience of the Palestinian problem, focusing the attention of the whole world on their plight.

The battle for the Beirut–Damascus road

Gaining control over the Beirut–Damascus road would provide Israel with the coveted strategic option of attacking from the flank the Syrian forces deployed around the road in the Beqa. In addition, in order to increase pressure on West Beirut in the central section, it was necessary to widen the encirclement around the city. Israeli control over the western part of the critical road would also allow it to move forces easily into the Christian mini-state north-east of Beirut, and thereby threaten Syrian positions in the northern Beqa and in central and northern Syria itself.

All these objectives were envisaged beforehand, and hence the formulation of the war plan included those targets set for the Israeli formation operating in the central sector. The force failed, however, to accomplish these objectives during the first week of the war. During the second week there had been some limited military moves intended to secure these objectives, but they also failed because the forces allotted to them were too small. Sharon and Eitan were clearly operating under severe constraints: the Israeli Cabinet was not ready to allow further fighting against the Syrians.

By the third week of the war, Sharon had his opportunity. Prime Minister Begin went to Washington on a state visit. In his absence and without the Cabinet's authority (but possibly with Begin's endorsement, tacit or explicit), the Israeli army went on the offensive in the central sector. By that time, the Syrians had fortified their positions and sent in reinforcements. Consequently the fighting was heavy and costly. When it was over, Israeli control stretched along the Beirut–Damascus road from Beirut to the hilly slopes leading to the Beqa.

Siege and diplomacy

The siege corresponded with the mediation effort of Philip

Habib. His activities centred on resolving the Beirut problem. The objective was to arrange for the evacuation of the PLO from Beirut and the lifting of the siege.

Apparently it was not just the military actions which convinced the PLO that it had to withdraw. Equally important was its realisation that it was isolated not only inside Lebanon and Beirut, but also in the Arab world.[45] That the Maronites were critically opposed to the PLO was no surprise, but apparently opposition extended to include many of the Sunni and Shi'i Muslims in Beirut and in Lebanon generally. Their negative reaction towards the PLO resulted from both the traditional pattern in the Arab world in which each Arab nation or community is primarily concerned with its own interests, and from the ruthless way in which the PLO imposed its presence in parts of Lebanon and in West Beirut. Muslim disdain for the PLO became extreme as the severe Israeli punishment of Beirut made life there increasingly intolerable. The hundreds of thousands of Lebanese of all religious persuasions living in West Beirut reached the conclusion that the continued presence of the PLO in their midst might bring them unacceptable pain. Even those who continued to sympathise with the Palestinians were not ready to sacrifice their own well-being and possibly their lives for the Palestinian cause. They were ready to form coalitions with the PLO when it suited their interests in the political struggle inside Lebanon, but this readiness evaporated when the stakes for the defence of the PLO were raised.

It was not an easy task to achieve the evacuation of the PLO. Two main obstacles lay in the way. First, by evacuating Beirut the PLO would lose its main independent territorial base. The PLO was ready for this only under duress *and* at a price. It was seeking to make good its military defeat by snatching as it were a political success. As mentioned earlier, the salience of the Palestinian problem had increased several times over since the beginning of the war. But the most important objective was to secure official US political recognition of the PLO. As far as the sources open to the public are concerned, the PLO failed in this particular objective. At best, some points were scored on the scale of US perceptions about the Middle East situation in general.

The second obstacle was a very genuine concern about the fate of the Palestinian community in Lebanon in general and in Beirut in particular. The PLO were concerned about the possible revenge that the Phalangists might invoke against their families. Once the main core of the hardened fighters left Beirut, the Phalangists might enter and settle their bloody scores with those who remained behind.

A third concern related to the future of the PLO itself once it had evacuated Beirut. The PLO leadership knew only too well the suspicions held against them by the Arab states and how by the same token they were ready to utilise the PLO for their respective political objectives. Thus, the PLO leadership was concerned about the fate of the organisation once it was dispersed among the various Arab states.

Many of the PLO were not happy about the idea of an evacuation under any conditions. They assumed that Israel was unlikely to enter West Beirut. Even if it ultimately decided to do so, it would suffer many casualties, and this could be counted as a major success for the PLO. Furthermore, it was likely that the difficulties in conquering a large and modern city would prevent the Israeli forces from wiping out all the PLO fighters. Finally, in the process of occupying Beirut, Israel might arouse the hatred and animosity of many of the Lebanese living in Beirut, and this would also constitute a net benefit for the PLO.

For all these reasons, it was not at all clear that Habib's mission would be successful. That it did succeed was due to exhaustion on the part of the PLO, resulting from a unique combination of Israeli, Lebanese and Arab pressure. American pressure, and the obvious desire of the PLO to build bridges towards the United States, also played a role.

One month after the beginning of the siege, the PLO appeared to be willing to withdraw from Beirut. It did insist, however, that the withdrawal be preceded by an Israeli withdrawal from the outskirts of Beirut. Israel flatly rejected this demand. Another possibility raised at the time, and which continued to float around until the very last phase of the negotiations, was a PLO withdrawal from Beirut to other parts of Lebanon under Syrian control. Two areas were mentioned: Tripoli and the Beqa. Both Israel and the Lebanese Government rejected the idea. This dispute led to a halt in the negotiations and to continued bloodshed and suffering in Beirut.

By the sixth week of the siege, it appeared as if Habib was gradually approaching a breakthrough. The main difficulty remaining was to determine to which countries the PLO fighters would be evacuated. None of the Arab countries contacted appeared to be enthusiastic to receive the PLO evacuees. They were concerned not to open their gates to an element which was notorious for its radicalism and for its propensity to destabilise the situation in any host country. Jordan had in the past suffered at the hands of the PLO and had overcome them only through a bloody campaign. Indeed, Syria had also had to mount an operation against the PLO in Lebanon. Lebanon had suffered worst, and was rescued only through the external intervention of Israel. No Arab country seemed to be willing either to repeat (in the case of Jordan or Syria) that experience, or to try it for the first time. Moreover, past experience had demonstrated that once an Arab country had accepted the PLO and then tried to curb its activity, the other Arab countries tended to criticise that Arab state and refused to help resolve its difficulties with the PLO.

Obviously the danger resulting from the presence of the PLO could have been mitigated through the dispersal of the organisation in several Arab countries. The numbers in each state would have been small, and presumably their attempts to destabilise the domestic situations would have been ineffective.

In addition to these difficulties, the United States encountered yet another problem in its search for host countries. The country most likely to accept the PLO was Syria. Although Syria had several times struck at the PLO, and relations between the two were far from relaxed and amicable, it was nevertheless the closest state to them. Furthermore, part of the PLO was directly controlled by Damascus, and Syria was probably interested in their total control. This goal might be achieved were it to accept many of their members. Syria realised that it could obtain favourable terms from the United States in exchange for its readiness to accept the PLO evacuees. These terms largely revolved within the Lebanese context. The main one was to obtain an American guarantee for the continued Syrian presence in those parts of Lebanon which Syria considered important for its own security. It is not clear whether the United States acceded to this request. Publicly, it stood by its original objective of complete Syrian withdrawal from Lebanon.

Throughout these negotiations Israeli military pressure continued to mount. After a relative lull in which there were no major air and artillery bombardments of Beirut, there came brief periods of heavy shelling and intensification of the siege. The US Administration, while not pleased by these Israeli activities, recognised their utility in facilitating the negotiations with the PLO. The Administration also recognised the severe limitations on its own ability to restrain Israel.

In order to protect his withdrawing fighters as well as the Palestinians left behind, Arafat delightedly accepted the idea of third-power forces being deployed in West Beirut. According to this proposal, a third power with the trust of both sides was to be interposed between the two forces. The units of the PLO would withdraw from Beirut under cover of the third power. By late June the idea was circulating in Washington, and coincided with the apparent willingness of the PLO to withdraw under strong pressure from the Muslim leaders in Beirut. Indeed, by early July, the US Administration endorsed the idea of sending American forces to participate in the newly emergent multi-national separation force. On 3 July Arafat gave his consent to the withdrawal[46] following a stormy session with Shafiq el Wazan, Lebanon's Prime Minister, himself a leader of the Sunni Muslim community in Beirut. The Sunni oligarchy had welcomed co-operation with the PLO in the Civil War in 1975–6, but by 1981–2, it was disenchanted with the continued chaos in Lebanon, and unhappy about the role of both the PLO and the Syrians. The Sunnis nevertheless maintained close relations with the PLO.

The heavy Israeli bombardment of Beirut caused difficulties for Habib's mediation effort. A high-level American intervention became necessary. Consequently, President Reagan sent a terse letter to the Israeli Prime Minister demanding a cease-fire. Israel complied.

The new cease-fire was maintained for about ten days in the sense that there was no heavy bombardment of West Beirut. However, direct exchanges of fire between Israeli troops and the PLO militias continued. Moreover, it was precisely during the first half of July that the main Israeli decision-makers decided to attack and occupy the southern part of West Beirut. As mentioned earlier, they had refrained from it only because of reservations in the Cabinet. There was also a simultaneous increase in the exchange of fire along the Israeli–Syrian cease-fire line around Lake Qarun and in the Beqa valley. It is reasonable to assume that most of these encounters were initiated by PLO forces operating from within Syrian lines. The objective may have been to react to Israeli operations around Beirut, and to demonstrate that a continued Israeli presence in Lebanon would involve costs for Israel. On 22 July Israel reacted massively, causing heavy Syrian casualties. The Israeli retaliation led to a long period of quiet on the Israeli–Syrian line which, except for some very minor encounters, persisted until the Israeli withdrawal from Lebanon.

On the same day, Israel apparently decided to resume heavy attacks on Beirut. The air force was called in, as were Israeli naval units. On top of direct ground fire aimed at the PLO military positions along the front line, Israel resumed shelling and air strikes inside Beirut.

By late July, it appeared that the Habib mission was very close to success. The PLO had apparently made it clear that it was ready to withdraw, and the Americans were confident that some of the Arab countries would be prepared to accept the evacuees. However, it was just at this point that Israeli patience ran out. The Israeli leaders probably did not believe that the PLO would ultimately withdraw from Beirut. In addition, they were concerned about the extent of the political concessions that the American Administration might be ready to give the organisation. Some Israeli leaders, and primarily Defence Minister Sharon, were unhappy about the agreement itself and would have preferred to storm the city.[47] The long wait outside Beirut and the continued PLO propaganda about the courageous stand of the Palestinian resistance against the mighty Israeli army, caused deep frustration in Jerusalem. In mid July, Israel intensified its shelling and bombardment of the city and completely cut off the water and electricity supplies. This step aroused American suspicions that Israel was in fact trying to frustrate the process of negotiations.[48]

In early August Israel decided to apply the third strategy, that is, to occupy the southern part of West Beirut in phases. Israeli armour and infantry first captured Beirut airport, and then moved in a pincer movement to attack the main loci of resistance in the southern parts of West Beirut.

While the Israeli attacks developed, American frustration increased. The reports on Beirut appearing in the media, coupled with the growing resentment of their Arab allies, brought home to Washington the need to restrain Israel. This need became a necessity when Habib reported back to Washington that because of the Israeli attacks he could not proceed with his mediation efforts, which were otherwise on the verge of success.[49] President Reagan decided to intervene. In an impromptu press conference he voiced his impatience with the continued attacks on Beirut. In a meeting with Israeli Foreign Minister Shamir, he demanded a halt to the attack on the city. However, the Israeli decision-makers seem to have concluded that the President's demand still left them room for manoeuvre, and the attack persisted.

This led to further straining of Israeli–American relations. The President sent a firm letter to Begin demanding immediate adherence to a cease-fire and the return of Israeli forces to the pre- 1 August lines. The Israeli leaders accepted the cease-fire demand but did nothing in regard to the return to the old lines. Even the cease-fire did not hold for long.

Meanwhile, Habib's mission was approaching its positive conclusion. Habib and Lebanese government sources appeared to be optimistic. On 7 August things were moving quickly towards a settlement of the final details of the agreement.[50] These developments led to what seemed to be a division of opinion in the Israeli Cabinet. On the one hand, the Ministry of Defence seemed to be doubtful about the new plan. Leaks from the defence establishment in fact argued that the plan was 'a cheat'. On the other hand, sources close to the Prime Minister appeared to welcome it.

The approaching agreement probably led to a decision by Defence Minister Sharon to try and sabotage the plan at the very last moment, or at least to hit the PLO hard.[51] After three more days of small-scale, yet gradually escalating violations of the cease-fire, involving Israeli air force attacks, there followed two days — 11 and 12 August — of massive military attacks on West Beirut. These attacks included a heavy artillery bombardment, slow ground moves into parts of West Beirut and, most visibly, waves of air strikes.

The news of the renewed shelling caused deep concern in the Israeli Cabinet. For some time a group of ministers had been increasingly unhappy about the course of the war and particularly about the role of the Defence Minister. They felt that the Cabinet was merely following events rather than directing them. Some Cabinet members were angered when they learnt unofficially that a few days earlier Israel had mobilised an additional reserve unit and moved it into the Maronite mini-state in the north-east of Beirut. This move was not authorised by the Cabinet.[52] The brigade of paratroopers mobilised was to be used against West Beirut if the order to attack was given.

On 12 August, the day of the heavy shelling of Beirut, the Cabinet was convened in order to discuss a request by Sharon for another military operation, apparently against Beirut. He encountered strong opposition, and firm demands to halt the shelling of Beirut. This time, Begin sided with the critics. His position seems to have been influenced by three factors: the number of Israeli casualties resulting from the salami strategy, the growing opposition in the Cabinet, and concern about US reactions. Begin's position encouraged the other ministers, and they voiced their criticism in phrases perhaps harsher than they would have otherwise used. Not only were Sharon's demands for approval of further operations turned down, but the Cabinet also decided to stop the shelling of West Beirut.

When Begin left the Cabinet meeting he was told that President Reagan wished to speak to him. A rather tense telephone conversation ensued and the President voiced his 'rage' at the Israeli military activity in Beirut. The government had decided moments before to stop the shelling. Following Reagan's intervention a decision was made to adhere to a complete cease-fire.[53]

By then, Habib's mission had in fact already secured its objective. All sides were ready to reach an agreement. The problem of host countries for the PLO fighters and officials was resolved. Syria at long last decided to accept the largest contingent. Other willing countries were Jordan, Tunisia, South Yemen and Iraq. Syria agreed to accept all the *Saiqa* fighters, the remains of its own mechanised brigade No. 85, which had been deployed in Beirut, some PLA units, that had been trained in Syria, and some members of Fath. South Yemen was ready to accept members of the more radical groups, the Popular Front for the Liberation of Palestine and the Popular Democratic Front for the Liberation of Palestine,[54] and Jordan agreed to take the *Badr* unit, most of whom held Jordanian citizenship and had joined the battle in Beirut after the Israeli invasion began. Iraq agreed to host members of the pro-Iraqi organisations within the PLO, and Tunisia the political leadership, and part of the Fath fighting contingents; it emphasised, however, that it would tolerate only political (and not military) activity by the PLO. The same sentiment was voiced by the Jordanian authorities.

The evacuation of the Palestinians and the Syrian mechanised brigade from Beirut temporarily transformed the situation in Lebanon. Most importantly, Lebanese political realignment became possible with the decrease in PLO and Syrian influence.

The emerging *rapprochement* between the Maronite leadership and the Sunni oligarchy inside Beirut became a fact of life. The party with the most power was now one group within the Maronite community — the Phalangists under the leadership of the Jumayyil family. Another crucial development was Israel's established position as one of the two most prominent external powers in Lebanon. The combination of these two developments ostensibly promised a convenient context for the emergence of a more stable regime in Lebanon, with an Israeli orientation. The election of Bashir Jumayyil to the presidency with the backing (under a certain amount of pressure) of the majority of the members of Parliament was an outcome of these factors. Later events demonstrated that hopes engendered by these early developments were premature.

Once the presidential election was over, the basic facts of Lebanese political life were reaffirmed. The fundamental dilemma faced by Jumayyil was the problem of reuniting the country. To achieve unity he had to mobilise political backing from at least some of the ethnic and religious communities in the country. Crucial was the support of the Sunnis in Beirut and its environs, the Shi'is, the Druze, and the Sunnis of the Tripoli area led by Rashid Karami. Although he had control over the strongest militia in the country, the Phalangists, and enjoyed the backing of Israel, he realised that this would not be sufficient to impose his will on the entire country. The achievement of co-operation with the Sunnis in Beirut seemed the first task. However, the Sunni community, represented by Shafiq al-Wazan (but actually led by a group of dignitaries among whom Saeb Slam has been central), were ready to accept the new President only if their interests were to be protected. This they could secure only if they were not totally vulnerable to the Phalangists and Israeli power.

Paradoxically, the only guarantor with sufficient power to balance the Phalangists and Israel, was the Syrians. Very quickly, Damascus again became the fulcrum of the political balance. Only a system which could play off Israel against Syria could guarantee an internal balance within Lebanon. Moreover, even within the Maronite community, and indeed even within the Phalangists, there persisted the attitude (voiced primarily by the present President, Amin Jumayyil) that the link with Syria should not be cut. Within the Maronite community there were also strong voices pointing to the importance of maintaining links with the Arab world; the economic welfare of Lebanon depended on close and intimate relations with Saudi Arabia and with the Gulf oil states. An alliance with Israel was liable to terminate that link. In general, then, the Israeli notion of a close link between Beirut and Jerusalem was perceived negatively by most Lebanese communities. Even Bashir, who was considered Israel's closest ally, tried to pursue a cautious approach, balancing the new relationship with Israel on the one hand, while maintaining close relations with Saudi Arabia and other Arab countries on the other. Moreover, although Bashir and most of his followers supported Israel's attempt to expel Syria from Lebanon, they still sought some form of amicable co-operation with Syria. This ambivalent policy seems to have stemmed from a realistic assessment of Syria's power and influence within Lebanon and possibly from the notion that it was desirable to balance the growing Israeli power in their country.

These pragmatic assessments led Bashir to a crisis with Israel. The Israeli leadership, incensed by the reluctance of the Phalangists to fulfil their role in the military operations in Beirut, demanded an undertaking from Bashir that a full peace treaty with Israel be signed. Furthermore, Israel wanted to maintain the position of its ally, Major Hadad, in the south of Lebanon. Bashir apparently refused these demands in a secret and stormy meeting with Begin and other members of the Israeli leadership.[55]

A later meeting between Sharon and Bashir on 12 September seems to have eased relations somewhat, but failed to achieve any major new understanding. Agreement was apparently reached, however, on a lesser matter. It was agreed that once Bashir was formally sworn in as President, the Lebanese army in conjunction with the Phalangists would enter West Beirut and clear the city of Muslim militias (primarily the *Murabitun*) and whatever was left of the PLO forces.[56] This understanding may have stood partly in opposition to the agreement on the evacuation of Beirut, signed only shortly before.

On 14 September, the headquarters of the Phalangist party was destroyed by a large explosion. The news that Bashir Jumayyil was among the dozens killed was received with shock in many Lebanese quarters. Although Bashir had many enemies and was considered by them and others as a reckless murderer, he had nevertheless established himself as a firm and resolute leader, who it was thought might bring a measure of order to a troubled Lebanon. Moreover, the extreme caution he had displayed in his relations with Israel, might have indicated his desire for the evolution of an intercommunal national consensus. This had somewhat moderated the fear and suspicions that many of his enemies had felt for him.

The assassins seem to have come from the Syrian Social Nationalist Party (PPS), which by that time began to side with Syria. They may have enjoyed the backing, if not the actual direction, of the Syrian security services.

The murder of Bashir came as a major shock to the Israeli leadership.[57] Although he had seemed to put some distance between himself and the Israelis, he was still considered Israel's closest ally among the Lebanese leaders. There were fears that his murder might throw the Israeli position in Lebanon into turmoil and place question marks over all the Israeli successes. Most importantly, new presidential elections would have to be conducted, and Israel had to obtain positions of influence before they took place. In general, a situation of uncertainty had been created and Israel wanted to control any subsequent developments. The only way to achieve this seemed to be by the use of its preponderant military power. At a hasty meeting on the night of 14–15 September, Begin and Sharon decided that Israeli forces should occupy West Beirut.

The explanations and rationales for the operation vary. Publicly and in response to anxious American queries about the operation, Israel claimed that it was a limited operation intended only to impose calm on the city and to pre-empt any disorder. This was undoubtedly at least part of the truth. However, this explanation neglects the Israeli desire to hold the city and thus to manipulate more effectively political developments following the murder of Bashir. Another explanation relates to the objective of capturing all the PLO headquarters. While this was probably an additional objective, it seems that the real issue was the troubling thought that after all the sacrifices made by Israel in Lebanon, and given the deepening unrest inside Israel about the war, the possibility of accomplishing its objectives was liable to vanish completely.

In addition to the occupation of West Beirut, Sharon and the Phalangist leaders agreed that Phalange units would attack two Palestinian neighbourhoods — Sabra and Shatila. This decision was followed by a series of meetings in which plans were laid for co-ordination between the Israeli and Phalangist forces. In the meantime, the Phalangist command organised the units which were to participate in the occupation of West Beirut; these units received some equipment from the Israeli forces.

The decision to involve the Phalangist units operationally was brought to the attention of the Israeli Cabinet at a special session on the night of 16 September. The main subject of discussion at that meeting was the Israeli occupation of West Beirut. The decision to involve the Phalangists was only a marginal item on the agenda.

Once the decision was taken to occupy West Beirut (as we have noted on the night of 14–15 September) the Israeli army began a rapid concentration of forces, and the actual occupation was performed early the following morning, 15 September. The main resistance came from the *Murabitun* militia. By the afternoon of the same day, Israeli forces controlled all the important roads of West Beirut and almost all resistance had been eliminated.

The following afternoon, 16 September, Phalangist units penetrated Shatila. Their professed purpose was to clear the area of Palestinian guerrillas, capture the PLO headquarters and collect arms. Their true objective was probably to expel many of the Palestinians living in the area and to continue the evacuation in other neighbourhoods of West Beirut.[58]

It is not clear whether the Phalangists had prior plans to avenge the assassination of Bashir Jumayyil by the extensive murder of Palestinians in the area, or whether the mass killings began with no prior organisation. Be that as it may, hundreds of Palestinians, including women and children, were ruthlessly killed. One should add that this massacre was no exception to the long and bitter confrontation among the different communities in Lebanon. For example, similar horrors were committed by the Palestinians in Damur in 1975 and by the Christians in Tel-Za'ater in 1976. Indeed, in 1985, Shi'i militia ruthlessly attacked the same neighbourhoods, killing many Palestinian civilians.

The Israeli units were deployed outside the area. Fragments of information about what was happening inside Shatila became known to some Israeli commanders the following morning, Friday 17 September. There was confusion among the commanders. At one point, the local divisional commander demanded that the Phalangist liaison officer terminate the whole operation. The same afternoon the Israeli Chief of Staff arrived in Beirut and heard about possible Phalangist excesses. Nevertheless, he did not order the Phalangist units out of Shatila. On the contrary, he agreed to an extension of the operation, and allowed the entrance of another Phalangist unit into the neighbourhood of Sabra, which was also inhabited primarily by Palestinians. The Phalangists were finally ordered to leave the neighbourhoods by 5 a.m. the next day.[59] For some time the war in Lebanon had been losing popular support in Israel. The massacres brought this feeling to explosion point. Under tremendous public pressure, the government decided to appoint a committee of inquiry.

American and international reactions

The massacre in Sabra and Shatila led to a tremendous outcry thoughout the world. The frustration and anger that had been felt concerning the heavy shelling and bombardment of Beirut, culminated with the events in West Beirut. Criticism of Israel was severe. The international reaction demonstrated that Israel was perceived as part of the Western world, and as such should operate under different moral principles from Third World countries.

In the American case, the criticism was combined with deep-felt unhappiness about the Israeli move into West Beirut. This contrasted with the agreement reached only a few weeks before. When Washington demanded an explanation for the Israeli action, Jerusalem responded by emphasising that Israel occupied West Beirut so that law and order could be maintained. The massacre seemed rather to belie that claim.

Washington demanded an immediate Israeli withdrawal from West Beirut, even before the events of Sabra and Shatila were known. Israel rejected the American demand and probably would have persisted in its rejection. However, the tremendous outcry in Israel and abroad about the massacre and possible Israeli responsibility, considerably weakened the position of the government. Within a few days, Israel withdrew from West Beirut and units of the Multinational Force were again deployed in various areas of the city.

NOTES

1. This part of Chapter 4 was basically written in late 1982. Later publications on the war have not changed any of its theses, only added more details which, needless to say, were of great help. I found that my formulation of Israel's war objectives which I wrote in autumn 1982 is still fully valid and so I therefore chose not to modify it any way. It is based partly on various Israeli statements, but more so on my own interpretation of the motivations and 'operational code' of the principal Israeli decision-makers: Begin, Sharon and Eitan. Since writing it, I have been fortunate to have several additional sources to refer to, which I do in the notes. The most extensively researched account of the Israeli war objectives can be found in Shai Feldman and Heda Rechnitz-Kijner, *Deception, Consensus and War: Israel's Intervention in Lebanon*. Feldman and Rechnitz-Kijner, however, do not refer to two additional possible objectives, or rather contexts: a possible disruption of Syria and at least increased deterrence against it, and the role of Israel in the 'heart' of the Middle East. As Feldman and Rechnitz-Kijner have painstakingly assembled evidence for the other objectives, I shall refer the reader to their work when listing the various objectives. My analysis, however, sometimes differs from theirs as I have discussed some additional rationales for the same objectives and tried to point out their weaknesses.

2. For analysis of this particular point see Yair Evron, *The Demilitarization of Sinai*, and *Problems of Arms Control in the Middle East*.

3. Thus, for example, in a public speech reported in *Ha'aretz*, 15 July 1984, Eitan emphasised that Mubarak had inherited the peace with Israel from Sadat, but was only waiting for the appropriate chance to cut it off. In another talk, reported in *Ha'aretz*, 24 August 1983, Eitan lumped all the Arabs together and insisted that if only they had the chance they would erect extermination camps in Israel.

4. There have been many references to this. See, for example, the IDF spokesman's description on 18 June 1982 in *Mivtsa Sheleg: Hedgeshei Hasbarah* (IDF Publications). Similarly see IDF spokesman as quoted in *Ha'aretz*, 30 June 1982.

5. For a discussion of this point see Feldman and Rechnitz-Kijner, *Deception, Consensus and War*.

6. Thus, Sharon declared that he 'believes that now [viz. after the first stage of the war] the Arabs in Judea, Samaria and Gaza, will enter into negotiations [about autonomy]', see *Yedioth Ahronot*, 20 June 1982. Similar declarations were quoted in *Ha'aretz*, 21 June and 28 July 1982. Foreign Minister Shamir made a similar observation, see *Ha'aretz*, 21 June 1982.

7. For example, see Sharon's statements on 18 and 28 June 1982, quoted in Feldman and Rechnitz-Kijner, *Deception, Consensus and War*, p. 33.

8. One example was the famous phrase by Prime Minister Begin when he referred to PLO members as 'two-legged animals'.

9. This interesting analysis is contained in G. Ben-Dor, 'The Strategy of Terrorism in the Arab–Israel Conflict: The Case of the Palestinian

Guerrillas' in Y. Evron (ed.), *International Violence: Terrorism, Surprise and Control.*

10. On 28 June 1982, Sharon told the Committee on Foreign and Defence Affairs of the *Knesset* that it was well-known that he favoured a military clash with Jordan. He somewhat, but unconvincingly, modified his position when he added that that was his view when he was in the army. See *Ha'aretz*, 29 June 1982.

11. For Sharon's references to Jordan as the 'Palestinian State' see Arie Naor, *Cabinet at War*, pp. 29–31. Rumours about the transfer of the Palestinian refugees from Lebanon as one of the war's objectives have been a part of Israeli political gossip for quite some time. A recent reference to it appeared in a journal article covering the 1982 war; see Orit Shochat in the *Special Supplement* on the 1982 war appearing in *Ha'aretz*, 7 June 1985.

12. See, for example, Dan Shuftan, 'The War in Lebanon and the Arab World', *Ma'arachot*, September 1982, No. 284.

13. Even the confrontation in the air of 1979 was no exception. It was very limited, came primarily as a signalling process, and Israel then extended its activity far beyond the tacitly agreed limitations.

14. See, for example, Avner Yaniv and Robert Lieber, 'Personal Whim or Strategic Imperative? The Israeli Invasion of Lebanon'.

15. See, for example, Shiffer, *Snow Ball*, p. 25; Schiff, *Ha'aretz*, 7 June 1985.

16. *Ibid.* and interviews with Israeli officials.

17. Ze'ev Schiff and Ehud Ya'ari, *Milchemet Sholal*, pp. 27 and 110, and Schiff, *Ha'aretz*, 7 June 1985.

18. Schiff and Ya'ari, *Milchemet Sholal*, pp. 110–11, and interviews with Israeli officials.

19. He first made this public after his retirement, when he first appeared on Israel Television. See also Schiff and Ya'ari, *Milchemet Sholal*, pp. 119–22.

20. Interview with a retired official.

21. Details about General Sagui's reservations are included in Schiff and Ya'ari, *Milchemet Sholal*. Sagui also referred publicly to his reservations.

22. For a recent reference to Northern Command attitude and initial planning for an eventual operation long before the war began, see interview with Mordechai Tsipori, *Ha'aretz*, 11 April 1985. See also Schiff and Ya'ari, *Milchemet Sholal*, p. 71.

23. Indeed, Eitan pointed out that the plans for the war on the level of the General Staff were already drafted in a framework form a year and a half before the war started. See interview with General Eitan, *Ma'ariv*, 2 July 1982.

24. See *Ma'ariv*, 22 July 1982, and Shiffer, *Snow Ball*, p. 118.

25. Sharon's own view, according to retired officers who knew him well, has been that Israel should from time to time strike militarily at hostile Arab neighbours as this would destroy potential threats and/or enhance Israeli deterrence. That the latter point carries an internal and inherent contradiction is more fully developed in Chapter 6.

26. See the article by Joseph Kraft, 'If Israel Should Move on

Lebanon', *Washington Post*, 16 March 1982. The article was written after a visit to Israel. Kraft described the outline of the Israeli military plan, including a strike at the Syrian army in Lebanon, and added: 'The theory is that the PLO and the Syrians would be forced to quit Lebanon, with Assad toppled from office. In that case, Syria would . . . ? A Sunni Moslem regime would dominate the central spine of the country . . . The Alawites would hole up in their mountain stronghold . . . The Druze . . . would draw together in the sector of southern Syria . . .'

27. He referred to this from time to time. This also underlined his view of the extended strategic environment of Israel which should include the whole of the Middle East, Iran, Turkey, Pakistan, the Persian Gulf and north and central Africa. See on this his outline for an address for an International Symposium on Strategic Problems at Tel Aviv University, 14 December 1981.

28. See his article on 'Milchemet Brerah' (Optional War), *Ma'ariv*, 20 August 1982.

29. Begin was more attuned to American positions on another occasion, i.e. his decision not to attack the Syrian SAM sites in Lebanon in 1981.

30. For Israeli–American contacts prior to the war see, *inter alia*, Alexander Haig, *Caveat, Realism, Reagan and Foreign Policy*; William Quandt, 'Reagan's Lebanon Policy: Trial and Error'; Yair Evron, 'Washington, Damascus and the Lebanese Crisis'; Ze'ev Schiff, 'The Green Light'. The extent of American–Israeli understanding is a matter for debate. It is my view that it extended only to the 'Small Plan' and only if a PLO provocation preceded it.

31. Interviews with Israeli politicians.

32. See *Ma'ariv, Special Supplement: The War Which Did Not End*, 3 June 1983, and an interview with an Israeli ex-member of the Cabinet.

33. The factual account is based primarily on the following sources: *Ma'ariv, Supplement*, 3 June 1983; Ze'ev Schiff and Ehud Ya'ari, *Milchemet Sholal*; Shiffer, *Snow Ball*; Ze'ev Schiff, 'Junieh Station is not Responding', *Ha'aretz*, 7 June 1985, *Special Supplement* on the war; various interviews with Israeli retired officials, plus members of the Cabinet and leaders of the then Labour opposition. Interpretations and analysis have been added by me.

34. This account is based primarily on the *Special Report* on the war published in *Ma'ariv*, 3 June 1983. The main themes and details of this account are confirmed by Schiff and Ya'ari, *Melchemet Sholal*, which supplies much additional data and information. See especially p. 119.

35. Berman, one of the few members of the Cabinet who continuously and persistently opposed the operation all along, was not present at the meeting owing to other reasons. The same day he obliquely criticised the Cabinet's decision in a public appearance, pointing out that terrorism could be fought by other and more efficient means.

36. See, for example, the description by Ya'acob Erez in *Ma'ariv*, 3 June 1982, in which he points out that the order to begin the operation on Sunday 6 June, was given to Northern Command on the evening of 4 June (p. 31).

37. For a detailed account of the controversy about whether the

Cabinet discussed a plan which clearly delineated a 40 km limit of advance or not, see Arie Naor, *Cabinet at War* and Feldman and Rechnitz-Kijner, *Deception, Consensus and War*, pp. 10–12.

38. Hebrew text of the letter appeared in *Ha'aretz*, 7 June 1982.

39. This decision was probably also in consequence of Bashir Jumayyil's opposition to such a landing.

40. The acount of the order of battle of both sides and of the main military moves is derived in the first place from Lt. Colonel M. Benny, 'Milchemet Shlom Hagalil: Hamahalachim Hatzva'iim Ha'ikariim' ('The Peace for Galilee War: The Main Military Moves'), *Ma'arachot*, 1982/1983, pp. 25–48; see also Richard A. Gabriel, *Operation Peace for Galilee*. These sources were supplemented by various reports which appeared in the Israeli press. The interpretation of some of the Israeli military moves as well as of the Syrian strategic intentions is mine. For a Syrian account of the war see *The Israeli Invasion of Lebanon* (translation from the Arabic into Hebrew), published by the Israeli Defence establishment. The book was supervised by the Syrian Defence Minister, Mustapha Tlas.

41. For details of the air strike, see Gabriel, *Operation Peace for Galilee*, pp. 97–100.

42. See *Ha'aretz*, 16 June 1982 and *Ma'ariv*, 28 June 1982. See also Feldman and Rechnitz-Kijner, *Deception, Consensus and War*, pp. 17–19.

43. See Schiff and Ya'ari, *Milchemet Sholal*, p. 112. Also interview with an Israeli retired official. The latter pointed out that Bashir was very careful not to undertake any explicit undertaking about participation in the war.

44. A proposal to attack and occupy the whole of the southern part of West Beirut — about half the city (all the area up to the Corniche al-Mazra'a) — which comprised about 8,000 buildings, was submitted to the Cabinet in July. The Cabinet endorsed it only after the plan received the Prime Minister's strong backing. Even then, nine were in favour, with eight opposed. Begin decided then not to pursue that operation. When the operation was eventually executed, it was not submitted to the Cabinet. See Schiff and Ya'ari, *Milchemet Sholal*, pp. 261–2; Schiffer, *Snowball*, pp. 107–8. The latter source even argues that Begin found himself in a minority in the Cabinet.

45. When explaining the PLO withdrawal from Beirut, Abu Mussa referred to the fact that no Arab state came to the aid of the PLO in Beirut, as an important factor in the PLO's decision. See his interview in *Al-Mawaqaf Al-Arabi*, Lebanon (Cyprus), 21 March 1983.

46. See *New York Times*, 21 August 1982.

47. See, for example, *Ha'aretz*, 8 August 1982; *Yediot Ahronot*, 9 August 1982; *Washington Post*, 9 August 1982.

48. See, for example, *Ha'aretz*, 12 July 1982, quoting *Time Magazine*.

49. See Schiff and Ya'ari, *Milchemet Sholal*, p. 273, and *Ha'aretz*, 2 August 1982.

50. On the PLO decision-making process, and for a detailed account of the negotiators, see Rashid Khalidi, *Under Siege: PLO Decision-Making during the 1982 War*.

51. Speculation about this rationale is based on a combination of the following two observations: first, as already mentioned, Defence Ministry sources described the Habib plan as a 'cheat'; second, there was no rational explanation for what actually took place in Beirut on 11 and 12 August. American observers were convinced that Sharon was trying to torpedo the plan. For an overall background to Sharon's decisions see Naor, *Cabinet at War*. For American reactions see also Khalidi, *Under Siege*.

52. See *Ma'ariv, Special Supplement*, 3 June 1983, p. 16.

53. Schiff and Ya'ari, *Milchemet Sholal*, pp. 278–9.

54. Both organisations are among the eight political-military organisations (to which one should add the Palestine Liberation Army) which form the PLO. The PFLP is headed by George Habash, and the PDFLP, which split from it, is led by Naif Huweitma.

55. See Shiffer, *Snow Ball*, pp. 118–20.

56. On the meeting see Schiff and Ya'ari, *Milchemet Sholal*, pp. 307–8.

57. Although at least one Israeli old hand who followed Lebanese politics at close quarters predicted the murder as an inevitable one (interview with Reuven Merchav).

58. For Sharon's long-standing objective of removing the Palestinians from Beirut see Schiff and Ya'ari, *Milchemet Sholal*, p. 260.

59. This account is based on the Kahan report.

5

The Outcome of the War:
A Reversal in the Israeli–Syrian
Power Equation in Lebanon

The decline of Israeli power in Lebanon during the period 1983–5 and the corresponding rise in Syrian influence, was not a direct consequence of the Israeli–Syrian relationship. Rather, it was shaped by two other sets of interactions: Lebanese inter-communal rivalries, and the respective Israeli and Syrian relationships with the various Lebanese communities. The shift in the balance of power between Israel and Syria in Lebanon affected in turn both the specific and general Israeli–Syrian deterrence equations.

ISRAELI INTERESTS AND POLICY

Israeli policy during 1983–4 followed no set course. The ambitious objectives formulated just before and during the invasion of Lebanon disintegrated in the period following the war. By late 1984 Israel had reverted to the policy adopted in 1976. The roots of the latter development are to be found in the dilemmas that emerged in the wake of the war. In the first place, there was the possibility of another round of hostilities with Syria. In this context, it was initially assumed that Israel would be the initiator. In the late summer of 1982, and again during the winter, debates in Israeli political and military circles suggested that in the coming spring Israel would probably have to attack the Syrians in the Beqa and finish the task of expelling them from Lebanon. It was argued that this was the only means of guaranteeing a political climate in Lebanon conducive to Israeli interests. However, the conclusions of the Kahan Commission of Inquiry into the Sabra and Shatila massacres, submitted in early 1983, had an indirect restraining effect. The Commission's report aroused a domestic political storm and led to the resignation of Sharon as Defence Minister. In addition, the deep dissatisfaction inside Israel about the war and its consequences, coupled with the long and exhausting winter deployment of an army comprised partly of reservists, lowered the Cabinet's readiness to resume hostilities.

In the meantime, Israel and Lebanon, with the strong prompting and active intervention of the United States, began a long period of negotiations aimed at the signing of a peace agreement between the two countries. The negotiations were based on unsound assumptions and reflected the difficult and problematic situation in which all three parties — Israel, Lebanon and the United States — found themselves.

Initially, Israel clung to the four declared objectives which had been defined at the end of the first week of the war: security for northern Israel; withdrawal of all foreign troops from Lebanon (Syrian, PLO and Israeli); the establishment of a strong and sovereign government in Lebanon; and the signing of a full peace treaty between Israel and Lebanon. To abandon these objectives, or even to compromise on them, would render the invasion a total failure. Thus, despite the deep cleavage within Israeli society about the war and the widespread bitterness among part of the population, and under continued criticism from abroad, the Israeli Government persisted in its objectives which rapidly became less and less realistic.

The main problem which Israel faced was neither the Syrian opposition nor the negative influence of the other external actors. Though these were important, much more decisive were the breakdown of Lebanese society, and the failure of attempts to create a new Lebanese national consensus. If the latter had been successful, then some Israeli (and American) objectives might have been secured, although the signing of an Israeli–Lebanese peace agreement was never a realistic aim. But the national reconciliation did not take place.

Indeed, the new Lebanese President, Amin Jumayyil, whose power was based on a narrow coalition of part of the Maronite leadership and the Sunni elite of Beirut, was also not interested in a wide-based agreement that would threaten his position in Lebanon. He was forced into the negotiations under American pressure to which he had to accede, given his dependence on the

American commitment to his government. It should be noted, however, that American pressure on Jumayyil was itself the consequence of Israeli insistence on a formal agreement between the two countries, and that this was a precondition of any Israeli withdrawal. Thus, the United States initially became active in securing an agreement only with Israeli prompting.

In the early stages of these slow and exasperating negotiations, it became increasingly evident that not only were the Israeli objectives unobtainable through the mechanism of negotiations between Israel and Lebanon, but also that there were built-in contradictions between the various objectives. Security for northern Israel appeared at the time to depend either on a continued Israeli military presence in parts of southern Lebanon, or at least on the strengthening of pro-Israeli militias there, coupled with some freedom of movement for Israeli forces. The presence of UNIFIL in southern Lebanon was a poor alternative. However, a full Israeli withdrawal from Lebanon and the reimposition of Lebanese sovereignty in the south were the *sine qua non* conditions of any Lebanese agreement with Israel. These conditions implied that the Haddad militia be dissolved, and that the Lebanese regular army be deployed in the south. Thus, Israel's long-run objectives were contradicted by its immediate security concerns. It is worth noting here that later events were eventually to unravel this contradiction as Israel's deployment in the whole of south Lebanon proved costly and counterproductive. The negotiations dragged on without success until May 1983, but two factors eventually combined to force Israel to lower its demands and to accept many of the Lebanese conditions. Israeli domestic opposition to the whole Lebanese exercise mounted throughout the winter of 1982/3. Moreover, the consequences of the lack of cohesion of Lebanese society began gradually to make some impression on the Israeli decision-makers, and some began to doubt whether Israel could ever obtain its original objectives. It should be emphasised, however, that Begin, Sharon and Shamir, as well as other members of the Cabinet, and, needless to say, Eitan, were apparently still hoping to secure at least part of the original objectives and were not aware of the futility or costs of the attempt. Furthermore, it was impossible for them to accept that the whole Lebanese venture would turn out to be totally fruitless.

Another major factor behind the Israeli concessions was

American pressure on Israel. The United States had by this time set the accomplishment of its own objectives in Lebanon as a first priority. It seemed that these could best be achieved by major Israeli concessions. Israeli concessions would ultimately lead — so went the reasoning — to parallel Syrian concessions.

Israel then, weakened by its own doubts, was unready to quarrel with the United States over objectives which seemed in any case beyond reach. The outcome was the Israeli–Lebanese Agreement signed on 17 May 1983. The agreement fell far short of Israeli aspirations, but still achieved a few benefits. It allowed for some 'normalisation' in civilian fields between the two countries, and also recognised some elements of Israeli security requirements in south Lebanon. On the other hand, it was a far cry from the creation of a new context for amicable politico-strategic relations. Furthermore, the clauses regarding the security measures in south Lebanon were not in themselves a sufficiently effective instrument to protect Israeli security interests. However, notwithstanding the Israeli concessions, the agreement ultimately proved unacceptable to Jumayyil.

Moreover, Syria opposed the agreement vehemently on the ground that it contained several clauses which appeared to threaten Syrian security. Syria also perceived the agreement, which was signed without any apparent consultation with Damascus and probably on the understanding that it opposed it, as an affront. On this there have been conflicting reports. Some sources have indicated that a semblance of tacit Syrian acceptance of the agreement had been secured before it was signed. Other sources emphasise that Syria never gave even tacit approval and clearly opposed it all the way. In the event, Damascus rejected the agreement and refused to sign any parallel document with Lebanon.[1]

INTERCOMMUNAL CONFLICTS AND ISRAELI WITHDRAWAL

Following the signing of the agreement (which was never ratified by the Lebanese President and which Lebanon ultimately cancelled unilaterally), Israel found itself under increasing pressure to limit its presence in Lebanon. Guerrilla activities began in the winter of 1982/3 and escalated in the spring. At the time they were conducted primarily by Palestinians. They became a nuisance element and reinforced Israeli domestic opposition to its continued presence in Lebanon. While the situation was still unclear, Israel and the more extreme Phalangist leaders co-operated in a venture which ultimately turned into yet another catastrophe. The Shuf ridge of mountains, south-east of Beirut, is inhabited by a majority of Druze and by Christians. Throughout the Civil War and the subsequent internal anarchy, the Shuf remained relatively calm. Moreover, Syrian forces were deployed only on its outer perimeter. Following the resurgence of Maronite power after the war, the Phalangists decided to impose their control over the Shuf. Thus, instead of trying to seek Druze communal support for the new President, Phalange elements entered the Shuf, erected road blocks and in general made their presence felt. This was done with the backing of Israel. The Druze reacted violently, the situation began to deteriorate, and violent clashes spread throughout the region. These clashes posed impossible dilemmas for the Israeli forces, who found themselves caught in the cross-fire and whose role was reduced to unpopular policing functions. In addition, the initial Israeli support for the Phalangists in the Shuf prompted severe criticism from the highly respected Druze community in Israel. This community is well known for its loyalty to Israel, and many Druze serve with distinction in the combat units of the Israeli army. When Israel eventually adopted a more neutral position in the Maronite–Druze confrontation, it was blamed by both sides. Moreover, Israeli soldiers were being killed or wounded in their efforts to separate the two warring militias.

With the departure of Sharon and Eitan, following the Kahan Commission Report, Israel's intimate relationship with and commitment to the Phalange militia diminished. Henceforth, it became easier to form working relationships with other communities. The first of these new initiatives was directed at the Druze community. The positive relationship resulting from this effort enabled Israel to extricate its focus from the Shuf mountains in the autumn of 1983. According to the informal agreement reached with the Druze community under the leadership of Walid Junblatt, the Druze undertook not to allow Palestinian guerrillas to establish themselves in the Shuf, following the Israeli withdrawal. On the whole, the Druze have fulfilled this undertaking.

The Israeli forces retreated to a new line on the Awali River, which still allowed for an Israeli presence in an extensive portion of Lebanon. Moreover, the large town of Sidon was included in the area under Israeli control. Altogether about 750,000 inhabitants remained in the Israeli zone.

It was the Maronites who initially emerged as the strongest community following the 1982 War. However, their relatively small size in comparison with the Muslim population rendered their dominance highly precarious. There was only one means by which they could rationally exploit this temporary position of power: the recreation of a national consensus in which some Christian political privileges would be retained, but the other communities, particularly the Shi'is, would have a greater share of political power. However, Amin Jumayyil chose to align the Maronites exclusively with the Sunni oligarchy of Beirut and refused any concessions to the other communities.[2] The catastrophic consequences of this choice for the Maronite–Druze relationship in the Shuf have already been outlined. The decision had a similarly negative effect on Maronite–Shi'i relations.

Whatever the other consequences of the 1982 War, one thing appears clear: the Shi'i community in Lebanon was the chief beneficiary. The Shi'is had become the largest community in Lebanon some years before, and by the early 1970s had begun to organise themselves politically. However, until the war they remained the most backward and least cohesive faction in the country. Moreover, a large part of the community was under the direct and brutal rule of the PLO. Indeed, during the years prior to the war, there had been a slow escalation of clashes in the south between Shi'is and Palestinians, and the potential for a major armed confrontation between the two groups had developed. The war freed the Shi'is from PLO rule, and acted as a catalyst in the process of their political organisation. Apart from the emergence of the Amal militia as the main political Shi'i force, there was also an Islamic fundamentalist radicalisation among parts of the community.

The Shi'is' greater self-confidence was directed towards establishing a change in their relative political power in Lebanon. Eventually it was also directed against their new occupier — Israel. While the PLO occupied south Lebanon, there was a potential basis for co-operation between Israel and the Shi'is. But once Israel was firmly established in the south, many Shi'is began turning against it. The half-hearted attempts by Israel to win the co-operation of Amal (beginning in late 1983) came much too late and did not appear credible because Amal sus-pected that Israel was trying to annex south Lebanon or parts of it.[3] In 1983, the Shi'is began guerrilla operations against Israeli units. Israel reacted strongly against the local population and, in consequence, the possibility of co-operation with Amal dwindled even further. In brief, within two years, between late 1982 and 1984, Israel had 'succeeded' in creating a new and dangerous enemy which was quite willing to resort to terrorism and guerrilla warfare.

In the meantime several attempts were launched to achieve a political compromise among the various factions. By late 1983, the inability of the warring Lebanese communities to reach an understanding forced them, as it had in 1976, to reconsider the possibility of Syrian mediation. In the Geneva conference, held with the participation of all the Lebanese leaders, Syria emerged as a crucial actor.

Eventually however, the political negotiations were tempor-arily pushed aside while the military realities in the field were settled. With the withdrawal of the Phalanges from the Shuf, the Druze and Shi'i militias formed an *ad hoc* alliance aimed at securing their control over areas which were predominantly Shi'i or Druze. A combined offensive enabled them to gain control over the southern entrances to Beirut itself, and later over West Beirut. In fact, when Beirut was redivided, Lebanon was separated again into areas corresponding to the geographical distribu-tion of the various communities.

A *de facto* understanding between Israel and the Druze leader-ship guaranteed that Palestinian guerrillas and terrorists would not be deployed in areas under Druze control. Nevertheless, Shi'i and Druze militias, for their own particular reasons, tried with only partial success to prevent the return of the Palestinian organisations to West Beirut.

FINAL ISRAELI WITHDRAWAL

In the final analysis, the most important reasons for Israel's loss of the war was the political nature of Lebanon. Israel entered the war with the hope of establishing a new order thereby helping to create a regime allied to Israel. This hope was based on the assumption that the Maronite militias would be capable of imposing their will on the other communities, and that the latter were so tired of the Syrians and the Palestinians and of their own intercommunal fighting that they would welcome, or at least acquiesce in, Christian dominance. In any event, it was assumed that Maronite power would be effective in meeting any resistance, were it to arise. In addition, the Israeli leaders were confident that the emergent new regime would link itself to Israel. All these hopes proved to be unrealistic, and rendered Israel's grandiose objectives in Lebanon unattainable.

Attention now shifted to the security of northern Israel and the possible consequences of further Israeli withdrawals. If the military presence had had no attendant costs, then pressure for further withdrawals would not have mounted. However, from early 1984, in particular from the spring of that year, a serious campaign of guerrilla warfare, conducted primarily by Shi'is, was directed against the Israeli forces. It became clear that the deployment in Lebanon was demanding more and more manpower and diverting the army from its most important function — to prepare for a possible war with Arab regular forces. The mood in Israel, and in the army itself, was now clearly opposed to a continued presence in Lebanon. In addition, the Lebanese Government decided to cancel altogether the still unratified May 1983 agreement with Israel. Furthermore, the Israeli delegation to Beirut was closed down in July 1984. In a symbolic way this action demonstrated the final failure of Israel's grand design for Lebanon.

When the new Israeli 'national unity government' was formed in August 1984, it was evident that its main function (apart from a new economic policy) would be to extricate Israel from the Lebanese quagmire. The Likud leadership was still hoping to demonstrate that some benefit had accrued from the war. Hence, it would not openly admit that the war had completely failed to achieve its objectives. It preferred to argue that the exclusive purpose had been to obtain security for northern Israel, and that that objective had indeed been secured. Suspecting that complete withdrawal from Lebanon might lead to a removal of attacks on settlements in northern Israel, the Likud decided to oppose such a withdrawal. On the other hand, were withdrawal to take place, then the Likud could blame the Labour Party for any renewal of terrorist attacks on Israeli settlements.

The Labour Party was largely free from these emotional and political entanglements and once in government took active steps to extricate Israel from Lebanon. However, Labour also had to act under two sets of constraints: it had to consider the position of its partner in government, the Likud, and it had to take into consideration the possible domestic political effects of renewed terrorist attacks against northern Israeli settlements following the withdrawal. Hence Peres, the new Prime Minister, and Rabin, the new Defence Minister, initially tried to secure some new explicit security agreement with Lebanon, backed by tacit understandings with Syria.

These negotiations dragged on for a while against the background of a sharp increase in terrorist activity against the Israeli forces deployed in the western sector of southern Lebanon. The mood in Israel was now unequivocal. When Peres and Rabin presented their plan for a three-stage withdrawal from Lebanon, they succeeded in securing majority support in the government. Most members of the Likud still opposed the withdrawal, but one joined Labour as did some representatives of smaller parties in the government coalition. The decision on a three-stage, instead of one- or two-stage, withdrawal was attuned to these political cleavages. The continued terrorism and guerrilla campaign against Israeli forces during the implementation of the phased withdrawal further weakened the opposition from the Likud. A final vote taken in the government during the withdrawal itself obtained the clear backing of several Likud members. Thus, almost three years after the beginning of the operation, Israel withdrew from Lebanon save for a thin 'security belt'.

SYRIAN INTERESTS AND POLICY

In the post-war period, Syria sought first to protect its diminished assets in Lebanon, and then to re-establish itself as the main external actor in the country. Once this had been accomplished, it aimed at cancelling any advantages Israel had gained during the war. Because of the credible Israeli deterrence posture, Syria was careful not to engage Israel directly. Rather, in pursuance of its objectives it preferred to adopt a low-profile strategy vis-à-vis Israel, while cultivating relations with various disaffected Lebanese groups. The Syrian intelligence services were also active in inspiring terrorist activities against Lebanese opponents. The continued breakdown of the Lebanese polity, accompanied by intercommunal fighting, simplified Syria's task. Gradually one community after another turned to Syria for support. The Shi'i and Druze were the first to do so, and by late 1983 the Maronites had followed suit.[4]

In particular, the renewed Syrian association with the Maronites was a rather improbable outcome of long-standing Syrian preferences. Throughout the period 1976–84, the Syrians persisted in their objective of attaining dominant political control over Lebanon. However, this policy goal was qualified by a Syrian emphasis on maintaining only a limited direct involvement and the minimisation of attendant costs. In the Syrian view this end was best served not by an alliance with one specific group, but rather by maintaining a rough balance among all communities. Since the Christians stood now as weaker than the coalition of the other groups, prudent Syrian policy required the extension of aid to the Christians.

A related point was that the Maronite President remained the formal head and chief representative of Lebanon. A close relationship with him extended legitimacy to Syrian involvement in Lebanon. At the same time, the decline in overall Christian power convinced Damascus of the need to introduce changes in the constitutional *status quo*. These changes had to be more far-reaching than the proposals of 1976. Were the Christian President to oppose such changes, Syria would be equally willing to apply pressure on him, and to increase its backing of the Shi'i and Druze militias.

As far as the Shi'is were concerned, the Syrian posture was ambiguous. On the one hand, there appeared to be converging interests between Amal and Damascus. On the other hand, the radical fundamentalism of extreme Shi'i groups outside Amal threatened Syria in three ways: the extension of their influence into Syria itself, thus threatening the regime; their coalition with Iran with which Syria has a tactical alliance, but, in regard to Lebanon, a conflict of interests; and finally, the Shi'i independence of behaviour. The latter characteristic was of special concern to Syria, since uncontrolled activities against Israel threatened to trigger an Israeli–Syrian confrontation.

Another Syrian objective has been to impose its control over the Palestinian community and to prevent Fath under 'Arafat's leadership from re-establishing itself in Lebanon. This was partly accomplished in 1983 when a group within Fath, whose main leader was Abu Mussa, challenged Arafat's leadership.

Syria gave its military support to the rebels who began a process of military pressure on Fath units loyal to 'Arafat. There ensued a major military clash culminating in the final destruction of the PLO base near Tripoli and the evacuation of those functionaries who had backed the 'Arafat-led majority in Fath.[5] Following their withdrawal, Fath was split. Thereafter, the Shi'i and Druze militias undertook the task of pre-empting continued efforts by the various Palestinian organisations to re-establish themselves in the Palestinian neighbourhoods in Beirut or south Lebanon.

The continued efforts to reach a compromise among the various Lebanese communities has been a slow and exasperating process accompanied by sporadic outbursts of violence among the various militias. At the time of writing, a new compromise solution has been reached through Syrian mediation, but it is still opposed by President Jumayyil.

RE-EMERGENCE OF THE RED LINES SYSTEM

Since the end of the 1982 War, Israel and Syria have been careful to avoid a major military confrontation. This cautious behaviour signified the existence of a stable balance of general deterrence. More problematic seemed to be the question of re-establishing a system of specific deterrence which would define the limits of military behaviour. The war destroyed the previous system, and left the opponents with no guidelines as to their military activity. Through a process of tacit signalling intermixed with direct messages, Israel and Syria succeeded, by 1985–6, in recreating a system of specific deterrence.

During the 1982 War, Syrian forces were forced to retreat north of the geographical 'red line' defined during 1976. Once Israel began its phased withdrawal from Lebanon, the main problem was the definition of the geographical limitation of future Syrian deployment. In 1976 the red line based on specific deterrence was defined prior to the full-scale Syrian intervention. At that time, the threat of Israeli counter-intervention, were the Syrians to violate that line, appeared extremely credible. In 1984 the picture was quite different. The miserable Israeli experience, together with the strong consensus in Israel in favour of withdrawal, threatened to undermine the credibility of Israeli deterrence threats designed to impose limitations on the extent of Syrian deployment following the withdrawal. Nevertheless, the Israeli decision-makers signalled Israel's resolution to act against Syrian troop movements into areas from which Israeli forces had retreated. In parallel, Israel was persistent in signalling its intention to refrain from attacking Syria provided the latter respected the red lines system. The deterrence threats and the reassurances were conducted through two of the accepted channels of communication with Syria: public declarations[6] and the American conduit. One can surmise that the Israeli 'specific deterrence' threats were ambiguous and left open for interpretation the question as to whether the new 'red line' was identical with the one established in 1976 or rather should conform to the cease-fire line of 1982. In general, the Israeli deterrent threats met with success: when Israeli forces finally retreated from south Lebanon (except for the narrow 'security zone') Syrian forces remained in place.

As stated earlier, Syrian behaviour since the war has been aimed at cancelling whatever assets Israel gained during the war. It might therefore be presumed that Syria would consider a return to the 1976 geographical red line as the effective cancellation of one of Israel's war gains. However, Syria acted with great caution, and initially Syrian units remained in place. Only gradually and slowly did they move south. By the spring of 1986, it became known that Syria was preparing defensive positions for its tanks reaching south almost to the pre-1982 line. Syrian units, however, have not as yet been deployed there.[7] This move created a feeling of acute concern in Israel but did not lead to any counter measures. It appears that the Israeli leadership itself has not as yet defined the new geographical 'red line'. It seems likely, however, that the power of precedence is such that the 1976 'red line' would re-emerge as the southern extent of Syrian military deployment.

The other important 'red lines' established in 1976 (and which underwent limited modifications in 1979 and especially in 1981), related to Syrian and Israeli air activity in Lebanese air space, and to the non-deployment of Syrian SAM systems inside Lebanon or close to its border. Since 1979 when the Syrians increased their air activity, and up to the outbreak of the 1982 War, the Syrian air force flew only occasional and limited sorties over some parts of Lebanon and refrained from interfering with Israeli flights. In 1981 the Syrians had also set in place a series of SAM batteries deployed in the Beqa and inside Syria adjacent to the Lebanese border. During the war these batteries were destroyed and the

171

Syrian air force was forced out of Lebanese air space. For the next three years Syria acquiesced in the new situation which was virtually a return to that existing in Lebanon prior to the crises of 1979 and especially of 1981, as described in Chapter 3. Syrian caution in regard to the non-deployment of SAM systems inside Lebanon reflected its tacit acceptance of the 'red lines' established in 1976.

Israel, for its part, used the freedom of manoeuvre in Lebanese air space for two purposes: surveillance and intelligence gathering, and selective air strikes at terrorist and guerrilla installations located both within and beyond the areas controlled by Syrian forces. The reconnaissance flights over the Beqa near the Syrian border enabled it to obtain information about Syrian deployments in Lebanon and also inside Syria.

Syria undoubtedly resented Israeli aerial freedom but up to late 1985 was careful not to challenge established patterns of behaviour. At that point it initiated two responses. When Israeli surveillance aircraft flew over the Beqa, Syrian interceptor formations were launched with increasing frequency but flew only in Syrian air space. In parallel, Syria prepared sites near its border with Lebanon for possible future deployment of SAM batteries.[8] One interpretation of these steps has been that Syria was signalling its readiness to take military action should Israeli flights over the Beqa persist. Another view has it that the air activity was intended as a deterrent against possible Israeli penetration of Syrian air space. A third interpretation was that, should Israel strike at the Syrian interceptors, the SAM batteries would be moved immediately and deployed in the prepared sites. In any case, in November 1985, Israeli aircraft flying a reconnaissance mission over the Beqa identified a formation of Syrian interceptors moving in a flight angle which would have enabled them to strike at the Israeli craft. Such aerial confrontations are fraught with tension, given the enormous speeds and advanced weaponry involved. The Israeli pilots considered the Syrian flightpath to be hostile and in a split-second decision received permission from ground control to strike first. Two Mig 23s were shot down and crashed inside Syrian territory.[9] The Israeli action was governed solely by genuine concern over Syrian intentions and served no signalling function. Defence Minister Rabin later admitted that Israel had misconstrued the Syrian motive.[10]

Both Israel and Syria refrained from making the incident

public; Israel did not seek to embarrass Syria, and Syria in turn did not wish to appear to have lost face. Moreover, public silence was merely a prelude on the Syrian side to diplomatic preparations for a countermove; clearly Damascus was not prepared to lay the incident to rest. First, Syria notified the United Nations Secretary General of its right to respond. Next, it informed Western diplomats that the Israeli action was directed as a challenge to Syrian credibility at a delicate stage in the negotiations about a political settlement among the Lebanese communities. Finally Damascus broke the public silence with a statement that Syria would no longer tolerate the transformation of Lebanese air space into a 'Zionist' air space.[11]

With the diplomatic groundwork laid, Syria moved in the field. In a two-pronged manoeuvre it deployed SAM batteries inside Lebanon in two locations, and other SAM batteries in several new locations inside Syria close to the Lebanese border. Israel responded through the Washington channel and Assistant Secretary of State Richard Murphy undertook to mediate between the two sides. Through his efforts, Syria withdrew the SAM batteries deployed inside Lebanon.[12] However, the batteries newly deployed within Syrian territory remained in place.

Taken together, Syrian behaviour demonstrated a keen awareness of the intricacies of a deterrence dialogue (to be fully analysed in Chapter 6). In terms of the 'red lines' system, Damascus, on the one hand, violated the *status quo* created during the 1982 War. Syrian SAM batteries inside Syria but close to the Lebanese border, that had been deployed in the first days following the Israeli invasion, were later destroyed. Syria, as already mentioned, refrained from redeploying them until November 1985. On the other hand, once the SAM batteries deployed inside Lebanon in November 1985 had been removed, Syria retreated from the 1982 *status quo* and signalled its adherence to the original 'red line' established in 1976 (and violated only in 1981). This infringement of the post-war *status quo* could presumably be justified by Syria on three grounds: the new *status quo* had never been sanctioned by Syria; Israel had been the first to violate it by shooting down the two Migs inside Syrian air space; and finally, Israel was in no place to dictate to Syria how to act inside its own territory.

Syria did not publicly admit the withdrawal of SAM batteries from Lebanon; Israel publicised it, probably for domestic reasons.[13] This may have made further Syrian concessions more problematic. More serious from the Israeli point of view, was the increase in the Syrian air defence capacity. In order not to contribute to future potential escalations, Israel modified the pattern of its flights over the Beqa.

NOTES

1. Interview with Reuven Merchav.

2. Some Christian leaders, most notably Raymond Eddé, although insistent on the preservation of some elements of the constitutional *status quo*, essentially that the President should be a Maronite, have nevertheless called for major reform in all other aspects of the political system. They have sought the creation of a new Lebanon which would accommodate the desires of all the communities, while retaining some special characteristics of traditional Lebanon. Such a formula would secure for Lebanon an identity separate from that governing the Arab world and thus would not threaten the Christian existence as a separate cultural community. It would enable the Lebanese to reduce their dependence on external powers.

3. On this see the illuminating observation by Yitshak Bailey, 'Israel and Nabih Berry' (Hebrew), *Koteret Rashit*, 13 March 1985.

4. The Maronite strategy was succinctly stated by Bashir Jumayyil in the autumn of 1976 when he met the then Israeli Foreign Minister Allon. On being asked about the Christians' political and strategic objectives, Bashir answered candidly that survival was the first priority, that there was no final and ultimate objective but only changing constellations. This was clear testimony of Christian flexibility and readiness continually to update their policies. Very significantly, Allon advised him that the Christians should try and reach an accommodation with the other Lebanese communities, because a military victory was not sufficient. A *political* victory was necessary. Bashir did not respond to this suggestion; the advice was certainly never heeded.

5. For some reactions from Fath officials in regard to the fighting in Tripoli and Syria's role in it, see for example 'Arafat's interview in *al-Amal* (Egypt), 29 November 1983; Salim al-Za'nun *al-Wakta* (Kuwait), 25 November 1983. For a detailed analysis of the PLO following the 1982 war see Asher Susser, *The PLO After the War in Lebanon: The Quest for Survival* (in Hebrew).

6. See, for example, references to Rabin's interview on Israeli Television quoted in *Davar*, 4 April 1985, Peres as quoted in *Davar*, 11 April 1985, and Rabin as quoted in *Davar*, 18 April 1985.

7. See, for example, references and articles in *Ha'aretz*, during May 1986.

8. On these moves see, *inter alia*, *Ha'aretz*, 23 November 1985, and article by Ze'ev Schiff, *Ha'aretz*, 16 December 1985.

9. For a detailed description of the incident see *Ha'aretz*, 19 November 1985.

10. Rabin appearing on Israel Television, 15 January 1986.

11. See *Ha'aretz*, 19 November 1985.

12. See *Ha'aretz*, 16 December 1985, and Peres interview on *ABC* quoted in *Ha'aretz*, 4 January 1986.

13. Peres, *ibid*.

6

The Israeli–Syrian Deterrence Equation

Most studies of deterrence focus on the nuclear relationship between the superpowers. However, as has been apparent to a growing number of scholars, deterrence also operates in conventional environments. Indeed, it is in conventional environments that the various assumptions of the theory can be tested. As several scholars have already pointed out, research has two main tasks: further development of the theory, and even more importantly, empirical studies to test the theory. Over the past decade or so scholars such as Alexander George, Bruce Russett, Robert Jervis, Richard Ned Lebow and Janice Stein, among others, have conducted empirical studies of the application of deterrence. Most of these studies focused on deterrence failures. Yet the same scholars have called for further case studies in order to identify deterrence successes as well. The present study of the Israeli–Syrian deterrence relationship fits into this search. Indeed, it is the main contention of this book that deterrence is a valid policy instrument for the avoidance of war and that there are no inherent impediments to its successful application. Its failure or success depends on different sets of conditions, many of which can be manipulated by the deterrer. This chapter sets about identifying the conditions under which the generally successful Israeli–Syrian deterrence system has operated, while examining the conditions for the partial failure of Israeli deterrence in 1973 and of Syrian deterrence in Lebanon in 1982.

What is unique is that the success of deterrence (which is usually much more difficult to identify and prove than its failure) is in the present case proved by two sets of evidence: visible military behaviour and indirect diplomatic communications.

Both have been detailed in the previous chapters of this book.

Although deterrence has been discussed and defined almost *ad nauseam* (but, I would hasten to add, the subject is far from exhausted), the present writer will fulfil his scholarly obligation and begin with a definition of the concept[1] and a brief reference to some of the elaborations on the theory. The latter will focus primarily on those modalities of deterrence most relevant to the analysis of the Israeli–Syrian relationship.

Deterrence has been defined in many different ways but the essence of these definitions might be summarised as follows: *Deterrence is the threat to use force in a denying or punishing mode in order to dissuade a challenger from undertaking a certain course of action involving the use of military force.*[2] Several distinctions are relevant here. To begin with, deterrence should be distinguished from compellance which is the attempt to compel one's opponent to undertake positive political or military steps. Secondly, there is a difference between 'general' deterrence and 'immediate' or 'specific' deterrence. General deterrence denotes the build-up of military capabilities by the deterrer, for the ongoing deterrence of a whole range of potential moves by the challenger. General deterrence is, therefore, close to some aspects of the notion of the 'balance of power'. It is, however, a much more limited concept. Specific deterrence refers to a situation in which the deterrer perceives a potential or planned *specific* action by the challenger intended to change the *status quo*, and issues a deterrent threat. This distinction is based on a formulation suggested by Morgan.[3] He distinguished between 'immediate' or 'pure' deterrence, which refers to an imminent planned action by the challenger, and 'general' deterrence. The definition of specific deterrence suggested here includes immediate deterrence, but in addition encompasses other specific deterrence threats which might pertain to potential defined future challenging acts. The obvious case of such threats are definitions of *casus belli*.

Another central distinction turns on the concepts of 'deterrence by punishment' and 'deterrence by denial'.[4] Deterrence by punishment, which has been more thoroughly treated in the literature, refers to the threat to punish the challenger's society if the challenger undertakes his action. This concept is more applicable to situations of nuclear deterrence. Deterrence by denial, on the other hand, refers to the ability to deny the challenger a victory on the battlefield.

The formal theory of deterrence suggests that the success or failure of deterrence depends on a rational calculation by the challenger regarding the likely costs and benefits resulting from an intended military action. As such, theorists of deterrence focused on the military balance between opponents, and ignored political factors. However, some deterrence theorists, but particularly critics of the theory, have pointed to the profound effect of political factors on the outcome of a deterrence relationship. Indeed, it is a central argument of this book that the success or failure of deterrence depends to a large extent on complex political factors. This does not detract from the potency of deterring military threats in the management of conflict. It does mean, however, that the success or failure of deterrence depends on a complex interaction between political and military factors.

The process of deterrence can be divided in a schematic way into two parallel streams: the calculus of the challenger and the calculus of the deterrer. Bearing in mind the importance of political factors, the calculus of each side comprises, roughly speaking, the following elements:

(i) An assessment of the side's own interests in the issue under contention,[5] and of the importance of that interest to the other side.

(ii) An assessment of the balance of military power between the two sides, and of the opposing side's perception of that balance.

(iii) An assessment of the resolve of the other side to carry out the intended action (in the case of the challenger) or the deterring threat (in the case of the deterrer).

Deterrence theory holds that the outcome of the deterrence process depends on the credibility of the deterrence threat. Beyond this initial formulation it appears that once a commitment is made by the deterrer, the success or failure of the deterrence depends on the three balances described above, namely the 'balance of military power', the 'balance of interests', and the 'balance of resolve', and on the perceptions of these balances by both sides. The balance of military power takes into account military capabilities, but also encompasses mutual perceptions of that power. The balance of interests refers to political and strategic interests directly involved in the issue under consideration — what Jervis called 'intrinsic interests'.[6] The balance of resolve refers to the readiness of both sides to suffer for the defence of their interests. Although that readiness depends to a large extent on intrinsic interests, it also derives from other sources: the general values of the society and its elite, its martial tradition, and the need to uphold reputation, prestige and credibility.[7]

When intrinsic interests are well established, deterrence commitments follow more clearly. However, the credibility of these commitments varies according to the challenger's perception of the interests of the deterrer and the balance of military power.

The 'art of commitment', analysed in such a masterly way by Thomas Schelling, is intended to harden one's own resolve as well as to project resolve to the other side. It is in a sense a strategy aimed at bolstering images of resolve when the profile of intrinsic interests appears to be low.

While the relevance of political factors to the deterrence process has been noted in the literature, most writers on deterrence continue to focus primarily on perceptions of the military balance. In addition, the literature has as yet failed to address the distinction between intrinsic interests (the balance of interests) and the political context (defining a broader set of interests) within which the challenger and the deterrer operate. The impact of these two distinct sets of factors on deterrence may differ both analytically and practically.

Deterrence theory has come under criticism for a number of reasons: as a deductive theory with insufficient empirical testing; as assuming rationality which, according to this criticism, is usually lacking in decisions taken by statesmen; as ignoring the cognitive context of decision-making processes; as overlooking the emotional background of decisions; as oversimplifying extremely complex relationships between states; as ignoring domestic political and bureaucratic factors and processes. Some of these criticisms will be tested in this chapter in the light of the Israeli–Syrian deterrence relationship.

Two opposing schools of thought have also criticised the usefulness of deterrence theory as a guide to foreign policy formulation. One approach argues that by overstating the military factor deterrence militates against the use of diplomacy, and underrates the possibility of conciliation as a credible means of conflict management. Furthermore, the consequence of overemphasising deterrence might be escalation rather than stability.

The opposing approach holds that deterrence cannot succeed. The opponent is intent on aggression and war, biding his time for an opportunity to attack suddenly. Hence, one has to use any opportunity to strike first.

THE ISRAELI–SYRIAN DETERRENCE EQUATION

In the context of the Arab–Israeli conflict, Israel has generally adopted — with varying emphases — a posture of deterrence, because in most cases the Arab states have been the ones to challenge the *status quo*.[8] The Israeli–Syrian deterrence equation forms part of the overall Israeli–Arab relationship but has its own special characteristics. This chapter analyses this equation from the perspectives of the proponents and critics of deterrence theory. The analytical questions are addressed in terms of the narrative of the preceding chapters, describing the development of the Israeli 'specific' deterrence posture in Lebanon, Syria's response, Syria's own deterrence posture, and the partial failure of Syria's 'general' deterrence in Lebanon in 1982. This system of deterrence and response within the limited Lebanese context interacts with the 'general' deterrence equation between Israel and Syria. A discussion of this broader relationship, viz. 'general deterrence', while largely beyond the scope of this book, will therefore precede the more detailed analysis of the deterrence equation in Lebanon.

The following discussion seeks, on the one hand, to clarify the nature of the Israeli–Syrian deterrence relationship, and on the other, to test various deterrence theory assumptions. Some general inferences for deterrence theory will conclude the chapter.

The 'general deterrence' equation — 1949–67[9]

The dominant feature of the period between the end of the 1948–9 War and the 1967 War was the fact that although the two states were locked in a fierce conflict, they refrained from a full-scale engagement. Outbreaks of violence along the border were limited and controlled throughout. The Israeli reluctance to initiate a major war was understandable in view of its being a supporter of the *status quo*. But Syria also, despite its adopting a strong anti-Israeli posture and its vitriolic rhetoric, made no attempt to challenge the *status quo*. Even when Egypt was attacked by Israel in 1956, Syria did not resort to arms, and its behaviour in 1967 (to be discussed below) also betrayed an unwillingness to become fully engaged. This caution points to a deliberate policy preference not to challenge the *status quo* in order to avoid a major confrontation with a potentially high cost. This preference indicates that war against Israel was not considered as Syria's overriding policy objective. Allied to Syria's perception of Israel's military superiority, this preference helped to promote a credible Israeli general deterrence posture.

While a major engagement was thus avoided, there were outbursts of border violence. These clashes frequently resulted from local mutual grievances which were linked to conflicting interpretations of various clauses of the 1949 cease-fire agreement. Beginning in 1963 the border violence became an even more salient feature of the tense Israeli–Syrian relationship. This resulted initially from the nearing completion of the Israeli 'Jordan Water Project' and subsequent Syrian attempts to prevent its operation through the diversion of the sources of the Jordan River. This Syrian move met with strong Israeli military measures aimed at destroying the Syrian diversion equipment. Syrian military reaction led to Israeli countermeasures. For the following four years the violence increased as both sides at times escalated their activity, albeit in a controlled and measured way.

The controlled escalation interacted with a different set of factors affecting Syrian behaviour, namely inter-Arab states competition. The rise to power of the Ba'th regime in Syria in 1963 and, even more so, the advent of the military leadership of the Provincial Ba'th in 1966, deepened Syrian–Egyptian tensions.[10] Under both regimes, Syria tried to mobilise Egyptian military support in its confrontation with Israel. This quickly turned into a catalytic strategy aimed at involving Egypt and Israel in a major military encounter. If Egypt allowed itself to be dragged into war, both it and Israel would be weakened. If, on the other hand, Egypt refused to be pushed into a war not of its choosing, it would suffer loss of face and Syria would emerge as the sole campaigner for Palestinian rights. This would presumably enhance its prestige in the Arab world.

The military regime in Damascus also endorsed the then negligible activities of the recently founded Fath. The combination of clashes between the Israeli and Syrian regular forces, and Fath terrorist activities inside Israel, heightened Israeli concern and formed the psychological background for escalatory Israeli actions. In an effort both to restrain Syria and to deter Israel, Egypt, under the influence of strong Soviet prompting, agreed in November 1966 to sign a defence pact with Syria. However, it was this agreement that allowed the ultimate convergence of the two processes — border escalation and inter-Arab competition. Contrary to Egyptian expectations, Syria was not restrained and Israel was not deterred. When it appeared as if Israel was about to escalate the conflict, Egypt faced a dilemma: to try to deter Israel and face possible escalation to war, or leave Syria to its fate and suffer a major loss of prestige in the Arab world. In the event, Egypt moved its forces into the Sinai in a deterring move against Israel, thus igniting the 1967 crisis.[11]

When Israel attacked Egypt, Syria in characteristic fashion reacted very cautiously. Apart from heavy shelling of Israeli border settlements, a tactic occasionally resorted to in the preceding few years, and a half-hearted attempt to advance with a small force against one Israeli settlement, Syrian forces remained in their defensive positions awaiting the outcome of the Israeli–Egyptian campaign. Syrian military behaviour was the very minimum to avoid being branded as a hypocritical traitor to the Arab cause.

In summary, Syrian activity during the 1949–67 period reflected a commitment to conflictual behaviour restrained by caution. Indeed, at some stages in the 1950s Syria also demonstrated a hesitant readiness to seek a *modus vivendi* with Israel. The Syrian decision to avoid war demonstrated the success of the Israeli general deterrence posture: Syrian leaders made a realistic appraisal of Israel's military superiority and, in addition, war was in any case not at the top of their foreign policy priorities. To put it differently, Israel was perceived as capable of denying Syria any military success and in addition of dealing the Syrian army a heavy punishment which went beyond the threshold of Syrian readiness to absorb. This perception can be inferred from actual Syrian behaviour.

Taken together, Syrian behaviour from 1949 to 1967 accords with the assumptions of deterrence theory as moderated by some of its criticisms. Deterrence theory holds that the challenger evaluates the military balance and accordingly assesses the costs/benefits equation of its intended action. Syrian caution and reluctance to become involved in a war suggest that assessments of the military balance formed the basis of Syrian calculations. But the assessment of costs/benefits was modified by political considerations. The level of costs which Syria was ready to absorb was a function not only of the punishment which Israel could potentially bring upon it, but also of its own foreign policy preferences. It was this modifying factor which dictated the major Syrian decision — to avoid war. On the other hand, other political factors, viz. inter-Arab states competition, propelled Syria in the 1960s towards a strategy involving major uncertainties. This potentially escalatory strategy was sustained in spite of the perceived Israeli military superiority.

Failure of Israel's 'general' deterrence: 1973

The outstanding Israeli military victory of 1967 was perceived, until 1973, as considerably enhancing Israel's deterrence. The decisive and elegant victory strengthened the image of Israel's military power. This indeed was the image the Syrian leadership held of the military balance. In addition, Israeli forces were now in control of the Golan Heights, and thus in a position directly to threaten Damascus. This should have acted as a further constraint on Syrian readiness to challenge the new *status quo* militarily.

If traditional assumptions of deterrence apply, Syria should now have been deterred from any further military activity against Israel. A cost/benefit analysis of a military action of whatever form should have convinced the Syrian leaders that exercising a military option would carry enormous costs. Nevertheless Syria did go to war in 1973. Moreover, it was the first time since 1948 that it was ready to take part (with Egypt) in a war initiated by the Arab side.

Unlike its Egyptian counterpart, the Syrian decision-making process leading up to the war has never been made public. It seems, however, to have been guided by a parallel set of considerations.[12] As in the case of Egypt, the loss of sovereign territory had created a sense of heightened political grievance which far exceeded previous sources of anti-Israeli policy, such as the Palestinian problem and the fear of Israeli aggression. This change significantly affected the cost/benefit calculus; Syria was ready to absorb higher costs in a military action.

Furthermore, the acute political grievance forced the Syrian leaders to consider not only the cost/benefit calculus of military *action*, but also the political costs accruing through continued *inaction*. As both proponents and critics of deterrence theory have pointed out, decision-makers assess not only the costs and benefits of military action but also the relative political risks of military action and inaction. If the political costs of the *status quo* are perceived as very high, a war decision might be taken even when war appears highly risky and its outcome uncertain.[13]

Another consideration impinging on the Syrian calculus appears to have been the range of political bargaining. Janice Stein has noted that when that range is perceived by the challenger as limited, the latter's tendency to resort to arms is greater.[14] By 1973 Syrian decision-makers had probably concluded (as had the Egyptians) that there was no political alternative to military action. Israeli political demands were unacceptable to Damascus and, in any case, Syria probably concluded that Israel was so satisfied with the *status quo* that it would not retreat from the Golan Heights as part of any political agreement.

This change in the perception of the balance of interests pushed Syria in the direction of war, but did not completely override assessments of relative military capabilities. Syria's sense of military inferiority cautioned it against initiating hostilities on its own. It waited patiently for Egypt to decide on a general offensive. Even then, concern about Israel's military superiority was such that Syria decided to limit the war in two significant respects. Like Egypt, it set itself only limited territorial goals — in its case the liberation of the Golan Heights. Secondly, in contrast with the understanding with Egypt, it planned to terminate hostilities after 24–48 hours. The cease-fire was to be imposed by the United Nations. This was agreed between Syria and the Soviet Union on the first day of the war. Accordingly, the Soviet Union tried to convince Egypt to agree to the UN cease-fire, but President Sadat rejected the idea.[15] Finally, Syria counted on the element of surprise, hoping to accomplish its territorial objectives, or at least part of them, before the cease-fire was imposed and the bulk of Israeli reserves arrived on the Golan.

In summary then, the Syrian decision to go to war could not have been predicted under the more primitive assumptions of deterrence theory, because the military balance in 1973 was seen as favouring Israel even more than in 1967. Only by introducing more complex factors related to the balance of political interests could the decision be explained. This balance increased Syrian readiness to absorb the costs of war compared with the entire period of the conflict up to 1967.

Nevertheless, the military strategy actually applied by Syria fits with the notion of the centrality of military calculations in deterrence theory. However, these calculations must be refined in the following way. The Syrian behaviour demonstrates that decision-makers distinguish between different types of war, and try to choose that which promises to minimise expected costs. Thus, deterrence must be seen not as a dichotomical situation, namely war or no war. On the contrary, deterrence might fail in terms of the very decision to go to war. It partly succeeds, however, in terms of the type of war chosen, and the limited objectives defined by the challenger.

In this context, the question arises as to Israel's handling of the issuance of the deterrence threat, prior to the war. Could Israel have deterred Syria had it issued credible *specific* threats aimed at changing the Syrian perception of the costs of a military operation?[16] It appears that Damascus must have operated on the basis that Israel would use everything within its means to deny Syria military sucess and to punish it. Consequently Damascus undertook the war decision only when Egypt opted for war, thus dividing the Israeli military effort and forcing the greater part of the Israeli forces to be employed against Egypt. Secondly, Syria aimed significantly to limit the war so as to limit the expected costs. Third, it deployed a very thick air defence system to blunt the capacity of the Israeli air force to inflict punishment. These defences were supposedly designed to defend Syrian military assets as well as the Syrian rear, thus denying Israel the option of strategic bombing in a punishing mode. In the event, Israel proved that it was capable of overcoming these defences during the war and of inflicting some punishment on the Syrian industry and economy. But this is beside the point; most important to note is that the implied threat of precisely such action had existed as a tacit deterrent ever since Israel employed 'deep penetration' bombing tactics in Egypt in 1970. As for ground operations, the thick defences between the Golan and Damascus were earmarked to increase Israeli costs were Israel to launch a counter-offensive and threaten the Syrian capital. Thus, it seems difficult to envisage what other specific threats Israel could have issued in order to deter Syria. As stated, the problem was a political one — Syria's readiness to absorb costs increased considerably between 1967 and 1973, in inverse proportion to the perception of its interests. Israeli deterrence threats which might have been more than sufficient to deter Syria in 1967, had by 1973 lost their potency.

1973–82

The 1973 War seemed at the time to have weakened the Israeli 'general deterrence' posture. This was primarily due to a psychological change resulting from the collapse of the Arab 'fear barrier' referred to by Arab writers.[17] That Egypt and Syria were capable of limited military success in the first days of the war came as a tremendous relief following the self-perception of total military inferiority created in 1967. Translated into military reality, this weakening of Israel's general deterrence posture was reflected in the first lesson Syria drew from the war — namely, that a concerted Arab military effort might result in some limited military success, especially when starting as a surprise attack. However, this lesson was moderated by Israel's demonstrated ability to withstand a surprise attack by its two most powerful Arab neighbours (aided by Iraq and to some extent by Jordan)[18] and to launch a threatening counterstrike.

Syrian post-war military planning had to include not only the creation of the necessary preconditions for another military initiative, but also the development of a defence capability to limit its own vulnerability to an Israeli-initiated operation. Such a capability could serve as the basis for a credible deterrent posture.[19] The Syrian search for defensive deterrent capabilities can only be understood within the context of Syrian perceptions of Israeli intentions. Israel was seen as essentially an aggressive power. In addition, from 1975 onwards Damascus had to consider the possibility of escalation of the conflict resulting from the deteriorating situation in Lebanon. Finally, Syrian decision-makers sought to create a deterrent against Israeli-initiated escalation if Syria were to initiate a limited stationary campaign on the Golan Heights.

Syrian spokesmen coined the term 'strategic balance' or 'strategic parity' to describe the situation in which Syria had attained the capability for launching a military initiative against

Israel. References to these notions appeared, for example, in retrospective interpretations of the 1973 War. The war was seen as a demonstration that the 'Arabs' had regained a 'strategic balance' with Israel. From these references one might infer that a 'strategic balance' is a posture in which the Arabs are able to launch a military operation without the expectation of total defeat.[20] In other references Syrian spokesmen repeatedly mentioned the notion of 'strategic balance' as a precondition for the initiation of any military action.[21] This balance comprised the following elements: a considerable increase in Syria's independent military capacity; the formation of a war coalition of all Arab countries; and a favourable international political context.[22] If the 1973 War serves as a precedent, then the aim of a war under these ideal conditions should be limited and tailored to the prevailing political context.

It is, of course, difficult to draw definite conclusions from these references to 'strategic balance' or 'strategic parity'. They are flexible concepts and their meaning probably varies with circumstances. Moreover, verbal formulations are not necessarily true indications of the real strategic or political intentions of the Syrian regime. Nevertheless, such references are helpful in the analysis of policy when they correspond to an objective assessment of military capabilities and when they accord with actual policies undertaken by Damascus.

Following the 1973 War, Syria worked simultaneously on further developing its military capabilities, cementing an Arab military coalition, and strengthening its relationship with the Soviet Union while creating new openings towards the United States. Each of these efforts served Syrian objectives both within the context of the Syrian–Israeli conflict and within a wider regional framework: its ambition to attain a central position in the Arab world has been a very high priority since the early 1960s.

Syria opted for both qualitative and quantitative increases in its military capabilities. Until the aftermath of the 1982 War, however, the quantitative growth was less striking than the qualitative improvements. In 1982, the Syrian ground forces reached an order of battle consisting of six divisions (plus independent brigades and battalions). This was an increase of only 20 per cent over the five divisions (plus independent brigades) active in 1973. More importantly, by 1982 all six divisions were either armoured or mechanised, whereas in 1973

187

three of these divisions were infantry. This change was accompanied by the introduction of many new and advanced weapon systems for the ground forces. This process of increased capabilities extended over some nine years. It should be added that Israel's quantitative increase in the basic formations of its ground forces, viz. the armoured divisions, from seven in 1973 to eleven in 1982, exceeded the Syrian rate of growth.[23]

In view of the increased military imbalance between Syria and Israel, Damascus was forced to seek a military coalition with other leading Arab countries. However, it was to face one disappointment after another. From late 1973, Egypt began slowly to disassociate itself from Syria and the separation between the two countries was complete by 1977. Limited associations with Iraq and Jordan proved to be total failures. In the absence of external backing Syria recognised that it faced a difficult strategic situation. Not only was a campaign to regain the Golan Heights an unrealistic proposition, but defence, and consequently credible deterrence against Israel, were becoming less attainable. Some solace was eventually found in the Soviet Union with the signing of the Friendship and Co-operation agreement of 1980. This agreement strengthened Syria's deterrence against Israel, but also added another constraint on Syrian decisions to initiate hostilities against Israel.

Syria's military inferiority *vis-à-vis* Israel, coupled with its political isolation, dictated cautious military behaviour. This, indeed, was clearly seen in its search for understandings with Israel in regard to its intervention in Lebanon beginning in 1976. Israel's caution in dealing with Syria in Lebanon from 1976 was probably perceived in Damascus as a signal that Israel was not searching for opportunities to attack Syria. Consequently the need to continue the rapid increase in Syrian military capabilities for deterrence purposes diminished.

The Syrian grievance over the problem of the Golan persisted, but its urgency was considerably reduced in the light of developments in Lebanon. In the first place, Syria gained control over parts of Lebanon and general influence over the whole country. This probably compensated somewhat for the loss of the Golan. Secondly, the military intervention in Lebanon consumed much of Syria's foreign policy and military resources, thus limiting the capacity of Damascus to plan another military campaign against Israel.

The convergence of all the factors and processes mentioned

here, contributed to the emergence of a relatively stable strategic relationship between Syria and Israel which persisted until 1982 and which withstood the shifting sands of the political situation in Lebanon. This stability on its own part might have led Damascus to entertain the hope that the Golan could be regained by other than military means. Developments during 1981–3 again shattered this assumption, but it may have recurred since 1984.

The 1982 War — partial failure of the Syrian 'general deterrence' posture

Syrian deterrence against a general Israeli strike at the Syrian forces in Lebanon was based in the first place on a factor which was not sensitive to Syrian manipulation, namely Israel's assessment of its own interests in Lebanon and its consequent disinclination to apply massive force there. Three additional factors enhanced Syrian deterrence. First, an Israeli strike in Lebanon might lead to a Syrian counterstrike on the Golan. In the Golan, the Syrians could rely on their heavily fortified defences and resort to a stationary war of attrition, forcing Israel to escalate and thus raising Israeli costs. Second, a major Israeli attack on Syrian forces which was not preceded by Syrian provocation, might impel other Arab states to join battle against Israel. At the very least, it could undermine the Israeli–Egyptian peace agreement. Finally, should Syria be losing the war, and especially if the regime in Damascus were threatened, the Soviet Union might feel compelled to intervene.

As described in Chapter 4, by 1981 Israel had reformulated its politico-strategic objectives in Lebanon and was bent on a radical change of the existing *status quo*. The transformed objectives were accompanied by a reassessment of Syria's role in Lebanon. Thus, Israeli perceptions of the balance of interests between itself and Syria in regard to Lebanon had changed, and Israel was now more ready to run the risks of high costs in order to accomplish its new objectives. In parallel, two other factors enhancing Syrian deterrence were seen as less relevant. The threat of regional escalation was all but eliminated. Iraq was deeply involved in war with Iran, Egypt appeared determined to stay out of a war, and Syrian–Jordanian relations were so cool that a Syrian defeat would have almost been welcomed by

Amman. As for Soviet reactions, Israel perceived the commitment to Syria as applying — if at all — only should Israel invade Syria proper. In the event, Israel postponed its attack on the main body of Syrian forces until it had monitored the relatively moderate Soviet reaction in the first few days of the war.

Of the four elements enhancing Syrian deterrence, only the threat of a counterstrike on the Golan retained its original force. Israel, ever conscious of this threat, concentrated a very large force on the Golan, thus making a Syrian attack there a very costly endeavour for Damascus. Moreover, this concentration of forces signalled a possible Israeli plan to strike through the Golan towards Damascus, if Syria did indeed initiate hostilities on that front. In the event, the Syrian order of battle was insufficient to confront Israel both in Lebanon and on the Golan. Israel, for its part, signalled its intention to limit hostilities to Lebanon. Thus, by tacit understanding, the fighting between the two countries was to take place only in Lebanon.

It is significant that although Syria suspected that Israel was planning a military operation in Lebanon, it did not try to communicate 'specific deterrence' threats on the eve of the Israeli operation. One must conclude that Syria's assessment was that, even if a strike were to take place, it would be directed only against the PLO and would not aim at changing the whole politico-strategic situation in Lebanon.[24] It might be speculated that Asad and his advisers assumed that Israel would react rationally from its own point of view. Such rational behaviour would preclude an attack on Syrian forces and over-involvement in Lebanese affairs. These assessments were probably also based on past Israeli behaviour in Lebanon: as noted extensively in this book, Israel was careful all along, not to engage Syrian forces directly unless they violated the 'red lines'.

Sharon's casus belli

It is ironic that the Israeli decision to undermine the *status quo* in Lebanon with the resultant destabilisation of the Israeli–Syrian strategic relationship, came about against the background of an ostensible new Israeli commitment to deterrence. This commitment had to do with a new formulation of the system of *casus belli*.

In the 1950s and especially during the period leading up to 1967, Israel had incorporated a system of *casus belli* as an important element in its strategic posture. The *casus belli* were in fact exercises in 'specific deterrence', aimed at bolstering Israel's overall deterrence. Following the 1967 War, Israel abandoned this system as many of the *casus belli* became irrelevant.[25] However, in 1981, Defence Minister Sharon reintroduced the *casus belli* system into Israel's declared strategic posture. His position was that 'Israel has the ability to prevent the disruption of the territorial *status quo* in the neighbouring countries'. More specifically, Sharon defined seven contingencies which would require an Israeli response:[26]

(i) Any violation of the 1979 Peace Treaty clauses concerning the demilitarisation of the Sinai.
(ii) Any violation of the demilitarisation of areas in the Golan agreed upon in the 1974 disengagement accord with Syria. These two contingencies were included by Sharon in the same clause as if they were of essentially the same nature.
(iii) A massive introduction of Iraqi forces into south Syria or Jordan, or the introduction of Syrian forces into Jordan.
(iv) The deployment of a SAM system along the Jordan River.
(v) The movement of Syrian forces south of the line along which they were presently deployed in Lebanon.
(vi) The presence of nuclear weapons in a hostile Arab country or the capacity to produce them.
(vii) A campaign of terrorism originating in south Lebanon.

Within Sharon's formulation the only *casus belli* concerning Syrian military behaviour in Lebanon referred to the movement of Syrian forces south of the line along which they were deployed. Such a contingency was not infringed prior to Israel's invasion of Lebanon in 1982. As such, the strike at the Syrian forces was unrelated to any Syrian violation of defined Israeli *casus belli*. It did not conform to the criteria which Israel itself, through Sharon, had formulated for war with Syria.

Thus the war decision demonstrates either Sharon's lack of understanding of the nature of deterrence, or simply the absence of any serious intention to implement his own set of *casus belli*. Clearly, a formulation of *casus belli* has two objectives: to deter a potential challenger by threat of military action and to signal the intention *not* to act militarily if the challenger does not act. Indeed, the war undermined the new attempt to introduce a system of *casus belli*.

The 1982 War and the deterrence equation

The effects of the war were multifaceted. In the first place, as has been noted, the application of an anti-*status quo* strategy does not accord with a deterrence posture. As Robert Jervis[27] has pointed out, deterrence involves not only the threat of war if the other side takes prohibitive action, but also the promise of peace if it does not.

The operational implication of this general reflection was that Syria could no longer be confident that an Israeli-initiated war could be averted by Syria's adherence to the limits defined by Israel itself. Consequently, Syria had to increase its defensive capability in order to form a more credible deterrence posture. This it did through the adoption of two strategic decisions: first, to increase its order of battle at a much faster rate; and second, to invite a sizeable Soviet military presence in Syria. Within four years Syria enlarged the order of battle of its ground forces from six divisions to nine, all of which are armoured or mechanised.[28] Although it is likely that some of these units do not have a full complement, the rate of growth was nevertheless unparalleled. Even more impressive was the increase in air defence systems. The unavoidable conclusion is that this rate of growth was caused by the change in the Syrian perception of the Israeli threat which in turn derived from the latter's behaviour in 1982. Israel's argument that one of the objectives of the war was to destroy part of the Syrian army prior to a Syrian military initiative is ironic. In the event, the result was quite the opposite.

Syria's strengthened ground capabilities can be explained in terms of actual Syrian military requirements. The war in Lebanon demonstrated to Damascus that the Syrian army was not able or large enough to face the Israeli army on two fronts: the Golan and Lebanon. The threat of an Israeli flanking operation through Lebanon forced Syria to concentrate very large formations in the Beqa and along the Syrian–Lebanese border. In these terms, the increase in capabilities had primarily a defensive rationale. As such, it also added to Syria's deterrent posture.

The Syrian emphasis on enhanced air defence capabilities was also linked to a specific Syrian dilemma. The 1982 War demonstrated yet again the clear Israeli air superiority. Moreover, and in contrast with the 1973 War, the Israeli air force was also capable of overcoming efficiently and without cost the Syrian air defences. Syria had therefore to enhance and modernise its capabilities in this area. As in the case of the ground forces, this modernisation programme was undertaken with generous Soviet assistance. The extensive deployment of the SAM batteries in many parts of Syria was intended to increase Syrian defensive, and consequently, 'general deterrent' capabilities.

Syrian deterrence was also enhanced by what appeared to be deeper Soviet commitment. In the first place, the extremely generous Soviet arms transfers to Syria following the war, indicated the ongoing Soviet interest in Syria. This by itself, however, would not necessarily have indicated any consolidation of Soviet commitment to intervene militarily on Syria's side. Notice of such a development was given rather by the deployment of Soviet units to command and man the SAM sites, in particular the SAM 5. The signal implicit in such a deployment was that any Israeli strike at the SAM sites might involve the loss of Soviet lives, thus lowering the threshold of Soviet military intervention.[29] As before, the ground rules for possible Soviet military intervention were not explicitly stated, but, in the event of a major Israeli strike on Syria, it seemed that the Soviet Union would find it more difficult to refrain from some military intervention. These Soviet teams were gradually withdrawn from Syria, lowering apparent Soviet commitment to Damascus to the level existing before the war.

Apart from major increases in the armed forces, the Syrian leaders also assessed the performance of the two sides during the war. Their analysis clearly distinguished between ground operations and air battles.[30] Although typically coloured by propaganda needs and a measure of self-delusion, the analysis nevertheless reflected what superficially would appear to be the main characteristics of the military aspects of the war. Syrian spokesmen admitted the inferiority of their air force, although they argued that Israel's technological advantage was due to its American equipment and some objective constraints. The Syrians emphasised, however, that their ground forces had proved their mettle in an uneven battle against Israeli armour and infantry. The 1982 War served, it was claimed, as an additional demonstration that the Israeli ground forces were not invincible. The fear barrier which, according to Syrian spokesmen, had begun to crack in 1973, was further shattered in 1982. Syrian references to the ground battles in Lebanon were more enthusiastic than similar descriptions of the 1973 War.

Another important element in the Syrian analysis of the war

has been the emphasis given to its political context. Syrian spokesmen argued that Israel had failed to accomplish its political objectives in Lebanon. This failure has been perceived by Syria as a general strategic Israeli defeat. Since 1973, Syria has emphasised the close connection between the military and political realms. Against this background, Israel's politico-strategic failure in Lebanon seems to have led Syria to perceive dents in Israel's overall capability, and may have strengthened its own confidence, especially in the credibility of its deterrence posture.

Simultaneously with the growth in Syrian capabilities, Syrian leaders began to refer again to the notion of a 'strategic balance' with Israel. Syria's isolation during the war demonstrated the need independently to acquire such a balance with Israel. By early 1986, Syrian spokesmen had begun to claim that they had already acquired such a capability. President Asad stressed, however, that a 'strategic balance' meant not only equal numbers of tanks and aircraft, but also Syrian equality with Israel in terms of social and economic capabilities and advancement.[31] Presumably, only these would create a solid base for a Syrian offensive initiative.

The significant qualitative and quantitative increases in Syrian military capabilities since 1982, coupled with repeated references to the notion of 'strategic balance' or 'parity', created deep concern in Israel. It was assumed that Syria might have reached the conclusion that an offensive action was within its capacity. In other words, it was increasingly argued by various observers that Israel's deterrence posture had been weakened. In more specific terms, one of the possible scenarios for a Syrian military initiative is that Syria might begin a stationary attrition war on the Golan, relying on its heavy defences in that area to deter an Israeli counter-offensive. Moreover, the thick Syrian air defences might lead the Syrian leadership to the conclusion that Israel would be deterred from counterattacking in the air. Another possible scenario that has been discussed is that Syria would rely on the element of surprise and try to gain control of the Golan Heights in a surprise first strike by relying on its standing forces, which are much larger than those of Israel.

The precise perceptions of the Syrian decision-makers, and foremost among them of Asad, of the deterrence equation are of course unknown. Nevertheless, on the assumption that the regime in Damascus is rational and cautious, it appears likely that the Syrian calculus of the cost/benefits of a military action continues to be based on the interaction between three factors: assessments of the military balance; the Soviet commitment; and inter-Arab relations. Syrian respect for Israeli military power does not appear to have been severely shaken. This explains, *inter alia*, the continued Syrian caution in Lebanon, including the readiness to accept (as mentioned in Chapter 5) a new system of 'red lines'. In addition, Syria's relations with its Arab neighbours have not as yet really improved. Then again it seems highly unlikely that the Soviet Union would endorse a Syrian offensive initiative. Since the level of Soviet commitment to intervene militarily to aid the Syrian regime would most probably vary according to the circumstances attendant on the initiation of hostilities, the Soviet position would act as an additional, though not ultimate, constraint. Finally, the continued involvement in Lebanon, as mentioned earlier, continues to divert Syrian attention and energy.

In terms of political interests, Syrian motivation to initiate hostilities in order to change the *status quo* in regard to the Golan remains high. To put it differently, Syrian readiness to pay a high cost for the restoration of territorial integrity appears to be high. (In contrast, other objectives such as the restoration of Palestinian rights or the accomplishment of territorial expansionary plans within the framework of various definitions of 'Greater Syria' do not appear to justify in Syrian eyes a readiness to absorb an Israeli punishment.) Nevertheless, because of calculations of the military balance as well as because of Syrian isolation in the Arab world, the potential costs involved in a future major war with Israel are probably perceived by Damascus as still too high to absorb.

In addition, as in the pre-1982 period, Syria's involvement in Lebanon affects its assessments of the balance of interests in a way that diminishes the urgency of the Golan problem. On the one hand, the Syrian perimeter of political influence has been widened and it now plays once more the central role in Lebanon. In fact, in annexing part of Lebanon, it has perhaps partly compensated for the loss of the Golan. Furthermore, Lebanese affairs continue to consume much of Damascus' energy and resources. Thus, Syria has at present two sets of competing demands on its attention and resources. This further complicates its costs/benefits calculus.

Moreover, the regime probably assumes that there is a remote possibility of regaining the Golan without resort to the use of arms but through a diplomatic compromise. There are two sides to this: Syrian readiness for political concessions in return for the Golan; and Syrian perception of Israel's readiness to give up the Golan under any conditions. As for the first, the official Syrian position is not clear and it is doubtful whether any definite conclusion could be reached on the basis of Syrian public declarations. On the one hand, the tenor of recriminations against Israel remains high, with continued accusations that Israel is bent on creating a Jewish empire from the Nile to the Euphrates.[32] On the other hand, there have been indications that Syria might be ready to sign a non-belligerency agreement (without full peace) if Israel were to return all the occupied territories and a Palestinian state was created in the West Bank and the Gaza Strip. Other declarations in very general terms have referred to Syrian readiness to act within the framework of all UN resolutions.[33] Indeed, President Asad has reportedly even mentioned the possibility of full peace with Israel if the territories are returned and a Palestinian state created.[34] Bearing in mind Syria's highly realistic approach to foreign policy, it appears that its most important condition for any kind of accommodation with Israel, is an agreement on the Golan Heights. Declared ideological formulas are less relevant for the Syrian regime.

Assessments of resolve and their impact on deterrence

The preceding discussion of Israel's and Syria's respective 'general deterrence' postures referred exclusively to assessments of military capabilities and possible strategies to employ them, on the one hand, and to perceptions of political and strategic interests as deciding the level of commitments on the other. Deterrence theory has repeatedly emphasised the importance of manifestations of resolve as enhancing deterrence commitments. To what extent did this factor affect the Israeli–Syrian 'general deterrence' equation?

As far as the initiation of a general war is concerned, demonstrations of resolve have played a lesser role than assessments of the military balance and of interests. Syria refrained from initiating war until after 1967 as a result of the interaction of its assessments of the military balance and the high priority it gave to other foreign policy issues over the war with Israel. It did go to war in 1973, although in 1967 and in later more limited encounters Israel had proved not only its military superiority but also its readiness to exercise that military power, thus demonstrating its resolve. The failure of Israel's general deterrence posture in 1973 had nothing to do with a failure to demonstrate resolve. Indeed, immediately before the war, Israel proved both its resolve and the superiority of its air force when in one encounter in September 1973 Israeli interceptors shot down 13 Syrian planes without one Israeli loss. Similarly, since 1982 Israel's deterrence against another Syrian-initiated war has been successful, not because of demonstrated resolve but as a result of Syrian assessments of the military balance and its isolation in the Arab world. In the same vein, resolve was not relevant to the success of Syrian deterrence against a limited Israeli strike on Syrian forces inside Lebanon. This success resulted from Israel's limited interests in Lebanon and its preference for the *status quo* over a military operation with uncertain political outcomes. And when Jerusalem decided to change its priorities in 1982, Syrian deterrence failed.

Indeed, neither Israel nor Syria need any demonstration of resolve to signal their readiness to fight in the case of an attack on their own territory. In that context, the Golan is perceived by both sides as an area for which Israel would fight. Thus, deterrence of a direct attack depends not on demonstrations of resolve but rather on the military balance, on the one hand, and, when possible, positive manipulation of the motivation to attack through conciliatory moves, on the other.

It may be argued, however, that demonstrations of resolve have been relevant in three contingencies related to the deterrence of war. Israel might have to communicate its resolve to widen the war and counterattack in the case of Syrian initiation of a stationary war of attrition on the Golan. A plan such as this could presumably be deterred by Israel signalling its resolve to turn such a campaign into a general war involving deep penetration into Syria, and its readiness to sustain high casualties provided the Syrian army is completely defeated. Another possible scenario — a surprise Syrian strike aimed at conquering the entire Golan before the arrival of the Israeli reserves — might be deterred in the same way. Syria, for its part, relied to a certain extent on the implied threat to initiate hostilities on the Golan in case of an Israeli attack on Syrian forces in Lebanon.

Whether the threat to escalate the conflict has been the basis of Israel's successful deterrence of a limited Syrian initiative since 1973 is difficult to prove. However, bearing in mind the Syrians' continued references to the notion of 'strategic balance', it seems that Syrian concern focuses on assessments of overall military capabilities rather than the threats involved in specific Israeli escalatory moves.

The Syrians, however, seek to acquire military assets which they presumably consider sufficient to deter Israel from escalation. This, one might speculate, serves as a pure defence-cum-deterrent purpose or alternatively might detract from Israel's deterrence against a limited Syrian attack on the Golan.

These military assets comprise heavy fortifications of the area between the Golan and Damascus, and a significant increase in air defence capability. Here, however, the Syrians may encounter an inherent problem which in turn results from a dilemma haunting Israeli strategic planning: if Israel can sustain a longish defensive campaign in the Golan without resorting to an escalatory strategy, then the Syrian objective itself will be defeated. If, on the other hand, Israeli leaders were to come to the conclusion that they could not sustain a lengthy stationary campaign on the Golan, then the logic of their position would direct them to adopt an escalatory strategy even if the attendant costs were high. If this is indeed the case, then it is not a question of the demonstration of resolve which is needed to enhance Israel's deterrence, but Syrian understanding that, whatever defensive assets they may have accumulated, Israel will nevertheless have to escalate because of its strategic dilemma. As for the other contingency of a surprise Syrian strike destined to overcome the whole of the Golan, it appears that the main deterrent is not Israeli resolve to escalate but rather its capability to deny Syria success. This in turn depends not on resolve but rather on military capability. It should be added that because of the large Israeli formations permanently deployed in the Golan, a Syrian strike would in any case turn immediately into a major battle and escalation is highly likely.

'SPECIFIC DETERRENCE' IN LEBANON — AN ANALYTICAL DISCUSSION

The Israeli–Syrian deterrence relationship in Lebanon as defined by the 'red lines' system falls into the category of 'specific deterrence'. While connected in some respects with the general deterrence equation obtaining between the two countries, it is not identical with it and has its own special characteristics. Its evolution and continued success since 1976 were determined by the following variables: Israeli and Syrian assessments of the overall military balance obtaining between them; their respective perceptions of the balance of their political and strategic interests in Lebanon; the overall political context and constraints within which they operate; the force of precedent and the impact of mutually accepted patterns of military behaviour; the role of the United States as an interested intermediary; and finally, to a lesser extent their respective estimates of each other's resolve.

As described in Chapter 2, Israeli deterrence threats to Syria in regard to Lebanon passed through several stages during the critical period from late 1975 to February–March 1977. Initially the threats were general and ambiguous as Israel indicated its concern about the possibility of any Syrian intervention in Lebanon. At the same time, there were some, though vague, indications of a delineation of different levels of threat. South Lebanon was increasingly mentioned as an area of crucial importance. By January 1976, three developments had taken place. First, the Israeli threats had become more clearly defined and limited; south Lebanon was increasingly defined as the area of vital importance. Secondly, the United States appeared as a channel of communication between Israel and Syria. Thirdly, the identification of south Lebanon as the area of vital importance for Israeli security somewhat weakened the Israeli deterrence threat against Syrian intervention in other parts of Lebanon.

In February–March 1976 there was another very significant development: Syria modified its position and moved closer to the forces supporting the *status quo* inside Lebanon. This modification was correctly perceived, first by the United States, and then by Israel. This had two results. First, the relationship between Israel and Syria in regard to Lebanon was somewhat decoupled from the overall conflict system between the two countries, as they came to recognise the existence of some coincidental interests in Lebanon. This recognition, in turn, added some elements of tacit co-operation to their conflict relationship inside Lebanon.

The second result was that the US came to take a much more

active role in efforts to stabilise the situation in Lebanon. Even before the switch in the Syrian position Washington was gradually moving towards the view that Syria might be a stabilising factor in Lebanon. However, it took the change in Syrian policy for it to be finally convinced. Washington sought to arrange an indirect understanding between Israel and Syria which would allow Syrian military intervention in Lebanon without an Israeli countermove. By late March the set of 'red lines' had been communicated to Washington, and from there to Damascus. By April 1976, the three-way dialogue between Israel, the United States and Syria was well established and had become the main feature of the developments that took place in Lebanon.

The Syrian invasion in late May–early June was conducted with indirect Israeli acquiescence and with the backing of the United States. It appears that the three powers generally adhered to their understandings. The Syrians, however, with tacit American and Israeli 'acceptance', went beyond the Israeli-defined limitations: both the size of the invading forces and the weapon systems used failed to correspond to the Israeli-stipulated limits. Admittedly, Syria notified Washington beforehand of the possible need for this extension. But most importantly, three of the 'red lines' were scrupulously adhered to by the Syrians: the geographical limitation of their deployment; the non-use of combat aircraft; and the non-introduction of surface to air systems.

In November 1976, Syria sought, via the United States, an Israeli 'green light' to extend the deployment of its forces into south Lebanon. Israel rejected the probe, however. In January–February 1977, Syria did send a limited unit to Nabatiyya. The Syrian action was undertaken with caution. It involved only a small unit that was part of the ADF and was ostensibly sent under the directive of the Lebanese President. The unit's objective was to act against the PLO, a move which Israel should have welcomed. Israel, however, refused to modify its tolerance threshold. Strong deterrence threats and active American mediation led to a Syrian withdrawal. The withdrawal was conducted in such a way as not to humiliate Syria.

The deterrence balance in Lebanon came under strain on several occasions: the above-mentioned Nabatiyya encounter; the Litani Operation; the air clashes of 1979; and, most critically, the Zahle and 'missile' crisis of 1981. Nevertheless it withstood all these encounters and collapsed only with the Israeli invasion in 1982. Once the war was over and the two sides again sought to regulate their military behaviour, they had to resort to a similar system of specific deterrence thresholds. The success of this system in the pre-war period was due, as mentioned earlier, to the interaction of several factors, which will now be discussed.

Perceptions of the military balance

Syria was keenly aware of the imbalance of military power vis-à-vis Israel and thus was careful not to pursue a policy which might lead to a direct military confrontation. Not only was it far inferior in terms of the respective size of the two countries' forces, but Israel would have been able to outflank the Syrian forces on the Golan Heights and attack Syria from Lebanon. Moreover, Syria was conscious of its isolation in the Arab world following the Sinai agreement and the deterioration of relations with Iraq. Thus, both in terms of a general war as well as in terms of a limited military encounter within Lebanon, it felt vulnerable to Israeli military power. Israel, for its part, was confident of its military power, but was not interested in a military escalation resulting from Syrian activity in Lebanon. Such an escalation might spill over on to the Golan Heights, causing a costly stationary war of attrition and necessitating rapid escalation to a mobile war. The latter would carry its own risks and costs, and might trigger a wider conflagration between Israel and other Arab countries. To put it differently, although Israel felt assured of the military outcome of another war with Syria, the potential political benefits appeared not to justify the expected costs. Israeli policy was to avoid a military confrontation unless critical strategic interests were threatened. Hence, despite Israel's military superiority, Syria could effectively deter Israel in Lebanon, provided it was careful not to threaten vital Israeli security interests.

This analysis underlines the centrality of perceptions of the military balance in deterrence. It was Israel's military superiority which assured the success of the 'red lines' system. To that extent, traditional assumptions of deterrence theory applied to the Israeli–Syrian relationship in Lebanon. At the same time, a deeper understanding of the workings of deterrence must take account of other factors, primarily political and security interests which critically affect the readiness of both challenger and deterrer to absorb costs. In addition, the military dimension is itself subdivided into different sets of considerations. Costs of a specific military action might vary according to both military and political circumstances. This applies in particular when there is a range of potential military responses, each with its resulting uncertainties and potential costs.

The balance of interests

As important as perceptions of the military balance in determining the success of specific deterrence, were the sides' respective assessments of their political and strategic interests. These interests can be divided analytically into three sets: the balance of intrinsic political and strategic interests under contention; the political context within which the deterrence process operates; and 'secondary' interests, viz. issues of credibility and prestige, what Robert Jervis termed 'strategic interests'.

Influencing political developments in Lebanon was a very high priority objective among Syria's foreign policy goals. In comparison, Israel's political stakes in Lebanon played a lesser role in its overall policy. This difference created an asymmetry in Syria's favour in the balance of political interests. Israel eventually came to recognise this advantage. Initially Israeli decision-makers were oblivious to the complexity and depth of Syrian interests in Lebanon and perceived them primarily as deriving from the ideological motivation to create a 'Greater Syria' and the urge to convert Lebanon into a 'confrontation state'. However, by early 1976, partly as a result of American communications, the Israeli leaders began to modify their perception of Syrian intentions in Lebanon. Though they remained suspicious of Syria, and identified the urge for expansionism in its plan for Lebanon, they nevertheless did recognise and accept that Syria had many other interests in Lebanon. Taken together, they sensed that the overall balance of interests favoured Syria.

It should be added here that the caution which Israel initially displayed in defining its deterrence thresholds, that is, during the latter part of 1975 and very early 1976, did not derive from a recognition of the assymmetry in the balance of interests. Rather, it resulted from Israel's other interests which lay beyond Lebanon and which imposed constraints on its freedom of manoeuvre. This will be enlarged upon later. Later, from March 1976, the Syrian advantage in the balance of interests played an important role in Israel's behaviour.

Israel, however, did define some vital security interests (the 'red lines') which it was ready to defend. Syrian observance of these lines demonstrated its cognisance of Israel's security requirements. The definition of the Israeli deterrence thresholds assumed credibility not only because of Israeli threats, but also because they were based on precedents which indicated long-standing Israeli concern. To begin with, Israel had operated militarily in south Lebanon since the 1960s and had repeatedly displayed its close attention to developments there. Similarly, Israel had for years used its aircraft extensively over Lebanon. Hence, Israeli air activity there appeared as a natural situation. Moreover, Israeli air superiority has always been a major factor in the Israeli strategic conception. Any measure which might detract from that advantage is construed by Israel as a significant strategic threat. Hence, the Israeli insistence that no Syrian aircraft operate in Lebanese air space and that no SAM batteries be deployed there, was the direct reflection of vital strategic interests. Thus, as far as these strategic interests were concerned, Israel had the clear advantage. Syria, acting in a rational manner, did not try to challenge these thresholds.

Israel and Syria were also affected by other interests and concerns which lie beyond developments in Lebanon. For Israel, its relations with the United States and overall regional interactions remained its highest priority. In regard to regional developments, Israel sought to foster the growing division in the Arab world resulting, among other things, from the Sinai II agreement, to hedge against an Egyptian–Syrian *rapprochement*, and, if possible, to cultivate further political connections with Egypt. All these were part of the overall political context within which Israel operated and, with the exception of security interests in south Lebanon and those which had been defined within the system of the 'red lines', they assumed priority over intrinsic interests in Lebanon. Thus, contextual political conditions operated as constraints on Israel's policy towards Syria in Lebanon.

Syria also operated under contextual political constraints. It was trying to diminish its isolation in the Arab world and to limit Egyptian movement towards further unilateral accommodation with Israel. It was also trying to improve the flexibility of its international position by an opening towards the United States. In some respects Syrian policy in Lebanon fitted well with its regional and international policies. Its presence and activity in Lebanon accorded with its new alliance with Jordan formed in late 1975, since both states were interested in crippling the PLO. More importantly, its dialogue with the United States became increasingly cordial as a result of American–Syrian co-ordination in regard to Lebanon during 1976. On the other hand, Syrian–Iraqi and Syrian–Egyptian relations were strained by the Syrian role in Lebanon, as were Syrian–Soviet relations. Thus, contextual conditions pushed Syrian policy in Lebanon in contradictory directions. However, unlike Israel, Syria perceived its own direct intrinsic interests in Lebanon as being more urgent and of higher priority than the contextual conditions.

Finally, there are two additional factors on the level of assessments of political and strategic considerations which affected the outcome of 'specific deterrence' in Lebanon. First, when Syria intervened, both Syria and Israel had simultaneously conflicting and coincidental interests in Lebanon. This moderated their positions and eased the way for the evolution of a stable deterrence system even in regard to conflictive issues. A second factor was the effect of decoupling. Initially, both countries tended to place each other's activities in Lebanon exclusively within the context of the rival's overall strategy in the conflict between them. Gradually they began to decouple developments in Lebanon from the overall conflict system. This further enhanced the development of a stable 'specific deterrence' system.

This analysis underlines the enormous importance of political and strategic interests in the calculus of deterrence. Israel modified its deterrence posture, abandoning the initial opposition to any Syrian involvement in Lebanon, once it recognised that the balance of interests tilted in favour of Syria, and that its military advantage might fail to deter Syrian intervention. On the other hand, Israel did define several deterrence thresholds which were clearly related to important security concerns. Syria recognised these Israeli concerns as legitimate. Thus, deterrence operated successfully because the definition of the thresholds took into consideration the perceptions of the opponent's balance of interests.

The mutual recognition of the 'legitimate' interests of the

rival has two implications. First, it lends credence to the threats issued by the deterrer; that is, the challenger realises that the deterrer considers the interests under contention to be vital. Secondly, once the deterrer implicitly or explicitly accepts the vitality of the challenger's interests, the latter tends to perceive his own grievance as diminished.

One of the criticisms of deterrence theory underlines the reflection that 'leaders are likely to pay attention to their own interests, interests that are psychologically salient, rather than to those of their opponent'.[35] Accordingly, the challenger, oblivious to the deterrer's interests, does not believe that the deterrer will fight when his interests are threatened. Consequently deterrence might fail due to the lack of its credibility.

In the Israeli–Syrian deterrence relationship in Lebanon, the situation was different. Both sides were aware that the other had important interests involved in Lebanon, but misperceived the nature of those interests. Israel suspected that Syria sought to annex Lebanon, and in any case to turn it into a 'confrontation state' against Israel. Syria suspected that Israel had its own territorial ambitions in Lebanon. Both sides gradually came to moderate their perceptions of the other's objectives, though they suspected that in the long run the rival would pursue his more extreme objectives.

When the deterrence thresholds were drawn, both sides clearly realised and accepted what they perceived as the immediate vital interests of the rival. Hence, the assumption that decision-makers focus only on their own interests was not borne out in this particular instance. On the other hand, the general implication of Stein's argument, viz. that deterrence might fail if decision-makers are unaware of the vitality of the interests under contention, is certainly applicable to the Lebanese situation.

Another analytical distinction seems most relevant here. Snyder and Diesing have suggested that a 'rational bargainer' distinguishes between his basic 'background' image of the opponent and his assessment of the opponent's immediate objectives. Hence his interpretation of information 'is based, not on what we "know" the opponent's fundamental characteristics and ultimate aims are, but on the specific pattern of his overt statements and actions this time'.[36] Both Israel and Syria were able to base their policies on the immediate actions and communications of the opponent and to distinguish the latter from what continued to be their assessments of his long-range policies.

The salience of accepted patterns of military behaviour

As noted, the very definition of the 'red lines' was partly based on accepted patterns of behaviour — Israeli air operations in the Lebanese air space, and Israeli ground operations in south Lebanon. Once these thresholds had been established in understandings with Syria, they assumed greater salience and became mechanisms for the stabilisation of strategic relations. But deterrence against their violation depended not only on military threats and definitions of interests, but also on adherence by Israel itself to 'accepted' patterns of military behaviour.

Syria adhered religiously to the 'red lines', with two exceptions — in the air clashes in 1979 and during the missile crisis of 1981. In both cases these violations came about as reactions to what might have been perceived as Israeli activity exceeding accepted limits. In 1979 Israel escalated its activity against the PLO; with a new level of ferocity, it attacked targets far beyond previous occasions. In 1981 the Phalangist operations around Zahle appeared to be threatening Syria's presence and influence in Lebanon and demanded strong Syrian reaction. When Israel shot down two Syrian helicopters, Damascus reacted with the deployment of the SAM batteries. It follows that Israeli 'specific deterrence' in Lebanon was predicated partly on another element, that is, that Israel itself would not change the pattern of its military behaviour.

With the above exceptions, Israel was careful up to 1982 not to provoke Syrian reactions by operating close to the geographical boundary defining Syrian military deployment. Consequently, Syria did not test this particular threshold.

In summary then, the success of Israeli 'specific deterrence' depended among other things, on Israel's avoidance of significant changes in the pattern of its own military behaviour.

The balance of resolve

When the Israeli–Syrian deterrence 'dialogue' in regard to Lebanon began in 1975 Syria suspected that Israel might use the Lebanese situation in order to impose its political design on Lebanon. As noted in Chapter 2, one of the reasons for Syrian intervention in Lebanon was in fact to pre-empt political developments there which might lead to partition, possibly with

Israeli endorsement. Both in connection with Lebanon and in general, Israel was perceived as aggressive and expansionist. Lack of resolve to use military force if the need arose was not part of the image that Damascus had of Israel. Consequently, one of the two main reasons for the Syrian approach to Washington in regard to the possibility of intervention, was its concern about Israeli military counteraction (the other being a desire to improve relations with the United States and insure its backing in the effort to stabilise Lebanon.)

In order to secure Israeli acquiescence in the Syrian intervention, Damascus sought to communicate its political intentions so as to modify the American and Israeli perceptions of Syrian designs for Lebanon. When Israel did indeed modify its perception of Syrian intentions and consequently modified its deterrence threshold against Syrian intervention, this did not affect Syrian perceptions of Israeli resolve. Hence, when Syria sought to go beyond the imposed limit, in the case of Nabatiyya in 1977, it first sought American and Israeli acquiescence in the move. It probably received what it thought was American tacit or explicit endorsement for that move, and assumed that under these circumstances, and in a move that would serve Israeli interests as well, Israel would not react. In this it was mistaken and Israeli reaction led eventually to its retreat.

Since that episode and up to 1982, Syrian behaviour could be interpreted as if Damascus continued to view Israeli resolve as a constant. Varying Syrian reactions to Israeli moves were decided not by perceived changes in Israeli resolve, but rather by changes in the pattern of Israeli military behaviour, as was the case in 1979 and again in 1981. As already mentioned, in both cases Syria was ready to violate two of the 'red lines' although it was clearly conscious of Israeli military superiority and also of Israeli resolve to react strongly were the 'red lines' to be violated.

When the 'missile crisis' of 1981 unfolded, one of the main arguments for an Israeli military action to destroy the Syrian SAM batteries was that otherwise Israel would demonstrate lack of resolve. As a consequence both its 'general deterrence' and its 'specific deterrence' in Lebanon against Syria would suffer, as Israeli military power would lose credibility. This did not take place, however. Although Israel did not strike at the batteries, Syria did not try further to erode Israeli 'specific deterrence' in Lebanon, nor to challenge Israel on the Golan. In fact, quite the contrary took place. It was Israel that attacked Syria in Lebanon in 1982.

One of the issues repeatedly arising in Israel has been the extent to which limited military actions are required in order to bolster images of resolve and consequently enhance credibility. The lessons of 'specific deterrence' in Lebanon lead to the conclusion that the most important variables for stable deterrence relate primarily to the challenger's perception of the interests to be protected as rational and 'acceptable' and the military capacity to protect those interests. Reactions to violations of 'red lines' should be measured and designed not to bring about escalation but rather to impress on the challenger the potential costs that might accrue if he were to continue in his violation. However, military actions exceeding those required for that objective, or that are unprecedented and divert from accepted patterns of military behaviour, rather than demonstrating resolve and enhancing credibility might lead to escalation and defeat the very purpose of deterrence.

Overall, then, resolve was relevant during the phase in which the 'specific deterrence' thresholds in Lebanon had been initially defined. Later on resolve became less relevant, since Syria already recognised the importance for Israel of these limits on Syrian military behaviour. The challenges to the 'red lines' then became related not to perceptions of lack of resolve to defend them, but rather to Israel's own military behaviour.

Furthermore, the lessons of deterrence in Lebanon indicate that there is no linkage between demonstrations of resolve through the use of force, designed to defend 'specific deterrence' thresholds, and the enhancement of 'general deterrence'. This fits with another criticism of the more primitive assumptions of deterrence theory. Critics of deterrence have repeatedly suggested that, in tests of deterrence, what mainly counts is not the demonstration of resolve, but rather the intrinsic interests under contention. Furthermore, they have noted that retreat by the challenger in one area of contention does not necessarily lead to loss of credibility in regard to other interests. In the American experience, these criticisms of deterrence theory have been primarily, if not exclusively, focused on issues of extended deterrence, viz. deterrence in defence of allies. The Israeli deterrence experience against Syria validates this criticism in regard to yet a further dimension of deterrence, viz. the linkages, or their absence, between 'specific deterrence' and 'general deterrence'.

To summarise, the success of Israel's specific deterrence in Lebanon was based on the interaction of several factors. In the first place, the Israeli–Syrian conflict system in Lebanon was decoupled from the overall conflict system between the two countries. At the same time, on the military level, Israel's general deterrence against Syria based on its superior military capacity, served as an important input into the deterrence system. The 'red lines' themselves were linked to important and rational Israeli security interests, and these were recognised as such by Syria. Deterrence was also predicated on Syria's freedom of military and political manoeuvre in much of Lebanon, where it had an advantage (recognised by Israel) in the balance of intrinsic political interests. In the background to this dialogue, Israeli resolve was well-established but the limited failures of 1979 and 1981 suggest that the long-run effectiveness of Israeli deterrence was predicated less on demonstrations of resolve, and more on Israel's avoidance of major changes in the pattern of its own military behaviour.

Syrian behaviour following the Israeli withdrawal in 1984 has demonstrated that it is ready to adhere to the recreated 'red lines' system. It appears that the same factors which determined the limits and success of the 'red lines' system prior to 1982 continue to direct Syrian and Israeli behaviour.

Israeli and Syrian extended deterrence postures in Lebanon

Over the years, Israel has hesitantly and gradually adopted a posture of extended deterrence in defence of the Maronite community. The Israeli commitment to the Maronites was a break with past Israeli strategic experience. Until then Israeli deterrence commitments had been limited to direct Israeli security interests and not extended to the defence of another allied state or sub-state community. The only partial exception was the tacit Israeli guarantee extended to Jordan concerning specific contingencies, which was amply demonstrated during the 1970 crisis when Syria invaded Jordan. However, that commitment differed from the one extended to the Maronites in two respects. First, the commitment to King Hussein was tacit and, secondly and more importantly, it was linked to a major security concern which up to 1967 had even been defined as a *casus belli*, viz. the introduction of massive foreign Arab forces into Jordan.

During the formative period of the Israeli involvement in Lebanon, Israeli decision-makers were delighted at the opportunity of having cordial relations with a Middle Eastern political community, but maintained their reserve as to the depth and scope of their commitment to the Maronites. In both its communications to Washington and its public deterrence pronouncements, Israel indicated its opposition to Syrian military intervention, noting disapproval of the possibility that Lebanon might become a confrontation state. The Maronite predicament played only a secondary role.

At the same time, in the developing relations between Israel and the Maronites a low-level commitment was created. In their direct contacts with the Maronite leaders in 1976–7, Israeli leaders were careful to emphasise that they could not hope to rely on an Israeli military umbrella, and that Israel would only 'help them to help themselves'. The Syrians, for their part, certainly knew of the Israeli–Maronite 'connection', and probably suspected that a Maronite attempt to divide Lebanon might receive Israeli backing. Similarly, they probably suspected that a direct attack on the Maronites might provoke an Israeli counteraction. In the event, the Syrians decided to co-operate with the Christians. Whether the Israeli deterrent threats played a role in that decision is not clear, because there were other political considerations prompting Syria in the same direction.

When Israeli planes broke the sound barrier over Beirut in 1978, in an attempt to deter Syria from further military pressure on Christian East Beirut, it signified a change in the level of Israeli commitment to the Christians. Admittedly, the Israeli commitment was far from open-ended and automatically binding. Two signals, however, had been communicated: a deterrence threat to the Syrians; and to the Christian militias, the possibility that, under some circumstances, Israel might be drawn into a military confrontation in their defence.

The commitment to the Maronites reached a new level during the Zahle encounter in the spring of 1981. The shooting down of the two Syrian helicopters signalled Israeli readiness to deter Syrian military activity against the Phalange militia even under ambivalent circumstances. However, as was discussed earlier in this chapter, this action went beyond accepted patterns of military behaviour and compelled Syria to violate one of the 'red lines' by the introduction of SAM batteries into Lebanon. Thus, the strategic stability between Israel and Syria had been affected by the activities of a third party — the Phalangists.

The deepening Israeli commitment to the Phalangists, as described in Chapter 3, combined with the political desires of the latter to end Syrian influence in Lebanon, made the Israeli–Syrian deterrence system to a certain extent dependent on the Phalangists. However, this point should not be overemphasised in the context of the events of 1981–2. When the main Israeli decision-makers (Begin and Sharon) decided in 1982 to execute the 'Big Plan', it was for objectives which went beyond the commitment to the Maronites. It was not the mechanism of 'specific extended deterrence' in defence of an ally which brought about the war, but a clear decision by the deterrer to change the basic political and strategic situation in the Israeli–Lebanese–Syrian context and to abandon the role of a deterrer.

Israel had undertaken another commitment in Lebanon: to the Haddad enclave in south Lebanon. That commitment differed from the one extended to the Maronite community at large: it was linked to an important Israeli security interest in south Lebanon; it was directed primarily against the PLO and not against Syria; and it involved a lower level of military activity and consequently lower risks of unintended escalation.

The Syrian relationship with the PLO was even more complex. The Syrian extreme declaratory posture in favour of the Palestinian cause created the impression of an unyielding military commitment to the PLO. In reality however, as noted earlier in this book, Syrian operations against the PLO at different conjunctions, such as in 1976 and 1983, and the persistent tension between the two sides, even during periods in which they ostensibly co-operated, signalled a lack of Syrian commitment to the PLO. Indeed, Israeli operations against the PLO, as in 1978 and again during the first days of the 1982 War, failed to provoke a Syrian reaction. Syria was ready to react only when Israeli forces threatened the Syrian deployment in Lebanon.

SYRIA AND ISRAEL AS RATIONAL ACTORS

Definitions of rational behaviour in foreign policy abound.[37] In the present context the term relates to three different levels. First, it refers to a 'reasonable' and prudent definition of objectives. Accordingly, rationality is not limited to the relationship between ends and means, but also includes the very choice of ends. A 'reasonable' definition of ends implies the following criteria: attention to constraints which limit the flexibility of one's foreign policy; being attuned to the risks and costs involved in the implementation of political objectives; and pursuing a self-interested policy which nevertheless takes account of international and moral considerations. This means, for example, that political aims should not comprise a total transformation of the *status quo*, especially when the costs attendant on such transformation are very high.[38]

A second level of rationality refers to the relationship between ends and means. Once the ends have been defined, the instruments for their implementation are chosen and assessed. The third criterion for assessing rationality is the procedure by which policy alternatives are sought, estimated and finally chosen. Crucial elements in the search for and assessment of policy alternatives are emotional detachment, avoidance of being captivated by the most salient alternative, and the continuous search for accurate information. A very extreme and ideal definition has been suggested by Janice Stein: 'To be fully rational, a decision-maker must be an efficient chooser [of alternative courses of action], an optimal estimator and a logical thinker'.[39] A more moderate yet highly relevant formulation is suggested by Snyder and Diesing in their categorisation of the characteristics of the 'rational bargainer'. One of the important characteristics of this type of actor is the ability to distinguish between his basic belief system about the opponent and the latter's immediate behaviour.[40]

Although neither Israel nor Syria was able to measure up to all the dimensions of these various demands, they nevertheless demonstrated a relatively high degree of rationality in their behaviour in Lebanon during the period 1975–81, and again since 1984. The definition of their aims in regard to Lebanon was 'reasonable'. They were aware of the regional and international constraints; they chose stability in Lebanon as their most important objective, and they refused to allow a complete breakdown of the *status quo* in that country. Furthermore, both Damascus and Jerusalem correctly assessed the balance of interests between them in regard to Lebanon, and their definition of aims allowed both to pursue a prudent policy with relatively low risks and costs.

Syria was the more active of the two, as was dictated by its vital interests in Lebanon. In pursuit of these interests it adopted flexible tactics and was prepared to search among several alternatives and to choose one initially with low salience — namely, co-operation with the Maronites coupled with an opening towards the United States, and most strikingly, an indirect understanding with Israel via Washington. Also significant was the process by which it tried to widen its understanding of Israeli intentions and probable reactions in case of Syrian military intervention. This process was evident in its use of the Washington channel and other intermediaries. Israel's reactions were also cautious, and were characterised by attempts to lower costs and risks. Israel gradually gained better understanding of Syrian behaviour.

The success of the Israeli–Syrian specific deterrence relationship in Lebanon was largely dependent on the relatively limited number of misperceptions about the short- and medium-term objectives of both sides. Both continued to suspect the long-term objectives of the opponent, but in operational terms this was less important than the said correct perceptions about the more immediate aims. One can add that the two sides' accumulated experience in low-level violence was also a contributory factor in enabling them to respond with restraint to minor outbreaks of violence.

SIGNALS AND COMMUNICATIONS

Communication between Israel and Syria was conducted through three channels: indirect explicit messages through the United States; public messages by means of declarations and the media; and tacit signalling through the deployment and movement of military units. Until January 1976 it seems that all communication between the two states was by means of the latter two channels. From then on, the US assumed an important intermediary role. The finely tuned system of 'red lines' which was established in March–April 1976 was achieved primarily through the agency of Washington. The other two channels were used to reinforce the Washington connection.

A major difference in using the Washington channel was the level of ambiguity; the messages delivered via Washington were much more explicit. Declarations and the movement of forces were apparently able to create only a general framework. This leads to the general conclusion that, when a detailed and specific system of deterrence thresholds is required, tacit bargaining is not sufficient, a trusted mediator becomes vital, and explicit signals and communications become necessary.

A further comment on tacit bargaining: once the 'red lines' had been established through the good offices of Washington, it was generally possible to maintain them by means of tacit bargaining and public communications. However, when the system of 'red lines' came under strain, as in the Nabatiyya case, American mediation again became necessary.

The above analysis does not negate the importance of tacit bargaining in defining specific deterrence thresholds in a situation of overall conflict. It does suggest, however, that under such conditions bargaining through a trusted third party is preferable. Such a procedure limits the danger of misunderstandings and hence involves fewer risks and lowers potential costs.

This final point should not, of course, go unqualified. Washington's mediation was attended by ambiguities. The relationship between Washington and Damascus was hardly intimate. Mutual suspicions might have created misperceptions. Even the Israeli–American relationship, though close, was complicated and allowed scope for suspicion. Indeed, it is not yet clear to what extent Washington manipulated the messages delivered to it by both Israel and Syria. Israeli and Syrian messages may have been 'doctored' by Washington in the interest of easing both sides into an indirect understanding. Ultimately, however, the American channel was effective in clarifying ambiguous tacit signals.

In his critique of deterrence theory, Richard Lebow has correctly pointed out the impediments to an accurate interpretation of deterrence signals.[41] For example, signals may be misunderstood because they are too complex and sophisticated, or because the recipients have an altogether different interpretation of the context, such as the political interests involved, and cannot understand that the other side has its own divergent interpretation.

Tacit signalling clearly increases the risk of such misunderstandings. Explicit signalling may not help either, because of contradictory interpretations of political interests. Third parties, on the other hand, may be able to clarify and remove some of these cognitive impediments. In the Israel–Syria context, Washington played precisely this role.

The US was able to fulfil its role as a 'clearing house' for the exchange of Israeli and Syrian messages only because it was *not* an uninterested party. It had an active interest in halting potential escalation between Israel and Syria and in stabilising Lebanon. It was also ready to use its power to demand certain policies and actions from both regional actors.

Recent contributions to the theory of third-party mediation in international conflicts have suggested that the successful mediator will not be neutral or disinterested. On the contrary, the mediator must be a power with strong interests in the issue *and* with the ability to apply pressure on the conflicting sides. Furthermore, as Touval has pointed out, the mediator should also act as an insurance company for the involved parties should costs be incurred in reaching a compromise or in the defection of one side from the agreement.[42]

The role of the interested third party might be transferable to informal bargaining processes, and even to the extreme case of deterrence. Washington's role in the Israeli–Syrian deterrence relationship in Lebanon serves as a clear illustration of such a pattern.

THEORETICAL INFERENCES

It has been suggested that deterrence is a 'primitive' human and social interaction.[43] It will be argued here that the success or failure of conventional deterrence, rather than being primitive, depends on the complex relationship between many factors. The seemingly 'primitive' nature of deterrence, as well as the lack of attention given by the theory to some of the factors affecting its outcome, led critics to deny altogether the importance of deterrence in inter-state relations, and consequently adopted an agnostic view of deterrence theory itself. The present study of the Israeli–Syrian 'general' and 'specific' deterrence equations suggests that deterrence is a central feature for the regulation of strategic and political relations between conflicting states. It also suggests that deterrence theory, as it currently stands, offers some useful tools for the analysis of deterrence successes and failures. However, traditional assumptions of the theory are far from sufficient fully to explain past behaviour or to predict the future outcomes of deterrence relationships.

Western deterrence theory has perforce focused on the ways

in which the United States could credibly deter attacks on its allies. Consequently, deterrence theorists have been preoccupied with the requirements of 'extended deterrence'. This emphasis allowed for the development of a relatively oversimplified postulate about the preconditions for the success of deterrence: viz. deterrence will succeed when a commitment to defend the *status quo* is clearly defined and communicated to the potential challenger. The credibility of the commitment depends on a favourable military balance and a demonstrable resolve to exercise adequate force. As Richard Rosencrance summed up this approach: 'strategic writers stress that deterrence is the product of capability and credibility'.[44] The theory also assumes rational behaviour by both parties. The present study argues that there is a need to add other theoretical postulates and distinctions to deterrence theory in order to strengthen its usefulness as an explanatory and predictive instrument. Some of these have already been suggested by some of the proponents and critics of deterrence theory and we shall attempt here to weigh their validity in the light of the specific case under discussion.

First, contrary to the requirements of extended deterrence, the very definition of a commitment to defend the *status quo* is not a central issue in situations in which the territorial integrity of the deterrer is threatened by a major attack. This commitment is in most cases a foregone conclusion and hence enjoys a very high credibility. The issue of miscommunication of commitments as a cause for the failure of deterrence is therefore not relevant. For example, in 1973, Syria did not doubt Israeli commitment to fight against any attack on its own territory, inclusive of the Golan. The failure of deterrence was not related to the miscommunication of commitments or their misperception by the challenger. This lesson is indeed shared by Lebow when he laments that 'Too much attention in theory and practice is probably devoted to the credibility of commitments and not nearly enough to trying to understand what might prompt an adversary to challenge a commitment'.[45]

Secondly, the centrality of the balance of interests in the outcomes of deterrence situations has already been recognised by some deterrence theorists, and more so by the critics of the theory. The Israeli–Syrian deterrence relationship is closely bound up with assessments of the balance of interests. The 'general deterrence' posture against Syria failed in 1973 because of a changed perception by the Syrians of the nature of the

216

conflict with Israel. The balance of interests may outweigh other considerations. This point underscores Lebow's observation as to 'the importance of motivation as the key to brinkmanship challenges'.[46]

Thirdly, and related to the previous observations, challenging the *status quo* is not a function of opportunity but rather, as Lebow points out, of perceived need. Decision-makers do not spend their time waiting for a sudden opportunity to attack. Rather, they feel compelled to act because of pressing and unavoidable political or strategic concerns. It should be added, however, that in high-conflict regions such as the Middle East the readiness to use force in a coercive mode is greater than in other regional sub-systems.

Fourthly, critics of deterrence theory, when discussing the interface between the balance of interests and resolve, have suggested that when the challenger's decision-makers are strongly motivated to attack, they tend to disregard the interests and resulting resolve of the other side.[47] The Israeli–Syrian 'general deterrence' experience suggests that this is not necessarily the case. When Syria attacked Israel in 1973, Syrian decision-makers were under no doubt that Israel considered the Golan as an area to be defended at all costs. The Israeli perception of its interests was clear to Damascus, but the attack was nevertheless carried out. Similarly, when Israel attacked Syrian forces in Lebanon in 1982, Israeli decision-makers (in particular Sharon) correctly assessed Syria's perception of its interests in Lebanon and its readiness to pay a high cost to defend them. The war decision was taken nevertheless. Israel decided to attack not because the *status quo* was unbearable but because it felt that it enjoyed a clear military superiority and hoped to use it to attain some gains and change the *status quo*.

The above analysis suggests that the challenger's correct perception of resolve is irrelevant to the success or failure of deterrence in the following cases: when the motivation to challenge the *status quo* is very strong because of pressing needs; or alternatively, when the challenger is bent on a change in the *status quo*, even without being motivated by a strong political grievance, but enjoys a clear military superiority which he is eager to test. In both categories, even if the resolve of the other side is correctly perceived, deterrence is likely to fail.

Fifthly, deterrence theorists have stressed the importance of 'secondary' interests such as 'reputation', 'prestige' and 'credibility' as being important in the postures undertaken by both deterrer and challenger. Stein, for example, has suggested that Egypt, and presumably by implication Syria as well, went to war in 1973, in the first place in order to regain its reputation and to re-establish 'Arab honour'.[48] The experience of Israeli–Syrian deterrence interactions suggests that 'secondary interests' do not determine the decision to launch a general war. Both in 1973 and in 1982, the main motivation for challenging the *status quo* derived from assessments of intrinsic interests. In 1973, Syria sought to regain its territorial integrity, whereas in 1982 Israel desired to impose a new political order in Lebanon and in the process also to destroy at least a part of the Syrian army.

Sixthly, 'secondary' interests have been mentioned in the literature, not only as powerful motivations for challenging the *status quo*, but usually as related to demonstrations of resolve on the part of the deterrer. Accordingly, the deterrer should not back down on one issue as this might be interpreted as a demonstration of lack of resolve in defending other issues. Some deterrence theorists as well as critics of the theory have argued that this need not be the case.[49] According to this critique resolve derives from the importance of the intrinsic interests under contention, and the loss of credibility in one place does not adversely affect the credibility of commitments in other places. The Israeli–Syrian deterrence relationship indeed justifies this latter modification of the theory. For example, that Israel did not strike at the Syrian SAM batteries during the 'missile' crisis of 1981 did not detract from the credibility of its overall deterrence against Syria.

Seventhly, a related and central issue is the extent to which forceful demonstrations of resolve, by military reactions to a challenger's limited probes, enhance the credibility of deterrence. In the Israeli–Syrian deterrence experience, the deterrence failures of 1973 and 1982 show that forceful demonstrations of resolve by both sides do not enhance general deterrence. As for 'specific' deterrence, their experience points in two directions. On the one hand, measured military reaction to probes which threaten specific thresholds did enhance the credibility of the specific threshold under contention. This happened, for example, during the Nabatiyya encounter in 1977, when military threats were issued although no shots were fired. It happened again in the summer of 1982 when Israel reacted forcefully to Syrian violations of the cease-fire. On the other hand, when

Israel or Syria at various times reacted disproportionately to limited probes by the rival, this usually led to escalation rather than the enhancement of stable deterrence.

Deterrence theory has indeed grappled with these issues, but only in the context of nuclear weapons. The nuclear deterrence scenario most relevant to the question of resolve is the deterrer's ostensible need to react forcefully (presumably with conventional arms) when minor issues are challenged, so as to enhance the credibility of the threat to use nuclear weapons if major challenges occur. This scenario is primarily applicable within the context of 'extended' deterrence. Thus, the notion of inter-dependence of commitments has become central in the theory. This notion has been criticised from three different viewpoints. The 'realists' do not foresee the military use of nuclear weapons[50] under any circumstances (with the exception perhaps of retaliation for a direct nuclear attack on the United States). Thus, the realist critique sees such demonstrations of resolve on minor issues as irrelevant. Others have argued that nuclear weapons do enhance deterrence and are 'usable', but the use of force on lesser issues does not enhance the credibility of nuclear threats. Nuclear threats, it is claimed, derive their credibility from the element of uncertainty.[51] Finally, the tendency in the American theory and practice of deterrence to emphasise the use of force for the sake of credibility has been seen more as the result of psychological and political-domestic factors than of nuclear deterrence require-ments.[52] The common thread connecting these three critiques relates to the enormous qualitative distinction between nuclear and conventional arms. Consequently actions taken within the conventional realm cannot affect the usability or non-usability of nuclear weapons. From the Israeli–Syrian experience one can infer that demonstrations of resolve through the use of force are problematic not only in nuclear but also in conventional environments. There is no necessary interconnection between the defence of 'specific' deterrence thresholds and the success or failure of 'general' deterrence.

Credibility in general is either less central or, to the extent that it is relevant, it derives from sources other than images of resolve. Similarly, there does not appear to be an interconnec-tion between the defence of one 'specific' deterrence threshold and the success or failure of other 'specific' thresholds.

Communication of firm commitments is required while new 'specific deterrence' thresholds are being defined. But deterrence succeeds to the extent that these thresholds correspond to important security concerns of the deterrer. More important than the demonstration of resolve is to define thresholds in such a way that they represent vital security interests. The Israeli-Syrian experience suggests that both sides correctly perceived the other's security priorities. The communication of priorities was not merely dependent on the subjective definition of the deterrer, but also on the objectively strategic situation. For example, that south Lebanon was of security importance for Israel was not merely an arbitrary decision taken by Israel, but also something which could be rationally and objectively justified. Once this is recognised, the credibility of the commitment to defend is considerably enhanced. In addition, deterrence thresholds should not violate important security interests for the challenger.

There are many and diverse motivations for war. These motivations relate to inter-state relations, to domestic pressures and to the nature of regimes and political elites. On the whole, Israeli-Syrian strategic relations have been characterised by what could be termed as 'pure' inter-state relations. Syria adopted a conflictive strategy *vis-à-vis* Israel because of reasons of state — its bilateral relationship with Israel, and competition with other Arab states. When Damascus at various times escalated the conflict, it was either in reaction to Israeli actions, or to compel Israel, or to gain points in the competition between Arab states. Since state interests rather than ideological reasons have been the chief factor in Israeli-Syrian strategic interactions, especially since 1967, the defender's ability positively to manipulate motivations for challenging the *status quo* appear to be more extensive than in the case of inter-state conflicts resulting from ideological or domestic causes. Indeed, the relative stability of Israeli-Syrian strategic relations in Lebanon became possible only because the two rivals acted purely according to 'states' interests'. This observation lends credence to the eighth inference concerning deterrence, viz. that strategic behaviour which is directed primarily by real state interests creates relatively better conditions for the evolution of stable deterrence systems.

When state interests are the issue, then the scope for positive manipulation of motivations for war is enlarged. Critics of deterrence theory have contended that it does not pay sufficient attention to potential positive inducements as an alternative to the threat of punishment. Indeed, the Israeli–Syrian deterrence experience after 1967 suggests that had Israel been ready to offer political concessions regarding the Golan, the Syrian motivation for war would have probably diminished. As Jervis has pointed out: 'Statesmen should usually combine threats with reassurances', although he cautions that the right mix of the two strategies is difficult to measure.[53]

The question of rationality is, needless to say, central in the deterrence process. Deterrence theory, developing as it did primarily within the context of nuclear deterrence, relied on the assumption of rationality. For this reason, deterrence came under severe criticism. One oft-repeated aspect of this criticism is the possibility of misperceptions arising from cultural and value differences between deterrer and challenger. For example, it has been argued that cultural differences between the West and the Soviet bloc, or differences between the industrialised countries and Third World countries, may lead to irrational or non-rational behaviour. This in turn would lead to deterrence failures.[54]

The Israeli–Syrian deterrence experience in general, and in particular the Israeli–Syrian 'specific deterrence' dialogue in Lebanon during 1976–81, suggests, however, on the contrary, that countries having completely different value systems may behave rationally at the strategic level. That is, Israeli and Syrian misperceptions did not exceed what could be expected among countries sharing the same cultural and ethical norms. The relative lack of misperceptions was an important factor in guaranteeing deterrence stability. Failures of deterrence, such as in 1973 and in 1982, were not due to lack of rationality and to misperceptions, but to other factors.

Furthermore, differences in systems of political values did not affect the rational choosing of limited objectives in Lebanon. Both Israel and Syria refrained from adopting total objectives and preferred limited targets which would not violate the politico-strategic concerns of the rival. They did not search for victory, but rather for the management of military behaviour.

Another criticism of the rationality aspect of deterrence theory argues that cultural differences may lead to misperceptions about the readiness of the challenger to absorb high costs for the accomplishment of foreign-policy objectives. In different cultures, so the argument goes, the tolerance thresholds for absorption of high costs for parallel foreign-policy objectives may vary considerably. Deterrence may therefore fail, not out of the deterrer's failure to understand the vitality of the interests under contention for the challenger, but from a basic misunderstanding of the challenger's readiness to absorb human costs.[55] The Israeli–Syrian deterrence experience suggests that this is not necessarily the case. In the first place, the two sides did not hesitate to escalate the conflict when their important security interests appeared to be threatened, even if that escalation might have incurred high costs. To put it differently, the two sides, though having very different systems of values, have been ready to absorb high costs in defence of their vital security interests. When deterrence failed, it was therefore not due to misperceptions of the cultural background of the other side, but rather to misunderstanding of the vitality of the rival's interests.

Whether this inference can be generalised is not at all clear. It may still be argued that tolerance thresholds for costs may vary from one cultural context to another. For example, messianic or fundamentalist regimes might not be deterred because of their readiness to spill blood for a cause.

It has been argued that because some regimes or societies are readier than others to absorb heavy punishment, the effort to deter them requires an extra demonstration of resolve. Thus, a rational deterrer when facing such a challenger must prove his own readiness to absorb costs. This may be achieved, for example, by a strategy of brinkmanship. Again, the Israeli–Syrian experience in Lebanon does not sustain this claim. Admittedly, demands were made in Israel, for example, for strong reactions against Syria in view of the cultural differences. It has been widely argued that a regime which was ready to massacre dozens of thousands of its own people (for example, in Hamma in early 1982) was ready to absorb high costs in human lives and could be deterred only by continued massive demonstrations of force which would among other things demonstrate Israel's resolve. In practice, brinkmanship and demonstrations of resolve were not the main variable in enhancing deterrence. More important was the rational delineation of security interests, in the event even recognised by Syria. The resolve to defend their interests was self-evident.

One of the main failures of deterrence theorists has been to overlook the motivations of the challenger. This has been referred to in the previous paragraphs dealing with various aspects of the balance of interests and the ways in which resolve may be communicated. Another central failure of the theory has been to consider deterrence all too often as exercised by only one side. In actual conflicts, however, the two rivals may reverse roles, or play simultaneously the roles of deterrer and challenger. Deterrence may fail in such circumstances not because of a lack of credibility or because the challenger decides to go to war in any case, but rather because of ambiguity about conflicting postures of deterrence.

This simultaneous playing of two roles is relevant to yet another lesson derived from the Israeli 'specific deterrence' experience in Lebanon. While Israel defined its deterrence thresholds, Syria gradually developed tacit deterrence thresholds of its own in Lebanon, which in a sense were the converse reflection of the Israeli deterrence thresholds. For example, while south Lebanon was defined as an important Israeli security area, and consequently Israel succeeded in deterring Syria from penetrating there, it became gradually 'accepted' by both sides that Israeli ground operations in the rest of Lebanon were 'unacceptable'. To an extent this became part of Israel's practice of self-denial, but it also gained some credibility as the function of an ambiguous Syrian deterrence posture. The main general inference from this experience is that the deterrer, when defining 'specific deterrence' thresholds, must observe self-imposed restrictions on his own military behaviour. At times, 'specific deterrence' might also lead to the creation of a mirror-image effect, that is of tacit 'specific deterrence' thresholds by the challenger which correspond to those defined originally by the deterrer.

As the Israeli–Syrian experience demonstrated, when an elaborate and relatively well-defined system of 'specific deterrence' is imposed, its relationship with the overall conflict system as well as with the 'general deterrence' system obtaining between deterrer and challenger, is complex. In order to succeed, the 'specific deterrence' system should be decoupled politically from the overall conflict system. On the other hand, the deterrer should have the overall advantage in military terms.

Deterrence theory in its first 'wave' focused on perceptions of the military balance as the central factor in assessments of the credibility of the deterrence threat. Later developments of the theory tended to emphasise commitments and demonstrable resolve as important factors in guaranteeing the success of deterrence. However, analysis of the Israeli–Syrian deterrence

223

dialogue shows that the credibility of deterrence threats stems primarily from respective assessments of different types of intrinsic interests, on the one hand, and from assessments of the military balance, on the other. The interaction between these two factors decides the stability of deterrence. The present case-study demonstrates that decision-makers tend to view realistically and rationally the military power balance. Military factors, when assessed in the context of intrinsic political and strategic interests, serve as the key to the success of deterrence. In this respect, deterrence remains a central determining factor in the relations between conflicting states.

Finally, strategic stability may develop out of the continued experience of successful deterrence. This, coupled with the diminution of political grievances, is a precondition for conflict management. In areas of intense conflict, strategic stability also requires other measures, such as arms control agreements. Deterrence theory should therefore be seen as an essential building block in a wider theory of conflict management and strategic stability.

NOTES

1. Contributions to the definition and discussion of the concept have been made by many people. The following list refers to some of the main contributors in the early stages of the theory: Bernard Brodie, Thomas Schelling, Alexander George, Glen Snyder, Bruce Russet, Morton Kaplan, Richard Rosencrance, George Quester, Thomas Milburn. For a comprehensive contribution, see Patrick Morgan, *Deterrence: A Conceptual Analysis*.

2. For a discussion of the various definitions of deterrence see Morgan, *ibid.*, Chapter 1.

3. *Ibid.*, pp. 25–43.

4. The distinction was first suggested by Glen Snyder, *Deterrence by Denial and Punishment*. His definition is somewhat different from the one used in my work.

5. This incorporates an important political component into the deterrence equation. Indeed, the literature on deterrence has given some attention to different aspects of the political factor. For example, Alexander George discussed the necessity for adjusting deterrence (and coercion) to various foreign policy goals; see Alexander George, David Hall and William Simons, *The Limits of Coercive Diplomacy*. Bruce Russet is also concerned with the political interests under contention in deterrence situations. See his 'The Calculus of Deterrence', and 'Pearl Harbor: Deterrence Theory and Decision Theory'. Richard Rosencrance

points to the centrality of political constraints in *Strategic Deterrence Reconsidered*. Patrick Morgan refers to it in *Deterrence: a Conceptual Analysis*, chapters 6 and 7. See also Steven Maxwell, *Rationality in Deterrence*; Robert Jervis, 'Deterrence Theory Revisited', and also chapter 3 of his *Perception and Misperception in International Politics*. See also Richard Ned Lebow, 'Deterrence Reconsidered: The Challenge of Recent Research', 'The Deterrence Deadlock: Is There A Way Out?' and *Between Peace and War: The Nature of International Crisis*.

6. Jervis, 'Deterrence Theory Revisited', p. 314.

7. The issue of resolve has been mentioned by many writers, usually as part of the issue of credibility. Oran Young discusses resolve and defines it as 'intensity of feeling'; see his *The Politics of Force*, pp. 33, 177–216. Jervis, 'Deterrence Theory Revisited', when discussing 'strategic interests' as distinct from 'intrinsic interests', refers to values which are related to the issue of resolve.

8. For studies of the Israeli strategic 'doctrine' see Yoav Ben Horin and Barry Posen, *Israel's Strategic Doctrine*; Michael Handel, *Israel's Political-Military Doctrine*; Dan Horowitz, 'Israel's Concept of Defensible Borders', 'The Israeli Concept of National Security and the Prospects of Peace in the Middle East', 'The Constant and the Changing in Israeli Strategic Thought' (in Hebrew) and 'The Control of Limited Military Operations: The Israeli Experience'; Nadav Safran, *Israel, The Embattled Ally*; Ephraim Inbar, *Israeli Strategic Thought in the Post 1973 Period*. For specific discussions of the Israeli deterrence posture see Horowitz, 'The Israeli Concept of National Security and the Prospects of Peace in the Middle East'; for a comprehensive analysis and evaluation of Israeli conventional deterrence, see Yair Evron, *The Middle East and Nuclear Weapons* (in Hebrew), chapter 3. On the Israeli deterrence calculus against Egypt between 1967 and 1973 see Janice Stein, 'Calculation, Miscalculation, and Conventional Deterrence II: The View from Jerusalem'.

9. Unfortunately no comprehensive detailed studies exist focusing on the Israeli–Syrian strategic interactions throughout this period. Partial references appear in various works, but do not provide a detailed account of the processes of limited escalation along the Israeli–Syrian border. See, for example, Ya'acov Bar-Simantov, *Linkage Politics in the Middle East: Syria Between Domestic and External Conflict, 1961–1970*; Nissim Bar-Ya'acov, *The Israeli–Syrian Armistice, Problems of Implementation 1949–1966*.

10. The best account of inter-Arab states' competition in this period is still Malcolm Kerr's *The Arab Cold War*. For analytical treatments of the complex relationship between inter-Arab relations and the Arab–Israeli conflict, see, *inter alia*, Gabriel Ben-Dor, 'Inter-Arab Relations and the Arab–Israeli Conflict', and *State and Conflict in the Middle East*, chapters 4 and 5; Yair Evron and Ya'acov Bar Simantov, 'Coalitions in the Arab World'.

11. The clearest statement of the Egyptian deterrence intentions in the first phase of the 1967 crisis was given by Nassir in an interview published in *Look* (New York), 19 March 1968, quoted in Geist, *The Six Day War*, chapter 13 fn. 31. Most observers, including Israelis, concur

that deterrence was indeed Egypt's strategy in its initial move into the Sinai in 1967. For a contrary argument see, *inter alia*, Theodor Draper, *Israel and World Politics: Roots of the Third Arab–Israeli War*.

12. For accounts of developments leading to the 1973 War and of its political and military aspects from different perspectives, see, *inter alia*, Avraham Adan, *On Both Banks of the Suez* (Hebrew); Michael Brecher with Benjamin Geist, *Decisions in Crisis: Israel 1967 and 1973*; Muhamad Hasenin Heikal, *The Road to Ramadan*; Ismail Fahmy, *Negotiating for Peace in the Middle East*; Henry Kissinger, *Years of Upheaval*; John Mearsheimer, *Conventional Deterrence*; William Quandt, *A Decade of Decisions*; Mahmud Riad, *The Struggle for Peace in the Middle East*; Anwar al-Sadat, *In Search of Identity*; Saad el-Shazly, *The Crossing of the Suez*; Avi Shai, 'Egypt Before the Yom Kippur War: War Aims and Plans of Attack' (in Hebrew), *Ma'arachot*, July 1976; Stein, 'Calculation, Miscalculation and Conventional Deterrence: The View from Jerusalem' and 'Calculation, Miscalculation and Conventional Deterrence: The View from Cairo', and ' "Intelligence" and "Stupidity" Reconsidered: Estimation and Decision in Israel, 1973'; Yair Evron, 'The Relevance and Irrelevance of Nuclear Options in Conventional Wars: The 1973 October War', Alexander George, 'The Arab–Israeli War of October 1973: Origins and Impact'.

13. The first to point out this aspect of the challenger's calculus was Albert Wohlstetter in 'Lectures on Strategy', University of California, Los Angeles, 1962, as quoted by Richard Rosencrance in *Strategic Deterrence Reconsidered*, p. 23. It appears that the main focus of Wohlstetter's analysis was the alternative military risks of a first strike measured against waiting to absorb a strike from the enemy. Rosencrance (*ibid.*) develops this formula to include political alternatives. For further discussions of this see also Rosencrance, *Deterrence and Vulnerability in the Pre-Nuclear Era*, pp. 14–20, 25; Janice Stein, 'Calculation, Miscalculation and Conventional Deterrence I: The View from Cairo', pp. 51–2.

14. See *ibid.*, pp. 49–51. On the importance of 'positive sanctions', for conflict management and by implication deterrence see David Baldwin, 'Power Analysis and World Politics'.

15. See Sadat, *In Search of Identity*, pp. 252–4, 256–9.

16. Stein, 'Calculation, Miscalculation and Conventional Deterrence I: The View from Cairo'.

17. See, for example, the analysis of the 1973 War by Syrian Defence Minister Tlas in his interview in *Tishrin*, 17 October 1981, p. 1.

18. Iraq sent one armoured and one mechanised division to the Golan, and Jordan sent two armoured brigades.

19. The first indication after 1973 of Syrian anxiety about Israel's growing military capability and the need to build a Syrian deterrence capability appears in an article by the former Syrian Chief of Staff Amin al-Nafuri, *al-Majala as-Askaria*, 25 October 1974. The emphasis on the air-defence system as a main deterrent against Israel is also developed in an extensive discussion in *Geish al-Sha'b*, 26 August 1975, pp. 26–9. On the 'strategic balance' as an instrument of Syrian deterrence against Israel, see also Hitam al-Ayubi in *Tishrin*, 30 May 1981.

20. See, for example, Mustapha Tlas, interview in *Tishrin*, 17 October 1981.

21. See, for example, an interview with al-Ayubi, *Tishrin*, 10 October 1981; and an interview with Abl-al-Assuf al-Qassam, Syria's Prime Minister, in *Tishrin*, 19 May 1980.

22. See, for example, an interview with Syria's Information Minister Ahmed Iskander in *al-Anwar*, 24 September 1980. Even more remarkable is the interview with Khaddam, *al-Mustakbal*, 6 February 1982. In an interesting interview with Ahmed Iskander, *al-Kfats al-Anabi*, 13 October 1980, he stressed the necessity for Arab unity and close political links with the Third World and the Soviet Union as preconditions for the 'strategic balance'.

23. For details see Mark Heller, Zeev Eitan, Dov Tamari, *The Middle East Military Balance 1983*.

24. See, for example, the report by Radio Monte Carlo's correspondent in Damascus on 6 April 1982. Damascus continued to hold to its opinion even in the first days of the war. See, for example, Radio Damascus, 6 June 1982.

25. For a discussion of the Israeli *casus belli* prior to 1967, see Michael Brecher, *The Foreign Policy System of Israel*, pp. 51 and especially 67. For unofficial definitions of the *casus belli*, see Yigal Allon, *Curtain of Sand* (Hebrew) and Shimon Peres, *The Next Phase* (Hebrew). For a study of these *casus belli* as deterrence instruments see Yair Evron, *The Middle East and Nuclear Weapons*, chapter 3.

26. See 'Israel's Strategic Problems in the 1980s', an address to the International Symposium on Strategic Problems at Tel-Aviv University, 14 December 1981; and *Ma'ariv*, 30 March 1982.

27. See 'Deterrence Theory Revisited', pp. 303 ff.

28. For details of the Syrian armed forces in 1985, see Mark Heller, Aharon Levran, Zeev Eitan, *The Middle East Military Balance 1985*. See also *The Military Balance 1985–86*.

29. There are many references to the deployment of the SAM batteries and their Soviet crews as deterrents against Israel. See, for example, interview with Mustapha Tlas in *El-Pais*, 19 May 1984.

30. See, for example, interviews with Mustapha Tlas, Syrian Defence Minister, in *a-Shark*, 9 April 1983 and in *Der Spiegel*, 10 September 1984. The main analysis of the war from the Syrian point of view is included in *The Israeli Invasion of Lebanon*. The book was written by a group of high ranking officers and some specialists under the overall direction of Mustapha Tlas.

31. See Asad's speech on 8 March 1986, broadcast by Radio Damascus on the same day.

32. President Asad's speech broadcast by Radio Damascus on 5 January 1985.

33. See, for example, President Asad's interview to ABC, broadcast on Damascus Television on 25 April 1984.

34. See, for example, Asad's interview with Patrick Seale, *The Observer*, 25 May 1984.

35. Stein, 'Calculation, Miscalculation and Conventional Deterrence: The View from Cairo', p. 39.

36. See Glen Snyder and Paul Diesing, *Conflict among Nations*, p. 335.

37. The literature on rationality in decisions on national security policy is very extensive. For references to the more important contributions see the list of references in Morgan, *Deterrence: A Conceptual Framework*, chapters 4 and 5; see also Janice Stein, 'Can Decision Makers be Rational and Should They Be? Evaluating the Quality of Decisions'.

38. This formulation is close to the interpretation given by Raymond Aron and the American 'realists' to *Realpolitik* and of the Realpolitik evaluation of the 'national interest' against other interests. See, for example, Raymond Aron, *Peace and War: A Theory of International Relations*, pp. 591–600. Reinhold Niebuhr, for example, emphasised that realism should not be cynical, and when referring to it he pointed out that 'It is a concern at one and the same time, with oneself and with the other, a concern in which the self maintains a proper respect for the opinions of humanity, derived from a modest awareness of the limits of its own knowledge and its own power'. He added that nations are egotistical but 'the sense of justice should keep prudence from becoming too prudent, in other words, too opportunistic in its manner of defining interest'. This text is included in Harry Davis and Robert C. Good (eds.), *Reinhold Niebuhr on Politics*, p. 332. Quoted in Aron, *Peace and War*, p. 594. Morgan's notion of the 'sensible' decision-maker comprises an element which is close to this definition of 'rationality'. However, he is mostly concerned with the process of decision-making rather than with the ends of policy. See Morgan, *Deterrence: A Conceptual Analysis*, chapter 4 and in particular chapter 5.

39. Stein, 'Can Decision Makers be Rational and Should They Be? Evaluating the Quality of Decisions', p. 319.

40. See Snyder and Diesing, *Conflict among Nations*, pp. 334–5.

41. See 'Deterrence Reconsidered: The Challenge of Recent Research'.

42. See Saadia Touval, *The Peace Brokers: Mediation in the Arab–Israeli Conflict 1948–1967*.

43. Morgan, *Deterrence: A Conceptual Analysis,* p. 9. Morgan of course goes on to demonstrate the complexity of deterrence.

44. See *Strategic Studies Reconsidered*, p. 23.

45. Richard Ned Lebow, 'The Deterrence Deadlock', p. 184.

46. *Ibid.*, p. 183.

47. See Stein, 'Calculation, Miscalculation and Conventional Deterrence I: The View from Cairo', pp. 40–1. Stein is not categorical in her discussion of the challenger's avoidance of attention to the deterrer's interests as affecting the success or failure of deterrence. Lebow is more explicit, when stating clearly that the challenger uses various psychological strategies to 'dismiss indications of an adversary's resolve'; 'The Deterrence Deadlock', p. 183.

48. Stein, 'Calculation, Miscalculation and Conventional Deterrence: The View from Cairo'.

49. See Alexander George and Richard Smoke, *Deterrence in American Foreign Policy*; Steven Maxwell, *Rationality in Deterrrence*;

Jervis, 'Deterrence Theory Revisited', and 'Perception and Deterrence'.

50. Among the adherents to this view, George Kennan has for many years been one of the foremost proponents. For a clear presentation of this view see McGeorge Bundy, George Kennan, Gerard Smith, and Robert McNamara, 'Nuclear Weapons and the Atlantic Alliance'. That, contrary to the prevailing view, the theory of deterrence does *not* fit the 'realist' tradition, see Patrick Morgan, 'Saving Face for the Sake of Deterrence'.

51. The emphasis on uncertainty as enhancing nuclear deterrence has been one of the main themes in deterrence theory. For a recent contribution to this approach, criticising the proposals for a shift to conventional deterrence as a recommended strategy for NATO, see Richard K. Betts, 'Conventional Deterrence: Predictive Uncertainty and Policy Confidence'.

52. See the illuminating analysis by Morgan, 'Saving Face for the Sake of Deterrence'.

53. Robert Jervis, 'Introduction' in *Psychology and Deterrence*, p. 9.

54. A common theme in the literature on nuclear proliferation is the irrationality of Third World leaders and elites. In parenthesis one might add that proliferation is fraught with dangers, but the above-mentioned theme is out of place in most contexts.

55. This argument has, for example, recurred in the American literature on the Soviet Union. It has become more fashionable since the mid-1970s in discussions concerning Soviet readiness to launch a first nuclear strike and to absorb a retaliatory American strike. Thus, for example, the Soviet civil defence programme, though capable of protecting only part of the Soviet population, is considered by this school of thought as sufficient in Soviet eyes to ensure success in a nuclear exchange.

Sources

BOOKS, MONOGRAPHS AND MANUSCRIPTS

Adan, Avraham, *Al Sh'tei Gdot Hasuez* (in Hebrew) (On Both Banks of the Suez) (Jerusalem: Edanim, 1979).

Allon, Yigal, *Masach Shel Chol* (in Hebrew) (Curtain of Sand) (Tel Aviv; Hakibutz Hameuchad, 1984).

Aron, Raymond, *Peace and War: A Theory of International Relations* (Garden City: Doubleday, 1966).

Bar-Simantov Yaacov, *Linkage Politics in the Middle East: Syria Between Domestic and External Conflict 1961–1970* (Boulder: Westview, 1983).

Bar-Zohar, Michael, *Ben Gurion* (in Hebrew) (Tel Aviv: Am Oved, 1977).

Ben David, Ofer, *Hamaracha Belevanon* (in Hebrew) (The War in Lebanon) (Private Publication, Israel, 1985).

Ben Horin, Yoav and Posen, Barry, *Israel's Strategic Doctrine* (Santa Monica: Rand Corporation R-2845-NA, September 1981).

Binder, Leonard (ed.), *Politics in Lebanon* (New York: Wiley Books, 1966).

Brecher, Michael, *The Foreign Policy System of Israel* (London: Oxford University Press, 1972).

Brecher, Michael (ed.), *Studies in Crisis Behavior, Jerusalem Journal of International Relations* (Special Issue) Vol. 3. Nos. 2–3, Winter-Spring, 1978.

Brecher, Michael, *Decisions in Israel's Foreign Policy* (London: Oxford University Press, 1974).

Brecher, Michael and Geist, Benjamin, *Decision in Crisis: Israel 1967 and 1973* (Berkeley: University of California Press, 1980).

Bulloch, John, *Death of a Country: The Civil War in Lebanon* (London: Weidenfeld and Nicolson, 1977).

Cobban, Helena, *The Making of Modern Lebanon* (Bolder: Westview, 1985).

Davis, Harry and Good, Robert (ed.), *Reinhold Niebuhr on Politics* (New York: 1960).

Dawisha, Adeed, *Syria and the Lebanese Crisis* (New York: St. Martin's Press, 1980).

Dayan, Moshe, *Avnei Derech* (in Hebrew) (Story of My Life) (Jerusalem: Adanim, 1976).

Draper, Theodor, *Israel and World Politics: Roots of the Third Arab–Israeli War* (New York: Viking Press, 1968).

Entelis, J., *Pluralism and Party Transformation in Lebanon, Al Kata'ib 1936–1970* (Leiden: E. J. Brill, 1974).

Evron, Yair, *The Demilitarization of Sinai*, Jerusalem Papers on Peace Problems, No. 16 (Jerusalem: The Leonard Davis Institute for

International Relations, The Hebrew University of Jerusalem, 1975).

Evron, Yair, *Problems of Arms Control in the Middle East*, Adelphi Papers, No. 138 (London: International Institute for Strategic Studies, 1977).

Evron, Yair (ed.), *International Violence: Terrorism, Surprise and Control* (Jerusalem: The Leonard Davis Institute of International Relations, The Hebrew University of Jerusalem, 1979).

Evron, Yair, *The Middle East and Nuclear Weapons* (in Hebrew) (Tel Aviv: Hakibutz Hemeuchad, forthcoming).

Fahmy, Ismail, *Negotiations for Peace in the Middle East* (London: Croom Helm, 1983).

Feldman, Shai and Rechnitz-Kijner, Heda, *Deception, Consensus and War: Israel's Intervention in Lebanon* (Tel Aviv: The Jaffe Centre for Strategic Studies, 1985).

Gabriel, Richard, *Operation Peace for Galilee* (New York: Hill and Wang, 1984).

Geist, Benjamin, *The Six Day War: A Study in the Setting and the Process of Foreign Policy Decision Making Under Crisis Conditions* (Ph.D. Thesis, Hebrew University of Jerusalem, 1974).

George, Alexander, Hall, David, Simons, William, *The Limits of Coercive Diplomacy* (Boston: Little Brown, 1971).

George, Alexander and Smoke, Richard, *Deterrence in American Foreign Policy* (New York: Columbia University Press, 1974).

George, Alexander, *Managing US–Soviet Rivalry, Problems of Crisis Prevention* (Boulder: Westview Press, 1983).

Gilmour, David, *Lebanon: The Fractured Country* (London: Sphere Books, 1984).

Golan, Galia, *Soviet–PLO Relations After Lebanon* (Research Paper No. 57, The Soviet and East European Research Centre, Hebrew University of Jerusalem, July 1984).

Gordon, David, *Lebanon: The Fragmented Nation* (London: Croom Helm, 1980).

Gordon, David, *The Republic of Lebanon: Nation in Jeopardy* (Boulder: Westview Press, 1983).

Haig, Alexander, *Caveat: Realism, Reagan, and Foreign Policy* (New York: Macmillan, 1984).

Handel, Michael, *Israel's Political-Military Doctrine* (Cambridge, Mass.: Harvard University Center for International Affairs, Occasional Papers, No. 20, July 1973).

Heikal, Muhamad Hasenin, *The Road to Ramadan* (New York: Quadrangle Books, 1975).

Heller, Mark, Eitan, Zeev, and Tamasi, Dov, *The Middle East Military Balance 1983* (Tel Aviv: Jaffe Center for Strategic Studies, Tel Aviv University, 1984).

Heller, Mark, Levran, Aharon, and Eitan, Zeev, *The Middle East Military Balance, 1985* (Tel Aviv: Jaffe Center for Strategic Studies, Tel Aviv University, 1986).

Horowitz, Dan, *Israel's Concept of Defensible Borders* (Jerusalem: Jerusalem Papers on Peace Problems No. 16, 1975).

Hourani, Albert, *Arabic Thought in the Liberal Age 1798–1939*

(London: Oxford University Press, 1962).

Hourani, Albert, *The Emergence of the Modern Middle East* (London: Macmillan Press, 1981).

Hudson, Michael, *Conditions of Political Violence and Instability* (Beverly Hills: Sage Publications, 1970).

Hudson, Michael, *The Precarious Republic: Political Modernization in Lebanon* (New York: Random House, 1968).

Inbar, Ephraim, *Israeli Strategic Thought in the Post-1973 Period* (Jerusalem: Israel Research Institute of Contemporary Society, 1982).

Israeli Commission of Inquiry into the events at the Refugee Camps in Beirut. *The Beirut Massacre: The Complete Kahan Report* (Jerusalem, 1983).

Jervis, Robert, *Perception and Misperception in International Politics* (Princeton: Princeton University Press, 1976).

Jervis, Robert, Lebow, Ned, Stein, Janice, *Psychology and Deterrence* (Baltimore: Johns Hopkins University Press, 1985).

Kass, Ilana, *The Lebanon Civil War 1975–1976: A Case of Crisis Management* (Jerusalem: Hebrew University, 1979).

Kerr, Malcolm, *The Arab Cold War: Gamal Abd Al-Nassir and His Rivals 1958–1970* (London: Oxford University Press, 1971).

Khalidi, Rashid, *Under Siege: PLO Decision-Making During the 1982 War* (New York: Columbia University Press, 1986).

Khalidi, Walid, *Conflict and Violence in Lebanon: Confrontation in the Middle East* (Cambridge, Mass.: Center for International Affairs, Harvard University, 1979).

Kissinger, Henry, *Years of Upheaval* (Boston and Toronto: Little Brown & Co., 1982).

Lanir, Zvi, *Hameoravot Haisraelit Blebanon* (in Hebrew) (The Israeli Involvement in Lebanon — A precedent for an "Open" Game with Syria?) Tel Aviv Center for Strategic Studies, paper no. 10, September 1980).

Lebow, Richard Ned, *Between Peace and War: The Nature of International Crisis* (Baltimore: Johns Hopkins University Press, 1981).

Leitenberg, Milton and Sheffer, Gabriel (eds.), *Great Power Intervention in the Middle East* (New York: Pergamon Press, 1979).

Ma'oz, Moshe, *Syria Under Hafiz al-Asad: New Domestic and Foreign Policies* (Jerusalem: Leonard David Institute for International Relations, The Hebrew University of Jerusalem, 1976).

Ma'oz, Moshe and Avner, Yaniv, *Syria under Assad* (London: Croom Helm, 1986).

Maxwell, Steven, *Rationality in Deterrence*, Adelphi Papers No. 50 (London: International Institute for Strategic Studies, 1968).

Mearsheimer, John, *Conventional Deterrence* (Ithaca and London: Cornell University Press, 1983).

Meo, Leila, *Lebanon Improbable Nation: A Study in Political Development* (Bloomington: Indiana University Press, 1965).

Morgan, Patrick, *Deterrence: A Conceptual Analysis* (Beverly Hills: Sage, 1977).

Naor, Arie, *Memshala Bemilchama* (in Hebrew), (Cabinet at War) (Tel-Aviv: Lahav Press, 1986).

Nir, Amiram, *The Soviet–Syrian Friendship and Cooperation Treaty: Unfulfilled Expectations* (Tel Aviv: Jaffe Center for Strategic Studies, Tel Aviv University, May 1983).

Owen, Roger (ed.), *Essays on the Crisis in Lebanon* (London: Ithaca Press, 1976).

Peres, Shimon, *Hashlav Haba* (in Hebrew) *The Next Phase* (Tel Aviv: Om Oved, 1965).

Quandt, William, *A Decade of Decisions: American Policy Toward the Arab–Israeli Conflict, 1967–1976* (Berkeley and London: University of California Press, 1977).

Quandt, William, *Camp David* (Washington DC: Brookings Institution, 1986).

Rabin, Itshak, *Pinkas Sherut* (in Hebrew) (The Rabin Memoirs) (Tel Aviv: Ma'ariv Library, 1979).

Rabinovich, Itamar and Zamir, Hanna, *Milchama Umashber Belevanon 1975–1981* (in Hebrew) (War and Crisis in Lebanon 1975–1981) (Tel Aviv: Hakibutz Hameuchad, 1982).

Rabinovich, Itamar, *The War for Lebanon 1970–1983* (Ithaca: Cornell University Press, 1984).

Rabinovich, Itamar, *Syria Under the Ba'ath 1963–66; The Army — Party Symbiosis* (Jerusalem: Israel University Press, 1972).

Riad, Mahmud, *The Struggle for Peace in the Middle East* (London: Quartet Books, 1981).

Rosen, Giora (ed.), *Milchemet Levanon — Bein Mecha' Lehaskama* (in Hebrew) (Lebanon War — Between Protest and Compliance) (Tel Aviv: Hakibutz Hameuchad, 1983).

Rosencrance, Richard, *Strategic Deterrence Reconsidered*, Adelphi Papers No. 116 (London: International Institute for Strategic Studies).

Rosencrance, Richard, *Deterrence and Vulnerability in the Pre-Nuclear Era*, Adelphi Papers No. 160 (London: International Institute for Strategic Studies).

Sadat, Anwar al, *In Search of Identity* (New York: Harper and Row, 1978).

Safran, Nadav, *Israel, the Embattled Ally* (Cambridge, Mass: Harvard University Press, 1978, 1981).

Salibi, Kamel Suleiman, *The Modern History of Lebanon* (New York: Praeger, 1965).

Salibi, Kamel Suleiman, *Crossroads to Civil War: Lebanon 1958–1976* (New York: Caravan Press, 1976).

Schelling, Thomas, *Arms and Influence* (New Haven: Yale University Press, 1966).

Schiff, Ze'ev and Ya'ari, Ehud, *Milchemet Sholal* (in Hebrew) (The Israeli War in Lebanon) (Tel Aviv: Shoken, 1984).

Seale, Patrick, *The Struggle for Syria: A Study of Postwar Arab Politics, 1945–1958* (London: Oxford University Press, 1965).

Sella, Abraham, *Achdut Betoch Perud* (in Hebrew) (Unity within Division (Jerusalem: Magnes Press, 1983).

Sharabi, Hisham, *Governments and Politics of the Middle East in the Twentieth Century* (Princeton, N.J.: Van Nostrand, 1962).

Sharabi, Hisham, *Nationalism and Revolution in the Arab World* (Princeton, N.J.: Van Nostrand, 1966).

Sharet, Moshe, *Yoman Ishi: 1894–1965* (in Hebrew) (Personal Diary) (Tel Aviv: Ma'ariv Library, 1978).

Shazley, Saad al, *The Crossing of the Suez* (San Francisco: American Mideast Research, 1980).

Sheffer, Gabriel (ed.), *Dynamics of Conflict: A Re-examination of the Arab–Israeli Conflict* (Atlantic Highlands, N.Y.: Humanities Press, 1975).

Shiffer, Shimon, *Kadur Sheleg* (in Hebrew) (Snow Ball) (Tel Aviv: Edanim, 1984).

Snyder, Glen, *Deterrence by Denial and Punishment* (Princeton, N.J.: Princeton University, Center of International Studies, Research Monograph No. 1, 1959).

Snyder, Glen and Diesing, Paul, *Conflict Among Nations: Bargaining Decision-Making and System Structure in International Crises* (Princeton, N.J.: Princeton University Press, 1977).

Stein, Janice and Tanter, Raymond, *Rational Decision-Making: Israel's Security Choices* (Colombus: Ohio State University Press, 1984).

Susser, Asher, *The PLO After the War in Lebanon: The Quest for Survival* (in Hebrew) (Tel Aviv: Hakibutz Hameuchad, 1985).

Tlas, Mustapha (ed.), *The Israeli Invasion of Lebanon* (translated into Hebrew) (Damascus: Tishrin Institute for Journalism and Publishing, 1983).

Touval Sa'adia, *The Peace Brokers: Mediation in the Arab–Israeli Conflict 1948–1967* (Princeton, N.J.: Princeton University Press, 1982).

Vance, Cyrus, *Hard Choices* (New York: Simon and Schuster).

Van Dam, Nikolaus, *The Struggle for Power in Syria* (London: Croom Helm, 1979).

Weitzman, Ezer, *Hakrav Al Hashalom* (in Hebrew) (The Battle for Peace) (Jerusalem: Edanim, 1981).

White, Jeffrey, *National Security Policy Decisionmaking in Israel* (M.A. Thesis, George Washington University, 1983).

White, Jeffrey, *Towards the Litani Operation: An Assessment of the Begin Government's Policy in Lebanon and the March 1978 Incursion* (Manuscript, 1983).

Yamak, L. Z., *The Syrian Social National Party: An Ideological Analysis* (Cambridge, Mass: Harvard University Press, 1969).

Young, Oran, *The Politics of Force: Bargaining During International Crises* (Princeton, N.J.: Princeton University Press, 1978).

Zamir, Meir, *The Foundation of Modern Lebanon* (London: Croom Helm, 1985).

ARTICLES AND CHAPTERS IN BOOKS

Aronson, Shlomo and Horowitz, Dan, 'The Strategy of Controlled Retaliation: The Israeli Example' (Hebrew), *Medina Umemshal*, Vol. 1, No. 1, Summer 1971.

Baldwin, David, 'Power Analysis and World Politics', *World Politics*, Vol. 39, No. 2, 1977.

Ben-Dor, Gabriel, 'Inter Arab Relations and the Arab Israeli Conflict', *Jerusalem Journal of International Relations*, Summer 1976.

Benny, M., 'Milchemet Shlom Hagalil: Hamahalachim Hatzva'iim Ha'ikariim' (in Hebrew) (The Peace for Galilee War: The Main Military Moves), *Ma'arachot*, 1982/1983.

Betts, Richard K., 'Conventional Deterrence, Predictive Uncertainty and Policy Confidence', *World Politics*, Vol. 37, No. 2, 1985.

Blechman, Barry M., 'The Impact of Israel's Reprisals on the Behavior of the Bordering Arab Nations at Israel', *Journal of Conflict Resolution*, Vol. 16, No. 2, June 1972.

Dawisha, Adeed, 'The Motives of Syria's Involvement in Lebanon', *The Middle East Journal*, Vol. 38, No. 2, Spring 1984.

Dawisha, Karen, 'The USSR in the Middle East: Super Power in Eclipse', *Foreign Affairs*, Winter, 1982–3.

Evron, Yair, 'The Relevance and Irrelevance of Nuclear Options in Conventional Wars: The 1973 October War', *The Jerusalem Journal of International Relations*, Vol. 7, No. 1–2, 1984.

Evron, Yair and Ya'acov, Bar-Simantov, 'Coalitions in the Arab World', *Jerusalem Journal of International Relations*, Summer 1976.

Evron, Yair, 'Washington, Damascus and the Lebanon Crisis' in Moshe Ma'oz and Avner Yaniv, *Syria Under Assad* (London: Croom Helm, 1986).

George, Alexander, 'The Arab–Israeli War of October 1973: Origins and Impact', in Alexander George (ed.), *Managing US–Soviet Rivalry*, Problems of Crisis Prevention (Boulder: Westview Press, 1983).

Hath, Paul and Russet, Bruce, 'What Makes Deterrence Work: Cases from 1900 to 1980', *World Politics*, XXXVI, No. 4, July 1984.

Horowitz, Dan, 'The War in Which the National Consensus was Broken' in *Lebanon War — Between Protest and Compliances* (Hebrew) (Tel Aviv: Hakibutz Hameuchad, 1982).

Horowitz, Dan, 'The Israeli Concept of National Security and the Prospects of Peace in the Middle East' in Gabriel Sheffer (ed.), *Dynamics of Conflict* (Humanities Press, 1975).

Horowitz, Dan, 'The Constant and the Changing in Israeli Strategic Thought' (Hebrew) in *Milchemet Breira* (Optional War) (Tel Aviv: Hakibutz Hameuchad Press, 1985).

Horowitz, Dan, 'The Control of Limited Military Operations: The Israeli Experience' in Yair Evron (ed.), *International Violence: Terrorism, Surprise and Control* (Jerusalem: The Leonard Davis Institute for International Relations, 1979).

Jervis, Robert, 'Deterrence and Perceptions', *International Security*, Vol. 7, Winter 1982–83.

Jervis, Robert, 'Deterrence Theory Revisited', *World Politics*, Vol. 31, No. 2, January 1979.

Jervis, Robert, 'Introduction' in Robert Jervis, Richard Ned Lebow, Janice Stein, *Psychology and Deterrence* (Baltimore: Johns Hopkins University Press, 1985).

Lebow, Richard Ned, 'The Deterrence Deadlock: Is There a Way Out?' in Robert Jervis, Richard Ned Lebow, Janice Stein, *Psychology and Deterrence* (Baltimore: Johns Hopkins University Press, 1985).

Lebow, Richard Ned, 'Deterrence Reconsidered: The Challenge of Recent Research', *Survival*, January/February 1985.

Lebow, Richard Ned, 'Windows of Opportunity: Do States Jump Through Them?', *International Security*, Vol. 9, No. 1, Summer 1984.

Ma'oz, Moshe, 'Hafiz al-Assad, A Political Profile', *The Jerusalem Quarterly*, No. 8, Summer 1978.

Morgan, Patrick, 'Saving Face for the Sake of Deterrence' in Robert Jervis, Richard Lebow, Janice Stein, *Psychology and Deterrence* (Baltimore: Johns Hopkins University Press, 1985).

Quandt, William, 'Reagan Lebanon Policy: Trial and Error', *The Middle East Journal*, Vol. 38, No. 2.

Russet, Bruce, 'Pearl Harbor: Deterrence Theory and Decision Theory', *Journal of Peace Research*, No. 2, 1967.

Russet, Bruce, 'The Calculus of Deterrence', *Journal of Conflict Resolution*, Vol. 7, March 1963.

Schiff, Ze'ev, 'The Green Light', *Foreign Policy*, 50, Spring 1983.

Shai, Avi, 'Egypt Before the Yom Kippur War: War Aims and Plans of Attack' (in Hebrew), *Ma'arachot*, July 1976.

Shuftan, Dan, 'The War in Lebanon and the Arab World', *Ma'arachot*, No. 284, September 1982.

Stein, Janice, 'Can Decision Makers Be Rational and Should They Be? Evaluating the Quality of Decisions' in Michael Brecher (ed.), *Studies in Crisis Behavior The Jerusalem Journal of International Relations* (Special Issue) Vol. 3, No. 2–3, Winter–Spring, 1978.

Stein, Janice, ' "Intelligence" and "Stupidity" Reconsidered: Estimation and Decision in Israel, 1973', *The Journal of Strategic Studies*, Vol. 3, September 1980.

Stein, Janice, 'Calculation, Miscalculation, and Conventional Deterrence II: The View from Jerusalem' in Robert Jervis, Richard Lebow, Janice Stein, *Psychology and Deterrence* (Baltimore: Johns Hopkins University Press, 1985).

Stein, Janice, 'Calculation, Miscalculation and Conventional Deterrence I: The View from Cairo' in Robert Jervis, Richard Lebow, Janice Stein, *Psychology and Deterrence* (Baltimore: Johns Hopkins University Press, 1985).

Yaniv, Avner and Lieber, Robert, 'Personal Whim or Strategic Imperative? The Israeli Invasion of Lebanon', *International Security*, Vol. 8, No. 2, Fall, 1983.

Young, Oran, 'Intensity of Feeling' in *The Politics of Force* (Princeton, N.J.: Princeton University Press, 1978).

Index

National Liberal Party 9, 91
Neibuhr, Reinhold 228n38
North Yemen 61
Nur al-Din al-Rifai 11

Operation Kadesh *see* Arab–
   Israeli Wars, 1956
Oranim 115
Ottoman Empire 3
Oziraq reactor 99, 118

Palestine Liberation Army
   (PLA) 34, 36, 40–2, 131
Palestine Liberation
   Organization (PLO) 7, 8
   activity against Israel 112
   attack on Israeli bus 74
   during Zahle encounter 98
   shelling of Galilee 122
   after Litani Operation 85
   and Arab world 29
   on Egypt–Israel peace
      agreement 67
   and Maronites 143
   and Muslims 48, 143, 146
   and Shi'is 61, 143
   and Syria 14, 67, 79, 200,
      211
   deployment prior to 1982 war
      129
   in Jordan 8, 9
   in Lebanon 1, 9, 22, 28–9,
      40, 45–56 *passim*, 91,
      97–8
   and status quo 12–13
   in Beirut 39, 61, 166, 170
   in South Lebanon 62,
      69–71, 81, 98, 170
   internal rivalries 169–70
   1982 War
      evacuation from Beirut
         142–53
      military operations 133–4,
         138–42
Pan-Arabism 6, 22, 27, 115
Parti Populaire Syrien (PPS) 6,
   10, 152
PDFLP *see* Popular Democratic
   Front for the Liberation of
   Palestine

Peace for Galilee 125; *see also*
   Israel, 1982 war; Arab–
   Israeli wars, 1982; Syria,
   1982 war
Peres, Shimon
   and Maronites 42
   background 58n29
   on deterrence 33
   on Lebanon 31
   on Syrian intervention in
      Lebanon 36, 39, 54,
      63
   1982 war 121, 128, 168
PFLP *see* Popular Front for
   the Liberation of Palestine
Phalanges
   and Israel 68–9, 92–3, 164,
      211
   and Syria 46, 69, 93, 150
   development 9, 91
   in Shuf 164, 166
   in 1975 civil war 10
   in 1982 war 139–40, 150,
      152–4
Phoenicians 25
PLA *see* Palestine Liberation
   Army
PLO *see* Palestine Liberation
   Organization
Popular Front for the
   Liberation of Palestine
   (PFLP) 10, 11, 149
PPS *see* Parti Populaire Syrien
Progressive Socialist Party 10
Protectors of the Cedar 10

Qlaia 70
Qarun, Lake 5, 146
Qassis, Sharbal 9–10

Rabin, Yitzhak
   background 58n29
   in USA 40–1
   Nabatiyya encounter 66
   on Lebanon 31, 33
   on Maronites 41–2
   on Syrian intervention in
      Lebanon 36, 39, 48–9,
      59n50
   resignation 70

as mediator
  between Israel and Syria
    39, 48, 65, 70, 88–9,
    96, 171, 199, 213–15
  in Israel–Lebanon peace
    negotiations 161–2
  of PLO evacuation from
    Beirut 141–53
  on Geneva Conference 67
  on Lebanon 37, 46, 72,
    199–200
  on Israeli policy 70, 75,
    77–8, 80, 95–6, 99,
    128, 137, 148, 154
  on Syrian policy 97, 200
  on PLO 89, 143
USSR 128, 184, 190, 192–5

Vancey, Cyrus 66
Vatican 11

Villages Association 109

War *see* Arab–Israeli wars;
  *for civil wars see individual
  country entries*
  types of 185
War of Attrition *see* Arab–
  Israeli Wars, 1969–70
War of Independence *see*
  Arab–Israeli wars, 1948
Weitzman, Ezer 71, 76, 78, 84,
  103–4
West Bank *see* Israel, on West
  Bank

Yom Kippur War *see* Arab–
  Israeli Wars, 1973

Zahle 34, 89–97
Zaharani River 79, 87

For Product Safety Concerns and Information please contact our EU
representative GPSR@taylorandfrancis.com
Taylor & Francis Verlag GmbH, Kaufingerstraße 24, 80331 München, Germany